The Constitution's Penman

AMERICAN POLITICAL THOUGHT

Jeremy D. Bailey and Susan McWilliams Barndt
Series Editors

Wilson Carey McWilliams and Lance Banning
Founding Editors

The Constitution's Penman

GOUVERNEUR MORRIS AND THE
CREATION OF AMERICA'S BASIC
CHARTER

Dennis C. Rasmussen

 University Press of Kansas

© 2023 by the University Press of Kansas
All rights reserved

Published by the University Press of Kansas (Lawrence, Kansas 66045), which was organized by the Kansas Board of Regents and is operated and funded by Emporia State University, Fort Hays State University, Kansas State University, Pittsburg State University, the University of Kansas, and Wichita State University.

Library of Congress Cataloging-in-Publication Data

Names: Rasmussen, Dennis C. (Dennis Carl), 1978– author.
Title: The Constitution's penman : Gouverneur Morris and the creation of America's basic charter / Dennis C. Rasmussen.
Description: Lawrence, Kansas : University Press of Kansas, 2023 | Series: American political thought | Includes index.
Identifiers: LCCN 2022030116 (print) | LCCN 2022030117 (ebook)
  ISBN 9780700634149 (cloth)
  ISBN 9780700634156 (ebook)
  ISBN 9780700640782 (paperback)
Subjects: LCSH: Morris, Gouverneur, 1752–1816. | Statesmen—United States—Biography. | Legislators—New York (State)—Biography. | United States—Politics and government—1783–1789. | United States. Constitutional Convention (1787) | Founding Fathers of the United States—Biography.
Classification: LCC E302.6.M7 R37 2023 (print) | LCC E302.6.M7 (ebook) | DDC 973.3092–dc23/eng/20220705
LC record available at https://lccn.loc.gov/2022030116.
LC ebook record available at https://lccn.loc.gov/2022030117.

EU Authorised Representative Details: Easy Access System Europe
Mustamäe tee 50, 10621 Tallinn, Estonia | gpsr.requests@easproject.com

For my teachers

Contents

Acknowledgments, ix

Introduction: Forgotten Yet Unforgettable, *1*

1 The Penman's Story: A Brief Biography, *10*

2 A Most Splendid Part: Morris at the Convention, *37*

3 A Representative of America: Federalism, *62*

4 Checking America's Aristocracy: The Senate, *79*

5 Property and the People's Branch: The House of Representatives, *94*

6 A Reluctant Architect of the Electoral College: Presidential Selection, *107*

7 An Office Fit for Washington: The Presidency, *122*

8 That Fortress of the Constitution: The Judiciary, *137*

9 The Curse of Heaven: Slavery, *150*

10 A Declaration of Motives: The Preamble, *164*

Epilogue: From Constitution-Maker to Aspiring Constitution-Breaker, *174*

Appendix: Morris's Great Convention Speeches, *185*

Notes, 193

Index, 245

Acknowledgments

As my research interests have migrated from the Scottish and French Enlightenments to the American founding, one of the greatest delights has been to get to know Gouverneur Morris. Morris played only a minor role in my last book, *Fears of a Setting Sun*, which focused on some of the more famous founders—Washington, Hamilton, Adams, and Jefferson—and their late-life disillusionment with America's constitutional order. Every encounter with Morris, however, left me more and more convinced that he is an important and utterly fascinating figure who deserves to be far better known than he is—hence the book that you currently hold in your hands.

My first and deepest thanks are to my family and friends, especially Emily and Sam, for their love, support, and willingness to put up with my curious obsessions. I reckon that Sam is one of the few nine-year-olds in the world who knows all about Gouverneur Morris, for which I apologize. I received a wonderfully warm welcome from the small but stellar group of Morris experts, both inside and outside the academy. Jack Barlow, Patrick Coby, Jonathan Gienapp, John Kaminski, Melanie Miller, A. J. St. Germain, and Bill Treanor all generously provided comments on the manuscript, as did two of my old graduate school friends, Bill Curtis and Ari Kohen. I was fortunate to have the opportunity to direct a small conference on Morris's constitutional vision in August 2021; I would like to thank Liberty Fund for hosting the conference and the participants for their keen insights.

The book is dedicated to my professors at Michigan State University's James Madison College and at Duke University, most of whom are now retired. None of them taught me anything about Morris, but they did teach me something about the Constitution, and more importantly they taught me to appreciate both the joys and the rigors of political theory and the scholarly life. For that privilege, I am more grateful than I can say.

Introduction:
Forgotten Yet Unforgettable

Who wrote the Declaration of Independence? Most American schoolchildren can tell you that it was Thomas Jefferson. Who wrote the nation's other key founding document, the Constitution? Strikingly few Americans know the answer, however well read they may be. Many assume that it must have been James Madison, "The Father of the Constitution." Others will correctly point out that the Constitution's provisions were hashed out over the summer of 1787 by dozens of different delegates at the Philadelphia Convention. Yet there was a single individual who put the nation's basic charter into its final form, choosing the arrangement and much of the wording of its provisions, not to mention composing the famous preamble ("We the people of the United States . . .") nearly from scratch. That individual was not Madison, but rather one of the least-remembered, but most colorful, of the founders: a peg-legged ladies' man with a wicked sense of humor, a staunch opponent of slavery and an unabashed elitist. He was Gouverneur Morris, "The Penman of the Constitution."[1]

It is, of course, something of an exaggeration to say that Jefferson "wrote" the Declaration of Independence.[2] He was part of a five-person drafting committee, and that committee met to discuss the Declaration's contents before choosing Jefferson to compose it.[3] When Jefferson did take up his pen, he drew on numerous sources, above all the Virginia Declaration of Rights that George Mason had written just weeks earlier, which included all of the famous self-evident truths of the Declaration of Independence—basic human equality, natural rights, government by consent, and the right to revolution—in much the same language.[4] Jefferson himself proclaimed that his aim was not "to say things which had never been said before," but rather to provide "an expression of the american mind."[5] Jefferson's draft of the document went through some changes when he showed it to John Adams and Benjamin Franklin, then more changes when it was brought before the full drafting committee (which also included Robert R. Livingston and Roger Sherman), and then still more changes—including quite extensive cuts—when it was considered by the Continental Congress as a whole. By the end of the process, around one third of Jefferson's original draft had been changed or eliminated, much to his chagrin.

It is similarly an exaggeration to say that Morris "wrote" the Constitution. The Constitution's provisions had been laboriously debated and voted on by the delegates to the Philadelphia Convention before he took up his pen, so his leeway in choosing the structure and powers of the proposed government was exceedingly minimal. And Morris, too, was a member of a five-person drafting committee that handed over the writing responsibility to him. Still, Morris singlehandedly reorganized the charter that the delegates had been crafting, consolidating twenty-three articles down to a neat seven, and he changed or chose a great deal of the wording on his own initiative, oftentimes in consequential ways. The preamble—the Constitution's ringing statement of purpose—was, by all appearances, Morris's own intellectual handiwork to a greater degree than the Declaration's celebrated opening paragraph was Jefferson's. And, in contrast to Jefferson's initial version of the Declaration, Morris's draft of the Constitution underwent very little revision before being finalized. All told, Morris was, far more than any other individual, the author of the Constitution—the charter by which Americans still live, and one of the most important texts in world history.[6]

Moreover, Morris's influence on the Constitution went well beyond simply penning the document. He also played a leading role in the debates at the Philadelphia Convention: Morris spoke more often, proposed more motions, and had more motions adopted than any other delegate. Of course, he by no means got his way in every instance. A number of the Constitution's features—particularly the structure of the Senate, whose members he argued should be appointed by the president and serve for life without pay—diverged rather sharply from Morris's own preferences. On the other hand, the same could be said of pretty much everyone who signed the charter, and Morris *did* have a sizable impact on the Constitution's substantive provisions, above all those relating to the selection and powers of the president. He was, along with James Madison and James Wilson, one of the Convention's three principal advocates of a powerful national government, and he was far and away the Convention's fiercest and most persistent critic of slavery, calling it "a nefarious institution" and "the curse of Heaven on the States where it prevailed."[7]

Joseph Ellis has remarked that "although Madison is usually described as the 'Father of the Constitution,' a plausible case can be made that Morris is more deserving of the title."[8] Similarly, Richard Brookhiser maintains that while Madison "is commonly called the Father of the Constitution," Morris "also deserves a share of the paternity."[9] Morris's claim to at least a share of that lofty moniker rests in part on the fact that Madison was not nearly as successful at the Convention or as enamored of the Constitution as is commonly supposed. In fact, Madison lost more battles than he won in Philadelphia, including a number of those that he deemed most important.[10] Hence, soon after the Convention's close, he wrote dejectedly to Jefferson that "the plan should it be adopted will neither effectually answer its national object nor prevent the local mischiefs which every where excite disgusts ag[ain]st the state governments."[11] To be sure, Madison played a number of critical roles both before and after the Convention in a way that Morris did not: he led the push for the Convention to be called in the first place, along with Alexander Hamilton; he helped to set its agenda by formulating the Virginia Plan; he wrote around a third of the essays in *The Federalist*; he led the forces in support of ratification at the critical Virginia convention in Richmond; he contributed more than anyone else to the drafting and ratification of the Bill of Rights; and his records remain the principal source of our knowledge regarding the Philadelphia Convention's proceedings. Nonetheless, during the Convention itself, Morris contributed more frequently to the debates than Madison did, was more successful in getting his proposals adopted than Madison was, and above all penned the Constitution itself.[12] Not bad for someone whose name most Americans would not even recognize.

The summer of 1787 was undoubtedly the high point of Morris's career in terms of subsequent influence, but it was just one moment in an exceedingly eventful and impactful life. Before the Philadelphia Convention, Morris supported the push toward American independence as a member of the New York provincial congress (1775–1777); was one of the principal architects of the first New York state constitution (1777); served in the Continental Congress, where he was one of General Washington's leading advocates and a signer of the Articles of Confederation (1778–1779); and helped to develop a national financial program that saved the revolution as the Confederation's Deputy Superintendent of Finance (1781–1783). After the Convention, he was urged (though declined) to contribute to *The Federalist*; went to London as America's first private agent to a foreign court (1790); followed in the footsteps of Benjamin Franklin and Thomas Jefferson as the American minister to France, where he was the only foreign diplomat to remain throughout the Terror (1792–1794); served as a Federalist senator during a critical period when the Republicans took power and the capital moved to Washington, DC (1800–1803); attended Alexander Hamilton's deathbed and gave his official eulogy (1804); was one of the guiding forces behind the grid layout of Manhattan (1807–1811) and the Erie Canal (1810–1816); and, as an elder statesman of the Federalist party, grew so disenchanted with the ascendancy of the Republicans and the War of 1812 that he eventually supported the secession of New England and New York from the union. Just for good measure, Morris accidentally killed himself using a whalebone to try to clear his infected urinary tract.

Even beyond his strikingly varied résumé, Morris was without question one of the most *interesting* of the founders. One scholar remarks of the gathering of notables at the Constitutional Convention that "Morris was easily the most colorful of the delegates present; he may have been the most colorful man in North America."[13] Morris was indeed a conspicuous figure wherever he went, thanks to his unusual first name (derived from his mother's family name), his aristocratic lifestyle (he had both a blue-blooded lineage and a gift for making money, and he lived like it), his massive frame (he served as the body double for Jean-Antoine Houdon's sculpture of George Washington), and especially his wooden leg (the result of a carriage accident—or perhaps, some whispered, a headlong flight to escape a jealous husband). Bold and irreverent, with a sharp intellect and an equally sharp tongue, he was quick to make both friends and enemies.

On the other hand, Morris took a more lighthearted approach to life than did most of his more famous contemporaries: he was just as devoted to witty conversation, fine wine, stylish clothes, and making money as he was to politics. He was particularly known—and frequently condemned—for his libertine lifestyle: Morris was an unapologetic devotee of sensual pleasures, and his fondness for women was legendary. He engaged in a long string of amorous adventures on two continents, including a protracted affair with Talleyrand's mistress, the countess Adélaïde de Flahaut, during his time in Paris. At age fifty-seven, Morris finally became the last of the founders to marry—to Ann Cary ("Nancy") Randolph, a fallen aristocrat more than two decades his junior who was then serving as his housekeeper, and who had earlier been accused of conspiring to murder her own newborn baby, fathered by her brother-in-law.

Morris's apparent frivolity has sometimes resulted in his being underestimated. One of today's finest historians has written that "James Madison can rest easy in his reputation as the true 'Father of the Constitution,'" since "Morris 'wrote the Constitution' only in the literal and limited sense that he led the committee on style that turned the convention's decisions into an official document. On the substance of the Constitution, Morris contributed precious little. In the debates, he spoke often but to scant, or negative, effect, preferring provocative rhetoric over meaningful compromise. . . . Truth be told, he was a political lightweight, a charming disappointment."[14] This book will endeavor to establish that Morris's contributions at the Philadelphia Convention and as the Constitution's penman were far more consequential than this assessment suggests.

As for the broader charge that Morris was a lightweight, perhaps it will be simplest to share the views of a few of Morris's contemporaries. No less a figure than George Washington rated Morris "a man of first rate abilities."[15] Alexander Hamilton, who was one of Morris's close friends, deemed him "a man of great genius."[16] Even after having frequently borne the brunt of Morris's stinging criticisms during his presidency, James Madison remarked late in life on "the brilliancy & fertility of his genius."[17] Another political opponent, Thomas Jefferson—who deemed Morris "a high flying Monarchy-man"— admitted soon after Morris's death that "genius has lost in him one of it's distinguished subjects."[18] Moving later into the nineteenth century, Theodore Roosevelt wrote a full biography of Morris in which he concluded that "there has never been an American statesman of keener intellect or more brilliant genius" and that "with all his faults, there are few men of his generation to whom the country owes more than to Gouverneur Morris."[19] If we can put any stock in the judgments of these figures, then clearly we should not allow Morris's effervescent worldliness to prevent us from appreciating the depth of his ideas or the size of his impact. He had many personal faults, but being a lightweight was not one of them.

William Treanor, the dean of Georgetown Law, has noted in an important recent article on Morris's authorship of the Constitution that "there is a great irony to Morris's place in history: he is both largely forgotten and seemingly unforgettable."[20] The longstanding neglect of Morris by historians, political theorists, and constitutional scholars alike has begun to be remedied of late: the past two decades have seen the publication of four biographies of him, a collection of his public writings, and critical editions of his later (post-Paris) diaries—all generally excellent.[21] Yet this minor renaissance has hardly put a dent in the general obscurity surrounding Morris. The distance between him and the "big six" founders—Benjamin Franklin, George Washington, John Adams, Alexander Hamilton, Thomas Jefferson, and James Madison—in the public consciousness is so vast that it can hardly be measured. There is no statue of Morris in the nation's capital, no mention of him in high school history classes, no city tour in New York that includes his grave, much less a place for his visage on our coins and bills, or a Broadway musical or HBO miniseries or substantial tourist industry dedicated to commemorating him. A recent panel of scholars ranked Morris third in importance—behind James Wilson and George Mason—even among the "forgotten founders" (i.e., those beyond the six just mentioned).[22]

Morris's handful of admirers, rightly perplexed by his continued obscurity, have offered a variety of potential explanations for it.[23] However, none of the proposed explanations seems entirely persuasive, at least taken in isolation. One common suggestion is that Morris's manifest elitism and criticisms of unfettered democracy are so offensive to our political sensibilities that we could never embrace him as one of our nation's key founders. He has long had a reputation as a reactionary, an aristocrat, or even a monarchist. Yet this reputation is quite misleading, as we will see, and in any case a whiff of political iconoclasm can just as often be alluring as off-putting. Alexander Hamilton remains a core member of the founding pantheon, for instance, despite being second to none in his misgivings about popular self-rule.

Another regularly broached possibility is that Morris's somewhat licentious lifestyle, combined with the fact that he devoted as much attention and energy to private life as to public life, undercuts the aura of gravitas that we expect from our venerable founders. This certainly explains why Morris was disdained by many during his lifetime, but one might expect that a predilection for fun, sex, and money would be less objectionable in our own, less censorious age—perhaps even a boon rather than a hindrance to his reputation. At any rate, Benjamin Franklin's eminence has not suffered as a result of his fun-loving and amorous ways. Morris's biographers also frequently note that he had little of the concern for posterity's judgment that so deeply marked the other founders, and thus that he did little to protect and burnish his posthumous reputation. Here too, though, one might expect that this kind of serene detachment would count as a positive rather than a negative in a culture that places such high value on authenticity and inner-directedness.

Still another potential reason for the lack of attention paid to Morris is that he never wrote a substantial work for scholars to pore over—certainly nothing on the scale of *The Federalist*, Jefferson's *Notes on the State of Virginia*, Adams's *Defence of the Constitutions of Government of the United States*, or even Franklin's autobiography. Of course, neither did Washington, and in any case, Morris left behind plenty of material to analyze: the recent collection of his political writings runs to well over six hundred pages, without including his private letters, extensive diaries, or speeches at the Constitutional Convention.[24] It is also true that Morris never held as high an office under the Constitution as the more famous founders did. (Franklin was too old and ill to hold high office by the time the new government was formed, but his fame as a founder had long since been secured by his services during the revolution.) As one scholar writes, Morris "played only a small part on the stage of honor he helped to build."[25] Then again, the posts that Morris did hold under the Constitution—minister to France and senator—were not exactly negligible. Moreover, it seems likely that Jefferson would be widely remembered today "merely" for having drafted the Declaration of Independence, even if he had never become president, whereas Morris's penning of the Constitution has not proven sufficient to assure his legacy.

A final common explanation for Morris's obscurity lies in his disenchantment with the state of American politics toward the end of his life, which eventually grew so deep that he advocated the secession of the North from the union. Melanie Miller, the editor of the Gouverneur Morris Papers, admits that "though Morris was passionate in his love of America . . . the faint tinge of 'traitor' seems to hang about him in his last years and has helped to push him off the stage."[26] As the present author has endeavored to demonstrate in a previous book, however, almost all the founders who lived into the nineteenth century—or even to the dawn of the new century, like Washington—grew deeply disillusioned with America's constitutional order; Madison was virtually the only exception on this score.[27] It is true that few of the other founders went so far as to support disunion, but even here Morris was not entirely alone. Jefferson, in particular, came very close to doing so.[28]

Perhaps the true cause of Morris's obscurity lies in some combination of these factors, or all of them, or perhaps it is simply a result of the vagaries of fortune. This puzzle is made all the more confounding, however, by the fact that Morris was a more forthright and eloquent critic of slavery than any of the founding "big six." In an age when we have become uncomfortable lauding Jefferson, Madison, or Washington too unabashedly because of their complicity in this institution, Morris would seem to be all the more attractive. Even leaving aside everything else that he did—which adds up to quite a lot—one would think that penning the Constitution and delivering the strongest antislavery orations at the Philadelphia Convention would be sufficient to assure Morris a place near the top of any list of the nation's most illustrious founders—at least on a par with, say, Aaron Burr, whose main claim to fame is having shot someone important. One can only hope that someday he will be given his due.

This book centers on Morris's contributions to the formation of the US Constitution. The Philadelphia Convention, it should be noted, was not Morris's only foray into constitution-making. He was also one of the chief framers of the New York state constitution of 1777; he proposed a number of reforms to the Continental Congress and signed the Articles of Confederation; and during his time in Paris, he both commented extensively on the French constitution of 1791 and drafted a potential French constitution of his own design. The following chapters occasionally draw on these efforts, as well as on Morris's other writings, speeches, letters, and diaries, in order to form a fuller view of what we might call his constitutional vision. The main focus, however, always remains on his speeches and actions in Philadelphia. The book begins with an overview of Morris's life (chapter 1) and role at the Philadelphia Convention (chapter 2). It then examines his views and contributions with respect to federalism and the role of the states (chapter 3), the Senate (chapter 4), the House of Representatives (chapter 5), presidential selection (chapter 6), the presidency itself (chapter 7), the judiciary (chapter 8), slavery (chapter 9), and the Constitution's preamble (chapter 10). The epilogue considers Morris's late-life disillusionment with the state of American politics, and the appendix includes the text of three of Morris's longest and most important speeches at the Philadelphia Convention—one on the Senate, one on the presidency, and one on slavery.

Although we now suffer from something of an embarrassment of riches as far as biographies of Morris are concerned, none of these works devotes more than a chapter to Morris's influence on the Constitution.[29] To date there have only been three extended studies of the topic: two unpublished doctoral dissertations and Treanor's lengthy law review article.[30] Given Morris's central role in shaping the Constitution, the paucity of work on the subject is striking.[31] Virtually every statement that James Madison ever made about the Constitution has by now been parsed nearly to death, and it seems only appropriate that the individual who has a fair claim to being the charter's other "father" be accorded at least a fraction of that attention.

Every reader will undoubtedly find something to dislike in Morris's constitutional vision. His privileging of property and wealth will surely be anathema to many on the political left, for instance, while his unflinching embrace of a powerful and far-reaching national government will just as surely rankle those on the right. (Those figures, like Morris, who were often deemed "conservative" among the founding generation would fit poorly within today's conservative movement.) Few observers anywhere on today's political spectrum would countenance senators, and perhaps even the president, serving for life. Morris's arguments were not always persuasive, and on a few occasions, they were not even plausible.

Still, there are many respects in which Morris's vision was astoundingly prescient. He saw as clearly as anyone in Philadelphia the need for a powerful executive with a popular mandate within America's constitutional order; the indispensability of an independent judiciary armed with the power of judicial review; the central role that parties would come to play in American politics; the myriad benefits that commerce and industry would usher in; and the unfathomable evils that slavery would visit on American life. As one commentator rather nicely puts it, "Though Morris' visage was never carved into a mountain, immortalized in marble on the National Mall, or emblazoned on legal tender, our America—this cosmopolitan, materialist, commercial republic we call home—is in no small part his monument. . . . The worldly patron Founder of cities, trade, materialism, wit, pleasure, and style, Morris stood athwart history and waved it in. . . . [Those] weary of churchy, censorious New Englanders and stiff-backed Virginians infatuated with their humid plantations, towering abstractions, and lofty but compromised ideals will find Morris' principled, jaunty cosmopolitanism a rush of fresh air."[32]

Regardless of how one ultimately assesses Morris's vision, it is impossible to fully understand the Constitution—or the government that has resulted from it—without appreciating the central role that he played in shaping it.

1. The Penman's Story: A Brief Biography

It is common for biographers to claim that their chosen subject's life contained all the elements of a great novel or movie. In Morris's case this claim happens to be quite true, although the movie would likely require an R rating. Morris's sixty-four years were marked by copious amounts of violence and political conflict, sex and love, money and foreign intrigue. He knew most of the great figures of the age—including not only Washington and Franklin, Madison and Jefferson, Hamilton and John Jay, John Marshall and James Monroe, but also George III and William Pitt, Louis XVI and Marie Antoinette, Lafayette and Talleyrand, Jacques Necker and Germaine de Staël—and counted many of them as close friends or political opponents (or both). He was an active participant in two of the great revolutions of the modern age, and through it all he lived with singular gusto. He scalded an arm and lost a leg, spent the winter at Valley Forge, earned a fortune, attended the convening of the Estates General, made love in a convent, advised a president and a king (and tried to help the latter escape his country), hid friends from the guillotine, planned a great city and an ambitious canal, and capped it all off by marrying a woman whom he loved and fathering a son whom he adored. Few lives have ever been fuller.

Morris was born on his family's manor in New York on either January 30 or 31, 1752.[1] His parents were Lewis Morris, an admiralty judge, and Sarah Gouverneur, Lewis's second wife. The Morris family had served at a high level in the colonial governments of New York and New Jersey for three generations, and the Gouverneurs were prominent landowners and merchants of Huguenot stock. As one scholar remarks, "It was as aristocratic a pedigree as anyone in the new world could claim."[2] Morris was christened "Gouverneur" after his mother's surname, and the foreign first name seems to have lent him a slightly exotic aura. It is not entirely clear, incidentally, how the name was pronounced. A distant descendant of Morris indicated that the pronunciation was anglicized to "Governor," while Abigail Adams, who sometimes spelled names phonetically, rendered it "Goveneer."³ At any rate, it does *not* seem to have been pronounced like the French *gouverneur*.

Morris had three half-brothers and a half-sister by his father—all more than two decades older than him—along with four full sisters. His oldest half-brother, also named Lewis, became a member of the Continental Congress and a signer of the Declaration of Independence, while another half-brother, Staats Long, became a general in the British army and a member of Parliament. Morris's half-siblings were displeased by their father's second marriage, and upon his death—which came when Gouverneur was just ten years old—the lion's share of the family estate went to them. Morris was thus left to the care of his mother, and to largely make his own way in the world despite his blue-blooded lineage.

The manor on which Morris grew up, Morrisania, was a magnificent one, encompassing the southwest portion of what is now the Bronx. The initial plot was procured by Morris's great-grandfather, yet another Lewis Morris, upon his arrival in the New World in the mid-seventeenth century, fresh from fighting in Oliver Cromwell's armies. (He purchased it from a Dutch farmer named Jonas Bronck, which is where the Bronx got its name.) The Morris family eventually expanded the estate to nearly two thousand acres, spanning the area from the Harlem River to the East River and stretching all the way up to what is now 180th Street. The two-story, nine-room manor house stood on a hill toward the south end of the estate and enjoyed a commanding view of Long Island Sound.⁴ Among the house's most impressive features was its library, which was one of the largest anywhere in America; Ezra Stiles, the president of Yale, judged at one point that Morrisania's library was second only to Harvard's, though it was later plundered by British troops during the Revolutionary War.⁵ The bulk of the property devolved on Staats Long when Morris's mother died in 1786, but Morris purchased it for himself soon thereafter and kept it for the remainder of his life; he would eventually die in the same room in which he had been born. Alas, Morrisania was torn down in the early twentieth century, though Morris also owned a summer house near what is now Gouverneur, New York, that still stands.

Relatively little is known about Morris's youth beyond the basics of his schooling. As a child he attended the French school of John Peter Tétard, a Swiss-born clergyman, in New Rochelle, where he learned the French language that would stand him in good stead later in life. At age nine he went on to the Philadelphia Academy, which had been founded by Benjamin Franklin a decade earlier and was one of the finest preparatory schools in the United States. He began attending King's College—now Columbia University—in 1764; at twelve years old he was the youngest student there, three years younger than most of his classmates. He does not seem to have been a particularly diligent student, but he was very bright and caught on quickly, excelling particularly in math and Latin.[6] Morris received a bachelor's degree in 1768 and gave a commencement oration on "Wit and Beauty"; three years later, when he received a (largely honorary) master's degree from King's, he spoke on "Love." It was during his college years, while visiting his family at Morrisania in 1766, that Morris suffered the first of his disfiguring injuries. A kettle of boiling water was accidentally overturned on his right arm, and the scalding was so severe that he was forced to spend the next year at home convalescing. He would have nothing but scar tissue on his forearm for the remainder of his life.

After college, Morris proceeded to read law at the office of one of the leading figures of the New York bar, William Smith. The position turned out to be a propitious one, as it enabled Morris to make some crucial connections: John Jay and Robert R. Livingston worked in Smith's office, and they both went on to become important political figures as well as Morris's lifelong friends.[7] During his time as a clerk Morris published his first essay, written in opposition to an issue of bills of credit—paper money—by New York's colonial legislature, which earned him a reputation as an expert on public finance despite his youth.[8] Morris was licensed as a lawyer in 1771, at the age of nineteen, at which point he plunged headfirst into the fields of law and business, as well as New York's social life, for the next four years.

Morris had much to recommend him on all these fronts. To begin with, he had a family name, a first-rate education, and a sharp mind; one historian describes him as a "fortunate amalgam of the aristocrat and the man of talent."[9] He also had good looks (aside from his arm), a rich voice, a powerful build, and an imposing stature. Like George Washington, Morris was well over six feet tall in an era when the average American man stood closer to five and a half feet. In fact, their frames were so similar that Jean-Antoine Houdon, the greatest sculptor of the age, later asked Morris to stand as the body double for a statue of Washington that had been commissioned by the Virginia state legislature.[10] (The original statue can still be seen in the rotunda of the capitol building in Richmond, and dozens of casts taken from the original have spread around the country and indeed the world—including the foyer of the building in which this author's office sits.) So striking was Morris's height that he was nicknamed "Tall Boy" in some circles. He was further graced with charisma, a keen sense of humor, and confidence to spare. Theodore Roosevelt writes that "he ranked as a wit among men, as a beau among women. He was equally sought for dances and dinners. He was a fine scholar and a polished gentleman; a capital storyteller; and had just a touch of erratic levity that served to render him still more charming."[11] Though Morris seemed destined for a life of comfort and ease, that destiny was soon upended.

Morris's world was torn asunder when he was just twenty-three years old by the outbreak of hostilities between Britain and the American colonies.[12] The war hit New York particularly hard thanks to repeated British attacks, a protracted occupation, and a deeply divided populace. Many of Morris's family members and close friends—including his mother, at least two of his sisters, and his mentor William Smith—remained loyal to the crown, and Morrisania stood behind British lines for most of the war. Morris's biographers frequently claim that, as a "conservative," he was slow to support the revolutionary cause, but in fact he embraced the idea of independence right around the same time as did the bulk of his fellow patriots.[13] From the surviving record, it appears that there was no one moment of epiphany for Morris, but that over the course of 1775 and the early months of 1776 he gradually came to the conclusion that continued subjection to British rule was no longer compatible with America's security, liberty, and prosperity.[14] Once his mind was made up he never flinched in supporting the American cause, even at great personal cost, though he was sometimes suspected of having Tory sympathies because of his family connections.

In the immediate wake of the battles of Lexington and Concord, Morris was elected to the first New York Provincial Congress, which convened in New York City in May 1775. Despite his youth, he served on a number of important committees, including one that greeted George Washington as he crossed the Hudson River on his way to take command of the Continental Army in Cambridge. This was Morris's first encounter with the individual whom he would come to admire more than any other; it would not be too much to say that Washington became Morris's hero.[15] In many respects they were an unlikely pair, with the Virginian's dignified reserve and unbending rectitude contrasting with the New Yorker's irrepressible boldness and worldly rakishness. However, Morris was always willing to fight vigorously for Washington's needs and interests, whether as general or as president, and Washington came to rely on and respect Morris's abilities. The two seem to have enjoyed each other's company as well, and eventually they became not just political associates but personal friends.

Morris also served in the third New York Provincial Congress, which met in Fishkill the following May. He advocated that they instruct the state's delegation to the Second Continental Congress in Philadelphia—a delegation that included Morris's half-brother Lewis—to support independence, but he could not convince enough of his fellow representatives to go along. (New York ended up being the only state to abstain from the vote for independence on July 2.) He did, however, help to convince the congress that a new constitution for New York should be drafted, and that a fourth congress should be elected to do it.

The fourth New York Provincial Congress, of which Morris was once again a member, met in White Plains on July 9, 1776. This time the congress voted immediately and unanimously to instruct New York's delegation to the Continental Congress to sign the recent Declaration of Independence, and the next day it resolved itself into New York's first constitutional convention. On August 1, a committee was formed to draft a new state constitution. Although the committee was comprised of thirteen members, the lion's share of the work was done by Morris, John Jay, and Robert R. Livingston—the three friends who had worked together in William Smith's law office. Jay prepared the initial draft, but Morris and Livingston also played critical roles in shaping the document.[16] The convention was harried from place to place by the movements of British troops, but the drafting committee eventually made its report in Kingston on March 12, 1777, and after five weeks of deliberation the convention adopted the new constitution with only one dissenting vote. New York's constitution was formulated slightly later than most of the other state constitutions, and it differed from many of the others in several respects, particularly in its inclusion of a strong executive, fairly high property qualifications for voting, and no separate bill of rights. Morris supported each of these distinctive features, though he fought for the governor's powers to be still greater than they ended up being.

While Morris's stance on the structure and powers of the new government exhibited his conservative side, on two crucial provisions related to civil liberties he was notably progressive. Whereas Jay wished to "erect a wall of brass around the country for the exclusion of Catholics," Morris successfully fought to preserve religious toleration within the state.[17] Morris was sometimes suspected of being a freethinker because of his playboy lifestyle, but in fact he seems to have earnestly believed in a benevolent God who intervened in human affairs, even if not the full panoply of Christian tenets.[18] Regardless, he was a firm and lifelong supporter of complete religious liberty. The following year he boldly declared in a public letter that "the religion of America is the religion of all mankind. Any person may worship in the manner he thinks most agreeable to the Deity . . . neither have we the least solicitude to exalt any one sect or profession above another."[19]

Morris also sought to include a provision in the New York constitution urging the state's future legislatures to "take the most effectual measures consistent with the public safety, and the private property of individuals, for abolishing domestic slavery within the [state], so that in future ages, every human being who breathes the air of this State, shall enjoy the privileges of a freeman."[20] This farsighted proposal—made all the more remarkable by the fact that New York had the largest enslaved population of any northern state—was supported by Jay but opposed by Livingston, who managed to kill the motion. New York would not pass a gradual abolition law until 1799, and slavery would not finally be eradicated from the state until 1827.[21]

New York's constitution ended up having as much influence on the US Constitution as any state constitution save that of Massachusetts, and Morris's extensive contributions to its framing would prove to be valuable experience for the Philadelphia Convention a decade later.[22]

Morris took his first major step onto the national stage in January 1778 when he became a delegate to the Continental Congress, which was then meeting in York, Pennsylvania. Upon taking his seat he departed almost immediately for Valley Forge as part of committee of five that was assigned to consult with General Washington about the army's considerable needs. Morris was shocked by what he saw at the camp: "The Skeleton of an Army presents itself to our Eyes in a naked starving Condition out of Health out of Spirits," he lamented to Jay. But his confidence in Washington and the troops remained undiminished, and he quickly added that "next Campaign I beleive [sic] we shall banish these troublesome Fellows"—that is, the British troops who were then occupying Philadelphia.[23] Morris worked tirelessly, both during the two months that he spent at the encampment and after his return to the congress, to reorganize the army's supply chain and to secure half-pay for the troops for seven years after the war's conclusion. Indeed, he was arguably Washington's most effective advocate in the Continental Congress during the two years that he spent there.

The congress returned to Philadelphia in July after the British withdrew from the city, and over the next year and a half Morris served on no fewer than sixty-five committees and was charged with drafting the reports for more than twenty of them.[24] He later recalled that "I led then the most laborious life, which can be imagined."[25] Among other assignments, Morris was charged with drafting the instructions for Benjamin Franklin upon his appointment as the first official American minister to France and with rebuffing the Carlisle Commission that was sent by the British to negotiate peace terms short of full American independence.[26] These labors did not, however, interrupt his usual extracurricular pursuits. Jay, who was also a member of the congress, reported to Livingston with a touch of both reproach and envy that Morris was "daily employed in making Oblations to Venus," the Roman goddess of love and sex.[27]

On July 9, 1778, Morris signed the Articles of Confederation—the first attempt at a national constitution for the United States—on behalf of New York, whose legislature had ratified the charter a few months earlier. Morris would eventually become one of only five individuals to sign both of America's national constitutions—the Articles and the Constitution itself—along with Daniel Carroll, John Dickinson, Robert Morris, and Roger Sherman. Morris regarded the Articles as an improvement on the existing, still somewhat provisional Continental Congress, but nonetheless woefully inadequate to address the nation's needs. Not long after signing this compact, he complained that the government's power "exists almost by meer courtesy and sufferance" of the state legislatures and that the union was in danger of becoming "what our enemies long since declared it was, a meer rope of sand."[28] To Nathanael Greene, the gifted general with whom he had worked at Valley Forge, Morris wrote: "That Congress have not proper powers I see, I feel, and I lament. Their Ministers have the arduous task before them to govern without power . . . They must persuade where others command, and the strong phalanx of private interest, with the impetuous sallies of private politics and party, encounters them at every step."[29]

In hopes of remedying this lack of "proper powers," Morris proposed a variety of ambitious reforms to the Continental Congress's methods of conducting business, including steps to institute a more vigorous executive, reorganize the treasury, consolidate the states' debts, establish a single national currency, and give the congress a more effective taxing capability.[30] These proposals were way ahead of their time, however, and none were implemented beyond the establishment of a new treasury board. Once again, Morris's political vision was far more expansive than those of most of his colleagues. It would take nearly another decade of ineffectual governance to persuade the country to accept a more vigorous national power akin to the one that Morris advocated in the late 1770s.

Although Morris was an able administrator, he was not well liked by everyone in the Continental Congress. As one of the youngest, most impatient, and most opinionated of the representatives, he rubbed some of his more seasoned colleagues the wrong way. One member of the New York delegation likened him to an "Elephant in War" that is often "more destructive to his Friends than his Antagonists."[31] Fittingly for someone of Morris's resolutely national vision, the New York legislature declined to reappoint him chiefly because they believed that he had neglected the state's parochial interests, particularly its disputed claims to the New Hampshire Grants—that is, the territory that eventually became the state of Vermont. Morris's tenure in the congress ended in November 1779. Given that New York City was still occupied by the British at the time, he chose to remain in Philadelphia, where he could continue his active social life and resume the law and business practices that he had put on hold at the outset of the war. Alas, all these pursuits would soon be interrupted once again, this time by a different kind of misfortune.

On May 14, 1780, Morris was setting out for a journey in his phaeton—a kind of light, open carriage—and, as one account had it, "the Horses taking a Fright ran away in the Street, struck the Carriage against a Post, broke it all to Pieces and in the Shock fractured Mr. Morris' Ancle to such a Degree that it became necessary to take off his Leg imediately."[32] The accident occurred near his lodging on the corner of High (now Market) Street and Third Street, just three blocks from the Pennsylvania State House where Morris would play such an important role seven years later. There were persistent rumors throughout Morris's life that the carriage accident was merely a convenient cover story and that he had actually shattered his ankle jumping out a bedroom window in order to avoid the wrath of an ill-timed husband; this latter version of the story cannot be disproven, but nor is there any evidence to corroborate it.

In any case, Morris's regular physician was out of town, and the two who were called in his stead recommended immediate amputation just below the knee, to which Morris submitted without a murmur. When his regular physician returned he was aghast at the decision and insisted that the leg could have been saved, but by that point there was nothing that could be done. Morris's good humor remained firmly intact despite the setback. The day after the accident, when a friend tried to console him by pointing out the beneficial effects that adversity often has on one's character, Morris replied, "My good Sir, you argue the matter so handsomely, and point out so clearly the advantages of being without legs, that I am almost tempted to part with the other."[33]

After a few months of recovery, Morris was fitted with a simple oaken peg, which became something of a hallmark for the remainder of his life. (The leg is now on display at the New-York Historical Society, alongside a leg brace that Franklin Delano Roosevelt wore on account of his polio.) Morris quickly adjusted to the wooden leg, and aside from an occasional slip in the mud, it did little to slow him down. He continued to walk long distances and to dance and ride with aplomb, and as late as 1807—when he was fifty-five—he shot the rapids of the St. Lawrence River in a canoe. Nor did the false leg curtail his appeal among women; on the contrary, for many it appears to have only enhanced his chic. When news of the incident reached John Jay, who was abroad by this point as the first American minister to Spain, he wrote to their mutual friend Robert Morris, "Gouvnrs. Leg has been a Tax on my Heart. I am almost tempted to wish he had lost *something* else."[34]

That other notable Morris of the founding era, Robert—no relation to Gouverneur—would play a key role in the next stage of our Morris's life. They had become fast friends while serving together in the Continental Congress, and they would both go on to represent Pennsylvania at the Constitutional Convention. Robert Morris was a financial whiz and perhaps the richest man in America, and in the summer of 1781 he was appointed the nation's Superintendent of Finance, a role that earned him the sobriquet "The Financier of the Revolution."[35] One of his first actions in this position was to bring Gouverneur on board as his deputy. The two Morrises would work closely together in the finance department for the next three and a half years, through the conclusion of the peace with Britain. Toward the end of this period Robert said of Gouverneur that "I could do nothing without him" and that "he has more Virtue than he shews & more Consistency than any body believes."[36] The pair quickly became the most powerful executive officers that the young nation had ever seen—though, given the state of the national government under the Articles of Confederation, this is perhaps not saying all that much.

The Morrises' task was nothing less than to save the national credit, and with it the revolution itself. By the time that they took up their posts, the paper money issued by the Confederation had depreciated to the point of near worthlessness, and the nation's ability to borrow money—and hence to keep the troops supplied and in the field—was in dire jeopardy. As Gouverneur wrote to Jay, "Finance my Friend. The whole of what remains in the American Revolution grounds there."[37] The Morrises worked together to forge a comprehensive financial plan that included the issuing of a temporary currency backed by Robert's own funds (known as "Morris notes"), a slew of new taxes, and above all a chartered national bank, the first in the United States. The plan not only had its intended effect of restoring public credit to a level at which the war could continue to be waged, but also served as a blueprint for the financial plan that Alexander Hamilton formulated a decade later. One historian describes the 1782 "Report on Public Credit," which was drafted by Gouverneur, as "the most important single state paper on public credit ever written prior to Hamilton's."[38]

Gouverneur also drew up a plan for a new national currency to replace the many different certificates and foreign coins that were then being used in various states. His proposal for a decimal system was the first of its kind, though it was somewhat complicated and would later be simplified by Thomas Jefferson before being implemented. He also, however, proposed that the term "dollar" (after the widely used Spanish dollar) be adopted for the basic unit of currency, and he invented the word "cent" to denote one of the smaller coins. As one scholar notes, this was surely "Morris's most influential contribution to the English language," surpassing even the preamble's "We the People of the United States."[39]

While the Morrises' efforts to rescue the nation's finances were vital to the revolution's success, the pair came perilously close to negating all the good that they had done through a colossal error in judgment. They had long hoped that their financial policies would serve as a springboard for the creation of a more vigorous national government, but whatever pressures toward centralization may have existed at the height of the war began to diminish as the war came to a close. In the early months of 1783, the two of them, along with Alexander

Hamilton, sought to capitalize on unrest among army officers about the continued absence of their promised pay—the so-called Newburgh conspiracy—in order to strengthen the national government's powers.[40] On New Year's Day of 1783, Gouverneur wrote to Jay noting that "the Army have Swords in their Hands" and hinting that they should use them, or at least threaten to do so: "altho I think it probable that much of convulsion will ensue yet it must terminate in giving to government that power without which government is but a name."[41] Historians have long debated precisely what role the Morrises and Hamilton played in this affair. It seems unlikely that they hoped for an actual military coup, but seeking to employ an angry army as a goad to political action was nonetheless the height of imprudence. Thankfully, George Washington managed to disarm the incipient cabal through a speech in which he famously donned his spectacles, thereby reducing his fellow officers to tears.

Morris left the finance department after the war's conclusion and devoted himself to private pursuits for the next several years. These pursuits were many and varied: with the British troops gone, he was able to visit his mother at Morrisania for the first time in nearly seven years; he returned to his law practice; he became a junior partner in many of Robert Morris's business ventures; he engaged in land speculation, purchasing large tracts in upstate New York; he became a charter member of Benjamin Franklin's Society for Political Inquiries; and he continued to enjoy the life of a bachelor in what was then America's largest city. Morris's mother died in January 1786, at which point Morrisania devolved on his half-brother Staats Long, who was then living in England. It took Morris some time to assemble the necessary funds, but he was finally able to purchase the manor for himself in April 1787, though he would not take up full-time residence there until after his return from Europe nearly a dozen years later. Until the beginning of 1787 Morris believed that he had left politics behind for good, but readers of this book already know that he was soon drawn back into the whirlwind.

In the summer of 1787, of course, Morris attended the Constitutional Convention, which would prove to be the most consequential few months of his life. Given that most of the remainder of this book focuses on these few months, however, we can forego discussion of them here. After the Convention's close, Morris hoped that the Constitution would be ratified, but he did little to fight on its behalf, for reasons that will be pursued in this book's epilogue. As

Alexander Hamilton set about assembling a select group of authors to write a series of authoritative essays in favor of the proposed constitution for the New York papers—the essays that became *The Federalist*—his thoughts naturally turned to his brilliant friend and fellow New Yorker, particularly since Morris was also close to Jay, another member of the team. Morris later recalled, "I was warmly pressed by Hamilton to assist in writing the Federalist, which I declined."[42] It was only after being turned down by Morris that Hamilton approached James Madison, who thereby became what one scholar describes as "the most consequential back-up choice in the history of political theory."[43] One can only speculate about how *The Federalist* might have turned out differently if Morris had agreed to contribute to it. It is likely that the project would have benefitted from his boldness and fire; it is certain that Morris would be far more famous today than he currently is.[44]

Morris did take one step, however, that he deemed as important as any other to ensure the Constitution's success. Just a month after the Convention's close, and well before any states had ratified the charter, he wrote to George Washington to urge him to accept his inevitable elevation to the presidency:

> Should the Idea prevail that you would not accept of the Presidency, it would prove fatal in many Parts. Truth is, that your great and decided Superiority leads Men willingly to put you in a Place which . . . they would not willingly put any other Person. . . . I will add my Conviction that of all Men you are best fitted to fill that Office. Your cool steady Temper is *indispensibly necessary* to give a firm and manly Tone to the new Government. To constitute a well poised political Machine is the Task of us common Workmen; but to set it in Motion requires still greater Qualities. . . . you therefore must I say *must* mount this Seat.[45]

Morris was soon able to press his case in person, as well, when he and Robert Morris stayed at Mount Vernon for a few evenings on their way to Richmond to attend to Robert's interests in the tobacco trade.[46]

Morris remained in Virginia for seven months, and toward the end of the trip he made time to attend some of the state's ratifying convention, which lasted from June 2 to 27, 1788. Virginia's was arguably the most momentous and illustrious of the state conventions, pitting James Madison, Edmund Randolph, and a young John Marshall against Patrick Henry, George Mason, and a young James Monroe, among others. Although the delegates agreed at the outset to proceed methodically through the Constitution, in fact they ended up ranging chaotically across time and space, thanks in no small part to Patrick Henry's Mad-Hatter style of oratory. The convention's intellectual wanderings prompted Morris to dash off an extemporaneous poem for John Marshall:

> The State's determined Resolution
> Was to discuss the Constitution
> For this the Members come together
> Melting with Zeal and sultry Weather,
> And here to their eternal Praise
> To find it's Hist'ry spend three Days
> The next three Days they nobly roam
> Thru ev'ry Region far from Home
> Call in the Grecian Swiss Italian
> The Roman Dutch Rapscullion
> Fellows who freedom never knew
> To tell us what we ought to do
> The next three Days they kindly dip yee
> Deep in the River Mississippi
> Nine Days thus spent eer they begin
> Let us suppose them fairly in
> And then resolve me gentle friend
> How many Months before they End.[47]

It was not uncommon for Morris to pen witty little poems, though they were more often romantic rather than political in nature.

Morris returned north in July, stopping at Mount Vernon for several days once again en route.[48] As autumn approached he decided to embark on an even more far-flung journey: he would travel to Paris in order to pursue various commercial ventures, both on his own behalf and on behalf of Robert Morris. Before leaving, however, he procured a bevy of letters of introduction from Washington to prominent figures in France, England, and Holland. Washington showed a rare touch of jocularity in his letter to the Marquis de Chastellux, remarking, "as for Mr Morris, only let him be once fairly presented to your French Ladies, and I answer for it, he will not leave the worst impression in the world of the American character, for taciturnity & improper reserve. I rely upon it he will make his way good."[49] Armed with these letters,

Morris embarked from Philadelphia in the midst of a snowstorm on December 18, just a few months before the new government formed by the Constitution would convene for the first time. Little did he know that he would remain in Europe for the next decade and play an active role in a second great political revolution—a much bloodier one—while he was there.

After forty dark, storm-filled days at sea, Morris reached the port of Le Havre on January 27, 1789, and made his way from there to Paris. His initial mission was simply to mend some of Robert Morris's now-floundering business affairs and to build his own fortune, principally through more land speculation and the purchasing of American war debt. In fact, however, he was about to undertake what one historian describes as "ten years of business, travel, diplomacy, love-making, and adventure in Europe that left even his friend Hamilton gasping with envy."[50] Happily for posterity's sake, soon after his arrival in Paris Morris began keeping a diary, which he continued to keep, with just a few interruptions, for the remainder of his life.[51] Morris's diary is remarkable for its candor, humor, and keen observations of people and events, and it has proven to be among the most valuable firsthand accounts of the French Revolution.[52]

With his connections, charm, and command of the French language, Morris quickly found a warm welcome at the salons, gardens, and dinner tables of the Parisian elite. One of his first orders of business was to seek out Thomas Jefferson, with whom he had "only a slight Acquaintance" before his arrival.[53] Jefferson remained in Paris for another eight months, and the two saw much of each other during that time.[54] They shared a taste for fine wines, lavish meals, and political gossip, though a mutual friend recorded that "Jefferson blushed to the temples at some of Morris's immodest expressions."[55] Morris also quickly found that, as he put it in his diary, "He and I differ in our Systems of Politics. He, with all the Leaders of Liberty here, are desirous of annihilating Distinctions of Order. How far such Views may be right respecting Mankind in general is I think extremely problematical, but with Respect to this Nation I am sure it is wrong and cannot eventuate well."[56] The two certainly did not see eye to eye with respect to the budding French Revolution, and they would be even more sharply at odds regarding American politics when Jefferson became president.

Morris's cool appraisals of his many prominent acquaintances from these years are a delight. In a letter to Washington he described King Louis XVI as a "small beer Character" who "at the slightest shew of Opposition . . . gives up every Thing, and every Person"; Jacques Necker, the finance minister, as "a very poor financier" whose plans were invariably "feeble and ineptious"; and the Count de Montmorin, the minister of foreign affairs, as a man who "means well, very well. But he means it feebly."[57] Morris was fond of the Marquis de Lafayette, whom he knew from their days at Valley Forge, but in the face of the unraveling of French society he worried that Lafayette was "very much below the Business he has undertaken and if the Sea runs high he will be unable to hold the Helm."[58] Upon meeting the soon-to-be-legendary (and notorious) diplomat Talleyrand, Morris presciently recorded in his diary that he "appears to me a sly, cool, cunning and ambitious Man. I know not why Conclusions so disadvantageous to him are formed in my Mind, but so it is and I cannot help it."[59] He thought more highly of Necker's daughter, the brilliant salon hostess Germaine de Staël, whom he deemed "a Woman of wonderful Wit and above vulgar Prejudices of every Kind," even if they frequently disagreed on political matters.[60] He wondered in his diary whether he might be able to "stimulate her Curiosity to the Experiment of what can be effected by the Native of a new World who has left one of his Legs behind him," though he does not seem to have succeeded in this endeavor.[61]

Morris's deepest attachment during his time in France was to the countess and salon hostess Adélaïde de Flahaut, with whom he had the most intimate and protracted romantic tie of his life, with the possible exception of his marriage.[62] The two met at Versailles in March 1789, and their somewhat tumultuous affair began a few months later. At the time she was twenty-eight, her husband sixty-three. Her young son had been fathered by her longtime lover, who was none other than Talleyrand. Morris's affair with "Adèle," as she was often called, lasted on and off for more than three years. During those years they devoted a substantial portion of their days to talking together, dining together, going on walks together, attending the theater and the opera together, and above all making love at every available opportunity—in her apartment in the Louvre (which, while it housed the royal art collection, was still mostly residential), in his carriage, in gardens and alleyways, even in the waiting room of the convent where Adèle's former governess was a nun. It is clear from his diary that Morris genuinely loved her, although at one point Adèle feared that she might be pregnant and proposed that they marry, and he quickly demurred. (It is unclear how she envisioned her current husband, who was still very much alive, fitting into this plan.) Eventually Adèle was forced to flee Paris in order to escape the guillotine, and she and Morris drifted apart.

After Adèle's departure Morris enjoyed a succession of erotic adventures as he traveled around Europe, taking full advantage of the fact that the boundaries of marriage were far more fluid there than they were in the United States.[63] Although Morris was proud of his prowess in the bedroom, it should be stressed that he was not simply a womanizer, at least by this point in his life. (This question is harder to assess with regard to his younger years, since without a diary the record is more sparse.) He sincerely enjoyed female companionship, and he was drawn to intelligence and wit more than to youth and beauty. Of course, he made no real stand for women's social or political equality, any more than the other American founders did, but he did respect women as serious thinkers and consistently seek out their views on politics and business in a way that Jefferson, for instance, never would have dreamed of doing.[64]

On May 5, 1789, just two months after his arrival in Paris, Morris attended the opening of the Estates General, having gotten a ticket at the last minute. This convening of the representatives of the clergy, nobility, and commoners for the first time in 175 years marked the beginning of the revolution that would engulf France, and indeed much of Europe, for the next decade. Jefferson welcomed the revolution with open arms and continued to champion it even through the Terror, but Morris was far leerier. Indeed, Hippolyte Taine, the great nineteenth-century French historian and critic of the revolution, claimed that Morris was one of just four observers who understood the character and scope of the revolution from the very beginning.[65]

Well before the revolution got underway, Morris sensed that a wholesale change in the nation's longstanding political order would unleash chaos rather than ushering in a new regime of ordered liberty. Back in February—a year and nine months before the publication of Edmund Burke's *Reflections on the Revolution in France*, one of the earliest and most famous attacks on the revolution—Morris had mused to William Carmichael, the American minister to Spain, "I have here the strangest Employment imaginable. A Republican and just as it were emerged from that Assembly which has formed one of the most republican of all republican Constitutions, I preach incessantly Respect for the Prince, Attention to the Rights of the Nobility, and Moderation not only in the Object but also in the Pursuit of it."[66] To be sure, Morris was far from an uncritical admirer of the old regime. On the contrary, he found the king and much of the nobility contemptible and the condition of the lower classes abominable, and he assured Washington that "the Leaders here are our Friends" and that the United States had "every Reason to wish that the Patriots may be successful."[67] However, Morris advocated gradual change toward a more limited constitutional monarchy rather than the sudden and sweeping change to a wholly republican order that the revolutionaries desired.

Many of these revolutionaries—and their American admirers, like Jefferson—assumed that France was simply following in America's footsteps by throwing off the yoke of a tyrannical monarchy and embracing free institutions, but Morris regarded the analogy with the United States as superficial and inapt. Whereas the United States had the benefit of a long history of self-government and a large middle class, France was saddled with a rigid social hierarchy and little but abstract theory to guide the new leaders. Morris remarked to Carmichael that the French seemed to "want an American Constitution . . . without reflecting, that they have not American citizens to support that constitution" and compared the revolutionaries who aspired to mimic the United States to "our young scholars [i.e., students], just fresh from the university, who would fain bring everything to the Roman standard."[68] He also wrote an extended essay elaborating on these points at the request of an unknown member of the Estates General.[69]

Morris continued to offer advice—some solicited and some not—to various French officials as they slowly set about drafting the nation's first written constitution, which was eventually adopted in September 1791. His advice was, however, emphatically not followed. Morris encouraged them to devise a constitution akin to Britain's, with a vigorous monarchy checked and balanced by a hereditary senate and a popularly elected assembly, but the National Assembly—the successor to the Estates General—instead settled on a weak monarchy and a unicameral legislature in an effort to better channel and implement the popular will.[70] Morris immediately declared to Washington that the new constitution was "inexecutable" and "good for Nothing."[71] He also wrote a memorandum for Louis XVI and his advisors and a draft of a royal speech that laid out the constitution's manifest flaws, but the king's counselors found the tone too severe and Morris's advice went unheeded.[72] Much as he expected, the constitution was scrapped in less than a year.

Morris's first diplomatic mission in Europe was far from a rousing success. The United States had not had a minister to Britain since John Adams's departure in February 1788, and there were a number of unresolved issues between the two nations involving trade, the continued British occupation of forts in the American northwest, and unpaid American debts to British creditors. President Washington asked Morris to travel to London to sound out the ministry about the possibility of reaching some kind of agreement on these matters, thereby making Morris the new nation's first known private agent to a foreign court.[73] Morris did his best, meeting and corresponding with Prime Minister William Pitt and the Duke of Leeds, Britain's foreign secretary, a number of times between March and September 1790. Little came of the negotiations, however, principally because the British had little to gain by an agreement with the United States at that point.[74] Morris ended up traveling to England a number of times during his decade in Europe, but he found the English "too cold, for my taste" and complained that "a tedious morning, a great dinner, a boozy afternoon, and dull evening, make the sum total of English life."[75]

Morris's next post would pose a far greater challenge—in fact, arguably as great a challenge as any American diplomat has ever faced—and this time he would carry it off as well as anyone could have reasonably expected. In January 1792, Morris was appointed the American minister to France, following in the footsteps of Benjamin Franklin and Thomas Jefferson.[76] His nomination was hotly contested in the Senate, both by Republicans who deemed him insufficiently friendly toward France and its revolution as well as by Federalists such as Roger Sherman who fretted that he was "an irreligious and profane man."[77]

The letter in which President Washington conveyed Morris's appointment also conveyed a series of warnings in the guise of reporting the charges that had been leveled against him in the Senate—for instance, that "the promptitude with w[hi]ch your brilliant, & lively imagination is displayed, allows too little time for deliberation, and correction" and that "it is indispensably necessary that more circumspection should be observed by our Representatives abroad than they conceive you are disposed to adopt."[78] In other words, now that he was an official American diplomat, Morris would need to be far more diplomatic. Morris quickly assured Washington that "*I now promise you that Circumspection of Conduct which has hitherto I acknowledge formed no Part of my Character*," although how fully he kept that promise is subject to debate.[79]

It would have been impossible for any foreign diplomat to have remained on good terms with the revolving door of factions that headed the French government during the heady days of the revolution, each more extreme and violent than the last. Over the course of the two and a half years that Morris served as the American minister, France had no fewer than eight different individuals at the head of foreign affairs, six of whom were denounced as traitors by the succeeding administration.[80] As Morris explained to Washington, "the Parties pass away like the Shadows in a Magic Lanthorn [i.e., lantern], & to be well with any one of them would in a short Period become Cause of unquencheable Hatred with the others."[81] Morris generally tried to remain aloof from the tumult while at the same time doing what he could to protect American citizens from arbitrary arrest, American commerce from unfavorable regulations, and American ships from French depredations. His regular reports to Secretary of State Jefferson and President Washington kept the American government abreast of the continuing flood of developments, and even today they remain among the most penetrating, faithful, and graphic accounts of the revolution to be found anywhere.

As Morris's ministry wore on, the chaos and violence that he witnessed were unspeakable. Near the end of his life he remarked, "My heart sickens at the recollection of those horrors which desolated France. That charming country, on which the bounty of heaven has lavished blessings, was the prey of monsters. To tell the crimes, everywhere and every hour perpetrated, would wound the soul of humanity, and shock the ear of modesty."[82] In the face of the Terror, Morris sheltered a number of imperiled individuals—among them Adélaïde de Flahaut and her son—in his home at various points, saving them from the guillotine. He was also involved in a series of attempts to help the king and queen escape Paris in the summer of 1792, though the king lost his nerve and the plot failed.[83] These acts of mercy may not have been as strictly neutral with regard to internal French politics as a diplomat should typically be, but it is difficult to fault Morris too severely for them, given the circumstances.

Morris himself faced some very real dangers. He was arrested twice, his house was searched on several occasions, and his mail was opened regularly, all in breach of normal diplomatic protocols. Given his known views on the unfolding revolution, it is not surprising that he was suspect in many quarters, and it took considerable courage to keep pushing for America's interests amid the bloodshed that surrounded him. Morris was in fact the only foreign minister who remained in France through the entirety of the Terror, although in May 1793 he did move from his house in Paris—488 rue de la Planche, on the left bank of the Seine in the Faubourg Saint-Germain—to a country house in Seine-Port, around thirty miles south of the city, in order to escape the chaos of the capital.

The various French ministries had long wished for Morris's recall, and Washington finally obliged them in the summer of 1794 as a sort of quid pro quo for the recall of the controversial French minister to the United States, Edmond-Charles Genêt. Morris was, frankly, thrilled to be "getting out of a wretched position," as he put it in a letter to the new secretary of state, Edmund Randolph, although he deemed his replacement as minister, James Monroe, "a person of mediocrity in every respect."[84] Many Republicans back in the United States had been displeased with Morris's appointment at the outset and remained so throughout the entirety of his tenure, but the individual whose opinion mattered most to him viewed his conduct far more favorably. "Whatever may have been his political Sentiments," Washington declared in a private note to himself a few years afterward, Morris "pursued steadily the honor & Interest of his C[oun]try with zeal and ability, & with respectful firmness asserted its rights."[85] Theodore Roosevelt later went even further, proclaiming that Morris's service as minister to France "forms one of the most brilliant chapters in our diplomatic annals," that "he successfully performed the most difficult task ever allotted to an American representative at a foreign capital," and indeed that "we have never had a foreign minister who deserved more honor than Morris."[86]

Morris departed France in the autumn of 1794, never to return. Rather than immediately head back to the United States, however, he spent the next four years traveling around Europe, spurred by a combination of business and pure curiosity. His wanderings took him through Switzerland, Hamburg, England, Scotland, the Netherlands, Prussia, Saxony, a variety of smaller German states, Bohemia, Austria, and Denmark. During his stops Morris frequently mingled with the political and social elite, including many French exiles. He spent time with Jacques Necker and Germaine de Staël in Switzerland, for instance, and while in England he met with King George III, William Pitt, and the young John Quincy Adams. In Austria he lobbied the emperor to release Lafayette from prison; Lafayette was eventually transferred to Hamburg, and Morris was present at his long-awaited discharge. (Morris also made a large personal loan to the Lafayette family, which was never repaid.)

Morris's hesitance to return to the United States appears to have stemmed in part from a desire to avoid being drafted into public service. In 1796, midway through his peregrinations, he wrote to his brother-in-law Samuel Ogden that "I am sure, that I could live more comfortably at Morrisania, than I can anywhere else," but "I had reason to apprehend being called again into public life were I in America . . . so long as I continue abroad, I can trust to the industry of my enemies for keeping me in a private station." Although Morris was still only in his mid-forties, he hoped to retire upon his return home: "Quietly to enjoy the advantages of those two constitutions, which I have had some share in framing"—that is, the constitutions of New York and the United States—"forms the summit of my ambition."[87]

Morris was right to surmise that his friends would want him to rejoin the political fray upon his return. In October 1798, Alexander Hamilton demanded of Rufus King, "Why does not Gouverneur Morris come home? His talents are wanted. Men like him do not superabound."[88] Morris departed Europe just five days later, and after a long and disagreeable journey he arrived in New York two days before Christmas. After spending two weeks in the city visiting with relatives and friends, including Hamilton, Morris returned to Morrisania and devoted the majority of the next year to unpacking his belongings, putting his affairs in order, and rebuilding the manor house. He also hosted a variety of visitors, some from abroad—including the Duc d'Orléans, the future King Louis Philippe—as well as a number of old friends. One of those old friends described Morris as "all hospitality. His wines are of superior quality and given with great liberality. His attachments to his own country and government have encreased by what he has seen in Europe."[89]

Morris's increased attachment to America's constitutional order did not prevent him from recognizing the difficulties that it was facing in the midst of the undeclared "Quasi-War" with France. During his absence the nation's political elite had divided into two parties that were sharply at odds with one another, the Federalists and Republicans, and the former group—with which Morris was naturally allied by outlook, temperament, and ties of friendship—was itself split between those who were loyal to President Adams and the "High Federalist" followers of Hamilton. Morris quickly recognized that this intraparty schism would pave the way for the ascendancy of the Republicans, and in December 1799 he turned to the one resource that he had always been able to count on, writing a desperate plea for Washington to emerge from his retirement and accept another nomination for the presidency.[90] Alas, Morris's great hero likely never even received this plea, for he died just five days later. The city of New York asked Morris to give its funeral oration, which he duly did on New Year's Eve of 1799.[91] Morris himself would soon reenter American politics, but he would prove unable to do what he believed only Washington could have done: save the Federalist party, and with it the nation's future.

One of New York's senators, James Watson, resigned his seat in March 1800, and the Federalist-controlled New York legislature selected Morris to fill the remaining three years of his term. Morris's reluctant return to American politics came just in time to participate in the move of the nation's capital from Philadelphia to Washington, DC. After relocating to the new, still-unfinished capital city, he told one European correspondent that "we want nothing here but houses, cellars, kitchens, well informed men, amiable women, and other little trifles of this kind, to make our city perfect . . . If then, you are desirous of coming to live at Washington, in order to confirm you in so fine a project, I hasten to assure you, that . . . there is no want of sites for magnificent hotels; that contemplated canals can bring a vast commerce to this place; that the wealth, which is its natural consequence, must attract the fine arts hither; in short, that it is the very best city in the world for a *future* residence."[92]

Morris's return to politics also came just in time for him to witness firsthand the spectacular and (as it turned out) permanent demise of the Federalist party, as the Republicans swept into the presidency and Congress in the election of 1800, where they would reign for the remainder of Morris's life and beyond. The presidential election ended up in an accidental tie in the electoral college between Jefferson and his running mate Aaron Burr, which was broken by the outgoing, Federalist-controlled House of Representatives. Many Federalists would have preferred to take their chances with the mercurial Burr rather than elevate their great rival Jefferson to the executive mansion, but Morris deemed the idea ill-advised—not, like Hamilton, because he regarded Burr as an unprincipled schemer, but rather simply because "it was evidently the Intention of our fellow Citizens to make Mr Jefferson the President" and "it seems proper to fulfill that Intention."[93] It took thirty-six ballots for the House to settle on Jefferson, and it is possible that in the midst of the balloting Jefferson made some kind of implicit deal with Morris in order gain the necessary Federalist support; certainly the two discussed the matter, but whether a deal was actually struck remains unclear.[94]

Morris was too independent-minded to always side with his party during his time in the Senate. He generally supported the Louisiana Purchase, for instance, even though most Federalists opposed it on the grounds that the states that would be carved out of the new territory would be overwhelmingly agricultural and Republican, thereby further diminishing the already-dwindling influence that commercial New England and the Federalist party wielded over national affairs.[95] For the most part, however, he was a harsh critic of President Jefferson, whom he accused of naively believing in "the perfectibility of man, the wisdom of mobs, and [the] moderation of Jacobins."[96] After dining with the president in April 1802, Morris commented briskly in his diary, "He is Utopia quite."[97] Like many Federalists, he also criticized Jefferson and the Republicans for hypocritically inflating the powers of the federal government and the presidency, which they had aimed to curb throughout the 1790s, now that they were in power. "When the Demos [i.e., Republicans] got into Power I ventured to foretell that they would do more to exalt the Executive in six months than the federalists would in as many years," he wrote to Hamilton in March 1802. "The fact has verified the Prediction."[98]

Morris's most noteworthy speeches on the Senate floor came in January 1802 in opposition to the repeal of the Judiciary Act of 1801. This act, passed by the Federalists in the waning days of the Adams administration, reorganized the federal judiciary and created a raft of new judgeships that Adams took it upon himself to fill with what became known as the "midnight judges." The judiciary was the last bastion of Federalist power within the federal government during the early years of Jefferson's presidency, and the Republicans sought to neutralize this stronghold by dismantling the Judiciary Act. Morris was horrified (for reasons that will be explored in chapter 8), and the issue brought forth two of his most passionate and powerful discourses.[99] One contemporary called Morris's first speech "a truly Ciceronian philippic" and said of the second that "his eloquence has never been surpassed, it is said, in either House of Congress."[100] Hamilton told Morris that the speeches were "truly worthy of you" and added, "You, friend Morris, are by *birth* a native of this Country but by *genius* an exotic."[101]

The Senate narrowly voted to repeal the Judiciary Act by a vote of sixteen to fifteen, and when the House supported the repeal as well Morris was despondent. This was the first of a long series of steps taken by the Republicans over the next decade and a half that eventually convinced Morris that America's constitutional order was doomed. His disillusionment with American politics will be treated more fully in this book's epilogue, so little more will be said about it here. Morris would not be able to combat the rising Republican tide from within the government, in any case, for his Senate term ended in March 1803. Even if he had wanted to be reappointed—which he did not—there was no chance of it happening, as the Republicans had taken firm control of the New York legislature in the years since his appointment. This would be his last political office.

Morris always kept an eye on what was happening in Washington, but politics was far from his only occupation during his later years. Although he was now in his fifties, his libido seems to have remained as strong as ever. After having tea at President Jefferson's one evening during his time in the Senate, Morris noted in his diary that he had encountered Dolley Madison at the gathering and surmised that she "has good Dispositions"—meaning that she was open to seduction—"which from the shrivelled Condition of the Secretary [i.e., Secretary of State Madison] are the less to be wondered at."[102] There is no indication in the diary that Morris's hunch about Dolley bore any fruit, though he did write "Pass the Evening with Mrs. Maddison" in an entry from the following year.[103]

Morris settled in at Morrisania after leaving the Senate, although he frequently ventured into the city and took trips upstate, where he owned large tracts of land on which he built a summer house in his final years. On July 11, 1804, he was informed that Hamilton had been killed in a duel with Aaron Burr. The next day he discovered that his friend had in fact survived the gunshot wound for the time being, so Morris hastened to Hamilton's deathbed, where he sat by his side until the end. (Not that that would be enough to earn him even a bit role in the musical.) There had long been a special bond between these two bold, charming, irreverent New Yorkers who had known each other since the Revolutionary War and who had similar politics, even if very different backgrounds. After Hamilton succumbed to his wound, his distraught widow Elizabeth said that Morris "was the best friend her husband had."[104] Morris wrote in his diary that evening that he had been "wholly unmanned by this Day's Spectacle."[105] At Elizabeth's request, he delivered the funeral oration two days later.[106]

Morris's life during his fifties and sixties was generally one of ease and retirement, interrupted by a few bouts of serious illness. As he described it in

1809, "I think of public affairs a little, read a little, play a little, and sleep a great deal. With good air, a good cook, fine water and wine, a good constitution, and a clear conscience, I descend gradually towards the grave."[107] All the same, Morris managed to find time for two more great projects. Starting in 1807, he played a leading role on a commission that was charged with planning the future streets of Manhattan, much of which was still rural but promised to develop rapidly. It took four years for the commission to formulate its report, which proposed a practical grid layout on a large and foresighted scale, running from Houston Street all the way up to 155th Street in Harlem. At this point New York was on its way to surpassing Philadelphia as the nation's largest city, and Morris's planning work helped to encourage that process.[108] In honor of his services a small street near the Battery was named Morris Street.

Much of Morris's energy during the last six years of his life was devoted to planning what became the Erie Canal. The idea of connecting the Great Lakes with the Atlantic had occurred to him as early as 1777, but it was not until 1810 that a commission was set up to pursue the idea. Morris chaired the commission and did a great deal of work for it, including drafting reports, advocating for the project in Washington and Albany, and even scouting routes himself, traversing the forests and swamps of western New York on his peg leg. Historians differ as to whether Morris or his fellow commissioner DeWitt Clinton most deserves the moniker "Father of the Erie Canal," but either way Morris's role was central. He rightly regarded the canal as a means of unifying the country, linking the eastern seaboard with the vast interior. The idea of forging such a link led him to exclaim to a friend that "the proudest empire in Europe is but a bauble, compared to what America *will* be, *must* be, in the course of two centuries; perhaps of one!"[109] He also believed that the "natural effect of the canal" would be "to make New York mistress of the union" by situating the nation's central trade route within its borders.[110] Morris did not live to see the canal built—construction began in 1817, the year after his death, and was not completed until 1825—but it eventually fulfilled his grandest visions. Spanning 363 miles from the Hudson River in Albany to Lake Erie in Buffalo, it was the second longest canal in the world (behind only China's Grand Canal).[111]

At age fifty-seven Morris finally left bachelorhood behind when he married the thirty-five-year-old Ann Cary Randolph.[112] Nancy, as she was generally known, came from the large and hugely influential Randolph family of Virginia; as a girl she was close friends with Thomas Jefferson's oldest daughter Patsy. In October 1792, when she was just eighteen, Nancy was accused of committing a lurid crime, which tarnished her reputation forever.[113] The details of the episode are complicated and remain somewhat hazy, but the basic charge was that she had conspired to murder her own newborn baby. At the time, she was living with her sister Judith and Judith's husband, their cousin Richard Randolph, at his plantation that was aptly named "Bizarre." Adding to the familial jumble, Nancy had been engaged to another cousin (and Richard's brother), Theodorick, who had died seven months earlier. One evening when Nancy, Judith, and Richard were visiting yet another cousin, Nancy delivered a baby that is now generally thought to have been stillborn. However, it appears that Richard was the only person present and that he disposed of the body, which led to allegations that he (rather than Theodorick) had been the father and that he and Nancy had killed the baby. The rumors quickly spread throughout Virginia, and the trial that Richard requested in order to clear his name was a sensation; Patrick Henry and John Marshall served as the defense attorneys. The charges were ultimately dismissed, but suspicions would follow Nancy for the remainder of her life.

Nancy continued to live at Bizarre until 1805, at which point she began to make her way northward, moving from place to place for several years. Morris hired her as a housekeeper in April 1809 and married her on Christmas day of that year—to "no small Suprize to my Guests," as he noted in his diary.[114] Morris later suggested that Nancy had divulged everything about her past before taking the position as housekeeper, and he breezily dismissed the sordid tales that continued to circulate about her behavior, past and present. When some relatives complained about the marriage, he responded with characteristic brass, "If the world were to live with my wife, I should certainly have consulted its taste; but as that happens not to be the case, I thought I might, without offending others, endeavor to suit myself, and look rather to the head and heart than into the pocket."[115] Morris's diary entries in his later years are exceedingly spare, but by all appearances the marriage was a happy one. They had a son, Gouverneur, Jr.—nicknamed "Gouverno"—in February 1813. Morris took great pride in the "little prattler," as he called him, though he did not live to see his fourth birthday.[116] Gouverno would go on to become a prominent railroad executive and an antislavery Republican.

Morris's last two years were marred by recurring episodes of gout as well as a fraud committed against him by his trusted nephew, David Bayard Ogden, which left his finances in a perilous state. Still, in the midst of his final summer he was able to write cheerfully to a friend, "Looking back I can with some little self complacency reflect, that I have not lived in vain; and at the same time look forward with composure, at the probable course of future events. At sixty-four there is little to desire, and less to apprehend."[117]

Morris's death was rather grisly. In the autumn of 1816 he suffered from a painful blockage in his urinary tract—a recurring problem for him, perhaps a result of venereal disease—and attempted to resolve it through a bit of ill-advised self-surgery. Taking a page full of italics, capital letters, and exclamation points from the do-not-try-this-at-home handbook, Morris attempted to use a whalebone from one of Nancy's corsets to clear the obstruction, and he died from the resulting lacerations. (He had successfully performed the same delicate maneuver a few years earlier using a flexible bit of hickory, but attempting it a second time was surely pushing his luck.)[118] The end came on November 6 in the same room in which he had been born, just shy of sixty-five years earlier.

Morris was initially buried in the family vault at Morrisania, but his son later had him reburied alongside Nancy outside a church in the Bronx, St. Ann's Episcopal, that Gouverno had commissioned in memory of his mother. The stone tablet listing some of Morris's many accomplishments—"The Man Whose Hand Wrote the Constitution of the United States . . . Washington's Minister to France during the French Revolution; Author of the Clause in the New York Constitution Providing Religious Freedom; Senator of the United States; Projector of the Erie Canal; Patriot, Scholar, Diplomat; A Statesman of Brilliant Genius; An American Through and Through"—can still be visited today, though it seldom is.

2. A Most Splendid Part: Morris at the Convention

Even after stripping away the mythology that has persistently surrounded it, the Philadelphia Convention of 1787 remains one of the most remarkable events in political history.[1] The importance of the Convention derives partly from the fact that its end result, the US Constitution, has proven so enduring and influential. The Constitution is the oldest extant charter of national government anywhere in the world, and regardless of whether one regards it as a blueprint for political freedom or a "covenant with death," it is difficult to dispute its impact on virtually every facet of American life. Rarely has a political document remained so deeply and immediately "relevant" for so long.

The Convention's importance also stems from the fact that when it met, the nation's fate was "suspended by a hair," as Morris later put it.[2] It was not at all clear in the summer of 1787 that the union of the thirteen states would persist indefinitely or that republican government could succeed on such a large scale. The delegates themselves were acutely aware of just how much was riding on their deliberations. James Madison declared matter-of-factly on the Convention floor that it was "more than probable we are now digesting a plan which in its operation would decide for ever the fate of republican government."[3] Alexander Hamilton quickly concurred, adding that "if we did not give to [the republican] form due stability and wisdom, it would be disgraced and lost among ourselves, disgraced and lost to mankind forever."[4] A few days later Rufus King of Massachusetts likewise posited that the Convention was "the last opportunity for providing for [the country's] liberty and happiness."[5] James Wilson commented that "when he considered the amazing extent of the country—the immense population which is to fill it—the influence of the Government we are to form will have, not only on the present generation of our people and their multiplied prosperity, but on the whole globe,—he was lost in the magnitude of the object."[6] Morris agreed with these assessments, going so far as to declare at one point that "the whole human race will be affected by the proceedings of this Convention."[7]

Close observers have long recognized the outsized role that Morris played at this singular gathering and the deep imprint that he left on the charter that it produced. No less an authority on the Philadelphia Convention than James Madison described Morris as "an able, an eloquent, and an active member" of that body, and no less an authority on the Constitution than Chief Justice John Marshall avowed that Morris "performed a most splendid part" in its framing.[8] Later in the nineteenth century, Theodore Roosevelt judged that Morris "was perhaps the most brilliant" even if "by no means the greatest" of the framers, while Henry Cabot Lodge proclaimed that "no man did better work in the great task of forming the Constitution than Morris."[9] One of the most venerable scholars of the Convention, Max Farrand, called Morris "probably the most brilliant member of the Pennsylvania delegation and of the convention as well."[10]

Another historian, Clinton Rossiter, divided the delegates into eight categories based on their contributions to the Convention, which he dubbed the Principals, the Influentials, the Very Usefuls, the Usefuls, the Visibles, the Ciphers, the Dropouts and Walkouts, and the Inexplicable Disappointments.[11] He included four individuals in his list of Principals: James Madison, whose contributions to the Convention were discussed in this book's introduction; James Wilson, the Pennsylvania lawyer who stood out as an advocate of a strong national government resting on a broad democratic base; George Washington, who hardly contributed to the deliberations at all, but whose role as president of the Convention conferred on it an aura of gravitas and popular legitimacy that it would not otherwise have had; and Morris.[12] Rossiter writes that

> the credentials of Gouverneur Morris as a giant of the Convention will always be slightly suspect to those who see him as a man too clever, too fickle, and too cynical 'by half.' Yet anyone who has traced and retraced his trail through the Convention—noting the frankness and superb timing of his important speeches, watching him shoulder most of the burden of committee work for his fellow Pennsylvanians, reading over his final draft of September 12—must recognize a magnificent contribution.[13]

The fact that Morris became one of the most important figures in Philadelphia is all the more striking given that he was not terribly well known on the national stage at the time, and was nearly not appointed as a delegate at all.

Although Morris was a native New Yorker who planned to return there eventually, by the beginning of 1787 he had been living full-time in Philadelphia for more than seven years and thus was considered a citizen of Pennsylvania. (He had also spent three years at the Philadelphia Academy during his youth and another two years in the state while serving in the Continental Congress.) When Pennsylvania's General Assembly met to select the state's delegates to the Constitutional Convention, Morris asked not to be included; he had withdrawn from politics more than three years earlier, after leaving the finance department, and he was preoccupied with gathering the funds to purchase Morrisania from his half-brother. However, the assembly selected him anyway, at a time when he was off in Trenton, New Jersey, on business. Morris reluctantly agreed to attend the Convention on the state's behalf, writing to Henry Knox, "Had the Object been any other than it is I would have declined. The Appointment was the most unexpected Thing that ever happened to me."[14]

Morris's selection was a close-run thing. Of the eight delegates chosen by the General Assembly he received the least support, just squeaking out a majority with thirty-three votes out of sixty-three cast. In addition to those legislators who voted against Morris in accordance with his stated desire not to be selected, many opposed him on grounds of both nativity and character. One commented that it was "improper . . . to choose an alien for he is certainly a [New] Yorker, beside the trouble he will give by his vanity & schemes."[15] However, Robert Morris, and perhaps also James Wilson, ultimately pushed hard enough to secure his inclusion. Their efforts were aided by the fact that Philadelphia was to be the Convention's host city. Each state could choose how many delegates to send, and Pennsylvania ended up sending the most of any state, partly because the individuals whom they selected were all already living in Philadelphia, so the state felt no obligation to pay them any salary or expenses. Had Robert Morris not been so convinced that Gouverneur would be a valuable asset at the Convention, had the Convention not been held in Philadelphia, or had Pennsylvania sent a slightly smaller delegation, Morris almost certainly would not have been included—and the Constitution may very well have turned out quite different than it did.

As it was, Morris was part of an extremely distinguished Pennsylvania delegation—second in importance only to Virginia's—that included Benjamin Franklin, James Wilson, and Robert Morris, among others. Pennsylvania had the second largest population among the states, even if its 434,373 inhabitants in the 1790 census were dwarfed by Virginia's 747,610, so it served as the unofficial leader of the northern states at the Convention. Pennsylvania was also notable for its relative cosmopolitanism, given that it was home to the nation's biggest city and to large populations of Quakers, German immigrants, and free Black people. The state's delegation reflected some of its diversity, with three immigrants (James Wilson hailed from Scotland, Robert Morris from England, and Thomas Fitzsimons from Ireland) and three transplants from other states (Benjamin Franklin was born in Massachusetts, Gouverneur Morris in New York, and Jared Ingersoll in Connecticut) joined by two born-and-bred Pennsylvanians (George Clymer and Thomas Mifflin).

Going into the Convention, Morris already knew a number of its leading lights even beyond the other members of the Pennsylvania delegation, including George Washington and Alexander Hamilton from the war and James Madison (somewhat less well) from the Continental Congress. That summer, Hamilton and the somewhat quixotic Elbridge Gerry of Massachusetts both took their lodgings at the boardinghouse where Morris had long been staying, Mary Dailey's on the corner of High (now Market) Street and Third Street, three blocks east of where the Convention met at the Pennsylvania State House (now Independence Hall).[16] At thirty-five years old Morris was on the younger side among the delegates, although many of the important figures—including Madison, Hamilton, and Edmund Randolph—were also in their thirties. (The delegates' ages ranged from Jonathan Dayton's twenty-six years to Benjamin Franklin's eighty-one, with a median age of forty-three.)[17] Of the fifty-five individuals who attended the Convention at one point or another that summer, fully forty-two had (like Morris) served in the Continental or Confederation Congress, and over half had (also like Morris) studied law. Somewhat surprisingly, however, Morris was one of only fifteen delegates with previous experience at a state constitutional convention.

Given how illustrious many of the delegates were, it was perhaps inevitable that the veneration—even deification—of the gathering began almost immediately. Writing from Paris that August, Thomas Jefferson remarked to John Adams that "it is really an assembly of demigods," and Madison suggested in *The Federalist* that the framers' deliberations had been guided by "a finger of that Almighty Hand which has been so frequently and signally extended to our relief in the critical stages of the revolution."[18] References to the Constitution as miraculous were commonplace from the time of the ratification debates onward. Morris, however, would have none of it. Soon after the Convention's close he wrote to a correspondent in France that "while some have boasted [the Constitution] as a work from Heaven, others have given it a less righteous origin. I have many reasons to believe, that it was the work of plain honest men."[19]

On the day that had been appointed for the opening of the Convention, May 14, only Pennsylvania and Virginia had the requisite number of delegates in attendance; it would take another eleven days to assemble a quorum of seven states thanks to the muddy roads from the unusually wet spring. On May 16, Benjamin Franklin hosted a lavish dinner for the delegates who were then in the city. Fortuitously, the attendees included a number of the individuals who were most deeply committed to a radical overhaul of the Articles of Confederation and the institution of a vigorous national government, including Madison, Washington, and Randolph from Virginia, and Wilson and both Morrises from Pennsylvania.[20] For the week or so after the dinner these individuals met regularly—at the State House each morning, while waiting to see who else would show up, and at the City Tavern or Indian Queen each afternoon—to formulate the blueprint that became known as the Virginia Plan, which provided a boldly nationalist basis from which the Convention would begin its deliberations. By all accounts Madison had the single greatest influence on the plan that this informal group drew up, but the contributions of the Pennsylvania delegates—especially Wilson and Morris—were substantial enough that one scholar has suggested that "the famous Virginia Plan would more accurately be labelled the Virginia-Pennsylvania Plan."[21]

The Convention formally opened on Friday, May 25, and the delegates spent that day and the following Monday laying down the assembly's ground rules. The Virginia Plan was introduced by Edmund Randolph—who was both the governor of Virginia and a much more capable orator than the quiet, somewhat shy Madison—on May 29. Morris was among the first and most vehement supporters of the plan when the Convention began to discuss it the following day, but then the day after that—May 31—he left for New York and did not return to the Convention until July 2. Morris had just completed the purchase of Morrisania on April 4, and he felt it necessary to be there in person to oversee some of the much-needed repairs and improvements to the estate.[22]

Morris's absence from the Convention for the entire month of June is striking in retrospect, but it was hardly remarkable at the time. Many of the delegates arrived late, departed early, or left for long stretches to attend to their personal affairs. Hamilton, for instance, missed nearly two full months of the deliberations. At no point during the summer were the fifty-five delegates all present; the average daily attendance was probably closer to thirty or thirty-five. In fact, there were never more than eleven state delegations on the floor:

Rhode Island refused to send any delegates, New Hampshire's did not arrive until late July, and by that point two of New York's had left in protest, thereby preventing Hamilton from casting an official vote for the state even when he was there. Given that the delegates saw themselves as deciding the fate of republican liberty for all time, not only within the United States but around the globe, the apparent nonchalance with which many of them—including Morris—attended the Convention is rather difficult to fathom.

In any case, the timing of Morris's absence may have been good for his sanity. Much of the debate that he missed centered on whether to propose an altogether new national constitution that would operate directly on the American people (as in the Virginia Plan) or to simply add a few powers to the existing Confederation (as in the New Jersey Plan), and Morris regarded the right answer as blindingly obvious. It is doubtful that the New Jersey Plan would have been rejected any more quickly or resoundingly had Morris been in attendance, and being spared that month's worth of frustrating disputation may have allowed him to husband his energy for the remaining two-and-a-half months of the Convention.

When Morris returned to the Convention on July 2, the delegates were, as Roger Sherman put it, "at a full stop," deadlocked on the question of whether representation in the Senate should be proportional to population (as many of the large state delegates advocated) or equal for each state (as many of the small state delegates advocated).[23] Morris immediately launched into one of his longest speeches of the summer, audaciously arguing that the Senate should be formed as an "aristocratic body" whose members would be appointed by the executive and serve for life without pay—a proposal that garnered little support from his colleagues.[24] After taking two days off for Philadelphia's elaborate Independence Day celebration, the delegates returned to forge what became known as the Connecticut Compromise.[25] This agreement, which was reached on July 16, granted the small states equal representation in the Senate, much to Morris's chagrin.

The Convention took a ten-day break between July 26 and August 6 so that the Committee of Detail could formulate a draft constitution incorporating all the decisions that the delegates had made up to that point.[26] During this interim, Morris went fishing with Washington. On July 30, the two set out for "the vicinity of Valley-forge to get Trout," as Washington recorded in his diary, and the next day, while Morris continued to fish, Washington visited the ruins of the encampment at which his army had spent that terrible winter a decade earlier.[27] From August 3 to 5, they went to Trenton on another fishing expedition, this time accompanied by Robert Morris and his wife.[28] This would be Morris's last respite of the summer.

Back in Philadelphia, Morris was as voluble and active as any delegate. In fact, despite missing the entire month of June, he spoke more often at the Convention than anyone else—173 times, according to James Madison's notes, which put him just ahead of James Wilson's 168 times and Madison's 161 times. Morris proposed 39 motions over the course of the summer, which was also more than any other delegate (Madison and Wilson were next with 35 and 31, respectively), and had 22 of his motions adopted, which was yet again more than anyone else (here he was followed by Wilson and Edmund Randolph, both of whom had 18).[29] In addition to being quite literally the leading voice of the Convention, Morris was an engaged participant in the committees that did so much of the crucial work that summer.[30] Morris proposed and chaired a five-member committee that recommended an initial apportionment for Congress (July 6–9); served on an eleven-member committee that reconsidered this apportionment question (July 9–10); served on an eleven-member committee that dealt with "unfinished parts," including the method for selecting the president (August 31–September 5); and did the lion's share of the work for the five-member committee that produced the final draft of the Constitution (September 8–12). He also proposed, but did not serve on, a committee on the slave trade and navigation laws (August 22–24). In all, only three delegates—Rufus King, John Rutledge, and Hugh Williamson—served on more committees than Morris.

William Pierce of Georgia recorded vivid descriptions of his fellow delegates in his diary, highlighting what he deemed most conspicuous about each individual—noting, for instance, that Madison "blends together the profound politician, with the Scholar" and is "the best informed Man of any point in debate"; that Hamilton "is deservedly celebrated for his talents" but "his manners are tinctured with stiffness, and sometimes with a degree of vanity that is highly disagreeable"; and that while "no Man has a better Heart or a clearer Head" than Roger Sherman, "yet the oddity of his address, the vulgarisms that accompany his public speaking, and that strange new England cant which runs through his public as well as his private speaking make everything that is connected with him grotesque and laughable."[31] Pierce left as full and brightly colored a depiction of Morris as of any delegate:

> Mr. Governeur Morris is one of those Genius's in whom every species of talents combine to render him conspicuous and flourishing in public debate:—He winds through all the mazes of rhetoric, and throws around him such a glare that he charms, captivates, and leads away the senses of all who hear him. With an infinite streach of fancy he brings to view things when he is engaged in deep argumentation, that render all the labor of reasoning easy and pleasing. But with all these powers he is fickle and inconstant,—never pursuing one train of thinking,—nor ever regular. He has gone through a very extensive course of reading, and is acquainted with all the sciences. No Man has more wit,—nor can any one engage the attention more than Mr. Morris.[32]

There are several things worth noting about this portrait of Morris, the first being Pierce's description of him as conspicuous in debate and captivating in speech. These qualities certainly shine through the notes that Madison and others took on Morris's contributions. Morris's prominence on the Convention floor derived partly from his robust frame and wooden leg, partly from the fact that he talked so frequently and at such length, and partly from his characteristic bluntness and provocativeness. Madison later recalled that Morris was "very frank in avowing his opinions when most at variance with those prevailing in the Convention" and spoke of Morris's "usual fondness for saying things and advancing doctrines that no one else would."[33] One historian describes Morris's demeanor at the Convention as that of "a passionate goad, a brilliant floater of trial balloons," and an "inveterate stirrer-of-pots," while another notes that "he was both an orator and an arguer; he could paint a glowing picture, or jab a rival in the gut."[34] The moral courage that was on display in Morris's strident criticisms of slavery, in particular, was without parallel at the Convention. Some delegates might have been moved by his eloquence while others were surely put off by his stinging repartee, but either way Morris was very difficult to ignore.

Pierce also characterized Morris as "fickle and inconstant," a charge that was frequently leveled at him throughout his life. However, at the Convention, at least, Morris's alleged fickleness was more the result of a laudable willingness to change his mind and to compromise where necessary than of some kind of innate capriciousness. Madison remarked that "to the brilliancy & fertility of his genius, [Morris] added what is too rare, a candid surrender of his opinions when the lights of discussion satisfied him that they had been too hastily formed, and a readiness to aid in making the best of measures in which he had been overruled."[35] Although Morris initially argued that the president should not be subject to impeachment, for instance, after listening to some more debate he announced that his "opinion had been changed by the arguments used in the discussion."[36] When William Paterson of New Jersey declared that "his resolution was fixed" regarding the necessity of equal state representation in the Senate, Morris retorted that "he had no resolution unalterably fixed except to do what should finally appear to him right."[37] While Morris was never shy about speaking his mind, he was frequently willing to compromise after he had made his point. More and more as the summer wore on, he abandoned the role of provocateur and adopted that of peacemaker. In one of the few retrospective comments that he made on his activity at the Convention, Morris declared that his overriding aim had been to "remove impediments, obviate objections, and conciliate jarring opinions."[38]

Throughout the Convention, Morris steadily pursued his basic goals—empowering the national government, particularly the executive and the judiciary; ensuring effective checks on the three branches as well as on the popular will itself; encouraging commerce and protecting property rights; restraining slavery—and simply adopted whichever tactic seemed best suited to reaching these ends at a given moment.[39] This combination of principle and prudence relates to another element of Pierce's character sketch, namely his assertion that Morris "has gone through a very extensive course of reading, and is acquainted with all the sciences." There is no question that Morris was a deeply learned man. His speeches at the Convention drew on not just the usual examples—the Articles of Confederation, the state governments, the histories of Britain and Rome—but also Sparta's ephors and the Holy Roman Empire's Aulic Council, the German Diet and the Polish Diet, the book of Ecclesiastes and King Rehoboam of Judah.[40] Yet Morris's overarching political principles appear to have been drawn less from his reading of some philosopher—John Locke or Montesquieu, David Hume or William Blackstone—than from history and concrete experience.

In fact, Morris tended to deride the application of abstract theory to political practice. In January 1790, he wrote of one faction in France that they "mean well" but "have unfortunately acquired their Ideas of Government from Books ... as it happens somewhat unfortunately that the Men who live in the World are very different from those who dwell in the Heads of Philosophers it is not to be wondered at if the Systems taken out of Books are fit for Nothing but to be put into Books again."[41] Later that year he wrote in his diary, "None know how to govern but those who have been used to it and such Men have rarely either Time or Inclination to write about it. The Books, therefore, which are to be met with, contain mere Utopian Ideas."[42] To be sure, Morris was not unremittingly hostile to political theory. In fact, back in 1776 he himself had penned a short, unpublished essay in which he explored the ultimate ends of government, particularly stressing the benefits of commerce and the primacy of civil liberty over political liberty.[43] Still, he believed that it was naïve in the extreme to expect that such musings could profitably be used to resolve specific public policy questions.

A final detail of Pierce's sketch that is worth highlighting is his remark that "no Man has more wit" than Morris. Judging from the notes that survive from the Convention, the framers were an unusually serious lot, seldom indulging in any kind of joking or raillery. Only a handful of moments of comparative levity have been passed down to us, and Morris was the source of the majority of them (although, true to form, Benjamin Franklin also contributed a few as well). For instance, at one point Franklin commented that "in free governments the rulers are the servants, and the people their superiors and sovereigns," so that for government officers to step down from their posts "was not to *degrade*, but to *promote*, them," to which Morris responded that he had no doubt that future presidents would have "too much modesty not to be willing to decline the promotion."[44] When Elbridge Gerry objected to making the vice president the president of the Senate on the grounds that "we might as well put the President himself at the head of the Legislature. The close intimacy that must subsist between the President and Vice President makes it absolutely improper," Morris retorted that "the Vice President then will be the first heir apparent that ever loved his father."[45] In making a (rather illiberal) case for a fourteen-year citizenship requirement before an immigrant could be elected to the Senate, Morris commented: "It is said that some tribes of Indians carried their hospitality so far as to offer strangers their wives and daughters. Was this a proper model for us? He would admit [recent immigrants] to his house, he would invite them to his table, would provide for them comfortable lodgings, but would not carry the complaisance so far as to bed them with his wife."[46] Of course, it was especially ironic for Morris, of all people, to express reservations about the bedding of another man's wife, given that he did so with some frequency himself.

Another story that allegedly took place during the Convention should perhaps be mentioned here simply because of its fame, even if it is very likely apocryphal. According to one version of the tale, Hamilton remarked to Morris that "Washington was reserved and aristocratic even to his intimate friends, and allowed no one to be familiar with him." When Morris responded that "that was a mere fancy, and he could be as familiar with Washington as with any of his other friends," Hamilton challenged him that "if you will, at the next reception evening, gently slap him on the shoulder, and say, 'My dear General, how happy I am to see you look so well!' a supper and wine shall be provided for you and a dozen of your friends." As the legend has it, Morris took up the challenge, but upon laying his hand on Washington's shoulder the latter "stepped suddenly back, fixed his eye on Morris for several minutes with an angry frown, until the latter retreated abashed, and sought refuge in the crowd. The company looked on in silence. At the supper, which was provided by Hamilton, Morris said, 'I have won the bet, but paid dearly for it, and nothing could induce me to repeat it.'"[47] Although there is little evidence that this incident actually took place, it has been repeated through the ages because it does appear to capture something about the staid and standoffish Washington and the playful and impudent Morris.

Although Morris influenced the decisions reached by the Convention in myriad ways, his single most consequential act that summer was actually penning the Constitution itself. This great responsibility devolved on him as a member of the committee that was charged with preparing the final draft of the charter. The committee had no official or uniformly accepted name: the journal that was kept by the Convention's secretary, William Jackson, referred to it as "a Committee of five to revise the style of and arrange the articles agreed to by the House" or more simply "the Committee of revision"; Madison variously described it as "a committee . . . to revise the style of, and arrange, the articles which had been agreed to by the House" or "the Committee of Style and Arrangement" or just "the Committee of Style"; James McHenry of Maryland called it "a committee of 5 to revise and place the several parts under their proper heads"; and Charles Pinckney of South Carolina called it "the Committee for revising the style and arrangement of the articles agreed on."[48] The committee is now generally called the Committee of Style, following Madison's most concise description of it, but it should be noted that some of the other descriptions—such as the Committee of Revision—suggest that its mandate went beyond the merely stylistic and that the delegates assumed that preparing a new draft was likely to have some substantive import.⁴⁹

In any case, the five committee members were chosen by ballot on September 8.⁵⁰ The chair was William Samuel Johnson—a well-respected lawyer from Connecticut who had recently been named president of Morris's alma mater, now rechristened Columbia College—and the other four members were Hamilton, Rufus King, Madison, and Morris. Madison and Morris were obvious choices, given their prominence at the Convention; King, too, had played a substantial role, and had served on more committees than any other delegate; and Johnson was regarded as a conciliatory figure. The choice of Hamilton is perhaps a bit more surprising, given how little of the Convention he had attended, but perhaps for this particular role his brilliant oratory outweighed his apparent lack of commitment in the minds of the other delegates.

While Johnson was a senior figure at age fifty-nine, the other four committee members were still in their thirties. The most striking thing about the committee's membership, however, was not its youth but rather its lack of geographical and ideological balance. On most committees there was a reasonable level of parity between delegates from the North and South, as well as between those who advocated a strong national government and those who favored reserving significant power to the states. The Committee of Style, however, had only one southerner (Madison), and its four younger members had been among the most forceful nationalist voices at the Convention, with Johnson alone having a reputation as a more moderate nationalist.⁵¹ The committee's nationalist bent may have been partly a result of who was left at the Convention to choose its members: many of the delegates who were hostile to a strong national authority had already departed in disgust by that point. The northern tilt is more difficult to explain. Perhaps the southern delegates felt comfortable with Madison representing their interests, and perhaps they also recalled that Johnson was a slaveholder who had consistently advocated giving the South a good deal of protection for its peculiar institution. Still, Morris and King were two of the Convention's harshest critics of slavery, and Hamilton was a member of the New York Manumission Society. Regardless of how exactly it came about, the committee represented a dazzling array of legal talent and eloquence.

Unfortunately, little is known about the activities of the Committee of Style. No records of it were kept, and no drafts of its proposed charter other than the final one survive (as they do for the Committee of Detail that composed the first full draft constitution earlier in the summer).⁵² The usual custom was for the chair to do a large portion of the committee's work, but in this case the actual writing of the draft was, by all appearances, left to Morris. Unfortunately, we know next to nothing about how much input, if any, he received from the other committee members at any stage in the process.

The primary evidence regarding Morris's role as the Constitution's drafter comes from three letters—one written by the historian Jared Sparks, Morris's first biographer; one by Madison, who was a fellow committee member; and one by Morris himself. When Sparks set out to compose his biography in the early 1830s, he wrote to Madison to inquire about rumors that Morris had penned the Constitution:

> I have been told by several persons, who professed to know the fact, that the constitution in its present form and language is from his pen; that is, after all debates were finished, and each particular had been adopted in substance, the instrument was then put into his hands to be wrought into proper phraseology & style. His friends here [i.e., in New York] are in the habit of thinking, that much is due to him for the clear, simple, & expressive language in which the constitution is clothed.⁵³

In his response, Madison confirmed that indeed

> the *finish* given to the style and arrangement of the Constitution, fairly belongs to the pen of Mr. Morris; the task having, probably, been handed over to him by the Chairman of the Committee [i.e., Johnson], himself a highly respectable member, and with the ready concurrence of the others. A better choice could not have been made, as the performance of the task proved. It is true that the state of the materials, consisting of a Reported draft in detail [i.e., the Committee of Detail's draft], and subsequent resolutions accurately penned, and falling easily into their proper places, was a good preparation for the symmetry and phraseology of the Instrument: but there was sufficient room for the talents and taste stamped by the author on the face of it.⁵⁴

Note that even as Madison sought to downplay Morris's contribution by remarking that many of the materials were already in place, he still described Morris as not just the stylist but also "the author" of the Constitution.

Further confirmation of Morris's role as the Constitution's penman comes in a letter that he wrote in December 1814 to Timothy Pickering, who was then a member of the House of Representatives from Massachusetts. Pickering had written to Morris to inquire about the debate within the Convention regarding a particular constitutional provision, to which Morris replied: "my dear Sir, what can a history of the Constitution [i.e., within the Convention] avail towards interpreting its provisions[?] This must be done by comparing the plain import of the words, with the general tenor and object of the instrument." After seeking to quash the use of original intent as a method of constitutional interpretation, and to encourage instead some combination of textualism and structuralism—as we might put his points today—Morris continued, with some justifiable pride: "That instrument [i.e., the Constitution] was written by the fingers, which write this letter."[55]

The obvious question is, why Morris? As we have just seen, Madison claimed that the task of composing the final draft of the Constitution was "probably . . . handed over to" Morris by Johnson, "with the ready concurrence of the others" on the committee. But why did Johnson choose Morris, rather than drafting the charter himself (as the committee's chair) or choosing one of the other three members, and why did the other members so readily concur in this choice? Unfortunately there is no clear answer, given the paucity of the record, but a few possibilities spring to mind.[56] Perhaps the choice was prompted by Morris's omnipresence on the Convention floor and within the Convention's committees from July onward. Or perhaps it was prompted by Morris's experience in this line of work: he was the only one of the committee members who had helped to write a state constitution, and he had also drafted many hundreds of reports and legal documents during his time in the Continental Congress and the finance department. Or perhaps it was prompted by Morris's well-deserved reputation for clear and eloquent expression. In the recent judgment of Richard Brookhiser, Morris was in fact one of only four great stylists among the founders, along with Thomas Jefferson, Benjamin Franklin, and Thomas Paine.[57] Of course, it is also possible that Morris was the only committee member to volunteer for the assignment, or that they simply drew straws. We do not know why Morris ended up penning the Constitution, only that he did.

What can be said with certainty is that Morris carried out his work exceedingly quickly. The Committee of Style was formed near the end of the Convention's session on Saturday, September 8, and copies of its draft constitution were ready for distribution on the morning of Wednesday, September 12, around ninety hours later.[58] Presumably Morris dedicated the bulk of the intervening three days to his task. The Convention never met on Sundays, and Morris was not a regular churchgoer, so he had September 9 free; the Convention met on September 10, but Morris is not recorded as having spoken (as Madison, Hamilton, and King did), suggesting that he likely skipped that day's debate in order to continue writing; and on the morning of September 11, the Convention simply adjourned in anticipation of the committee's report the following day.

What Morris accomplished over the course of these three days is remarkable. He began with the draft constitution that had been compiled by the Committee of Detail back in late July and early August, along with a list of the changes, additions, and deletions that had been voted on by the delegates in the intervening month and more of debate and committee work—a list that was, truth be told, rather messy and hard to decipher in the Convention's official journal.[59] Morris not only brought order and coherence to this jumble, but fundamentally restructured the charter in the process.

The Committee of Detail's draft constitution contained twenty-three articles, including seven on the legislature and just one each on the executive and judiciary. In this respect it mirrored the state constitutions, most of which included many dozens of articles, the bulk of them devoted to the legislature. Morris pared down the charter to seven articles, including the initial tripartite structure that we know today, with Article I on the legislature, Article II on the executive, and Article III on the judiciary. None of the state constitutions or the earlier plans at the Philadelphia Convention had employed this framework, so it appears to have been entirely Morris's doing. Giving each branch its own article was not only cleaner and simpler but also suggested to the reader that the three were coequal bodies in a way that the Committee of Detail's more convoluted draft did not. Morris devoted Article IV to the relationship between the federal government and the states and territories, Article V to the amendment process, Article VI to a few miscellaneous provisions (including the declaration that the Constitution would be "the supreme law of the land"), and Article VII to the ratification process.

In addition to giving the Constitution a more logical organization, Morris streamlined many of its provisions, cutting down the wordy verbiage that had pervaded the Committee of Detail's draft and replacing it with crisp, measured prose. As Morris himself later remarked, he sought to weed out "redundant and equivocal terms" and to render the Constitution "as clear as our language would permit."[60] (The most notable deviations from the document's usual clarity came in the passages dealing with slavery, where Morris, following the Committee of Detail, was forced to adopt tortured circumlocutions in order avoid using the words "slave" or "slavery.") There is hardly a provision in the document that was not touched by Morris's editing pen. For some of the passages the touches were light—a comma here or a new word there—but many of the passages were substantially reworked or even composed anew. Thus, when constitutional lawyers and scholars pore over the fine details of the document, searching for clues regarding its meaning, they have Morris to thank (or blame) for many of these details. Joseph Ellis remarks that "Morris's Constitution does not quite sing like Jefferson's Declaration, which had the rhetorical advantage of being about founding principles rather than about the political structure to implement those principles," but he did manage to "cast the Constitution into an elevated format that rose above the nettlesome details of its content" and to give the final draft "a clarity and accessibility that it had not previously possessed."[61]

The one part of the Constitution that *does* rise to the level of Jefferson's eloquence is the preamble, which was, so far as we can tell, almost wholly Morris's handiwork. The preamble in the Committee of Detail's draft constitution had been a mere roll call of the states: "We the people of the States of New Hampshire, Massachusetts, Rhode Island and Providence Plantations, Connecticut, New York, New Jersey, Pennsylvania, Delaware, Maryland, Virginia, North Carolina, South Carolina, and Georgia, do ordain, declare, and establish, the following Constitution for the government of ourselves and our posterity."[62] Morris, apparently on his own initiative, transformed this plain statement of fact into an inspiring rendition of the document's fundamental aims, one that is familiar across the country and indeed around the world today: "We the people of the United States, in order to form a more perfect union, to establish justice, insure domestic tranquility, provide for the common defence, promote the general welfare, and secure the blessings of liberty to ourselves and our posterity, do ordain and establish this Constitution for the United States of America."[63]

As if thoroughly remodeling the Constitution were not enough, Morris also appears to have written—or at the very least contributed to writing—another important document during this intense three-day stretch: the letter with which the Constitution was submitted to the Confederation Congress, which was then meeting in New York.⁶⁴ Although the letter was ultimately sent under the signature of George Washington, the Convention's presiding officer, the original version is in Morris's handwriting and was transmitted to the Convention by the Committee of Style on September 12 along with its draft of the Constitution itself.⁶⁵ This "cover letter," as it has been called, sought to put the delegates' work into context by reciting some of the problems that had led to the calling of the Convention in the first place, the challenges that the delegates had faced, their aims in constructing the Constitution, and their hopes regarding its reception and impact.⁶⁶ The letter was adopted by the Convention without revision or debate, and during the succeeding ratification debates it was reprinted far and wide alongside the Constitution itself.⁶⁷

Given that Morris chose the wording of many of the Constitution's provisions, observers have long wondered whether he was in any respect a "dishonest scrivener," to use the term employed by William Treanor—that is, whether he made any subtle but substantive changes to the resolutions that the delegates had approved during the Convention in an attempt to further his own constitutional vision.⁶⁸ The first and most prominent accusation to that effect came in June 1798 when Albert Gallatin, who was then a member of the House of Representatives from Pennsylvania—and who would go on to serve as treasury secretary under both Jefferson and Madison—claimed on the House floor that Morris had illicitly tried to change the punctuation and hence the meaning of the general welfare clause.

During the Convention the delegates unanimously approved a provision stipulating that Congress "shall have power to lay and collect taxes, duties, imposts, and excises, to pay the debts and provide for the common defence and general welfare of the United States."⁶⁹ According to Gallatin—who claimed to be "well informed" on this point, although he did not himself attend the Convention—Morris tried to sneak in a semicolon (and hence a sharper break) after the word "excises" in his draft, thereby effectively making the providing of the general welfare a separate power.⁷⁰ That is, the original provision had suggested that Congress had the power to collect taxes *in order to* pay debts, provide defense, and provide for the general welfare, but with Morris's semicolon the provision could be read as saying that Congress had to the power to collect taxes *as well as* (more generally) to pay debts, provide defense, and provide for the general welfare. If providing for the general welfare were read as a distinct power rather than a limitation on the taxing power, of course, then it could be used to justify any action that Congress deemed to be for the good of the country—an extraordinary expansion of the federal government's delegated authority. According to Gallatin, however, the "trick" was discovered at the Convention by Roger Sherman, and the punctuation was restored.[71]

We know that the broadside copy of the Committee of Style's draft constitution that was distributed to the delegates did include the semicolon, and we also know that it did indeed become a comma again in the final, engrossed Constitution that the delegates signed on September 17. However, it is not entirely clear whether the semicolon was an unsuccessful "trick" by Morris that was caught by Sherman. None of the notes taken at the Convention record any kind of exchange on this point, and Madison claimed late in life that the semicolon had been a mere transcription error—"an erratum of the pen or of the press"—that was duly corrected in the final version.[72] That said, it is noteworthy that Morris did favor reading the general welfare clause as a broad grant of power. James McHenry records having participated in a conversation on September 6—just two days before the Committee of Style was formed—about whether Congress should be given the power to erect piers in order to protect shipping, during which Morris suggested that this could be done under the general welfare clause. "If this [clause] comprehends such a power," McHenry noted in horror, then it would also grant sundry other powers to the legislature, such as the power "to grant exclusive privileges to trading companies etc."[73] We have no record of Morris commenting on the punctuation of the general welfare clause, so it is impossible to prove that the semicolon was a deliberate "trick" on his part (as Gallatin charged) rather than a mere "erratum" (as Madison suggested), but if it was the latter then it was a rather striking coincidence.[74]

We know that quietly smuggling changes—or at least ambiguities—into the Constitution's text was not beyond Morris, for we have two statements from his own pen in which he admits having done so. In the letter to Timothy Pickering in which he declared that he sought to render the Constitution "as clear as our language would permit," Morris immediately went on to acknowledge that "a part of what relates to the judiciary" represented an exception to this rule: "On that subject, conflicting opinions had been maintained with so much professional astuteness, that it became necessary to select phrases, which expressing my own notions would not alarm others [i.e., the other delegates], nor shock their selflove."[75]

Morris appears to be referring here to the judicial vesting clause, which had initially stated that the judicial power "shall be vested in one Supreme Court, and in such inferior courts, as shall, when necessary, from time to time, be constituted by the Legislature of the United States," but which Morris tweaked so as to state that this power "shall be vested in one Supreme Court, and in such inferior courts as the Congress may from time to time ordain and establish."[76] In addition to making the passage much simpler and cleaner, Morris subtly shifted the language to suggest that Congress was *required* to establish lower federal courts, or at the very least that it could do so at its own discretion—not just when it found such courts to be "necessary."[77] Back in mid-July the delegates had debated whether or not lower federal courts should be constitutionally mandated; Morris contended that they should be, but the delegates ended up voting to "empower" (but not require) Congress to establish such courts.[78] Morris admitted in the letter to Pickering that in drafting the Constitution he sought to "select phrases" regarding the judiciary that would be subtle enough to "not alarm others" but that would still convey his "own notions"—that is, his belief that the creation of lower federal courts should be encouraged if not required. Moreover, as a senator Morris argued that the judicial vesting clause as he constructed it did indeed mandate the creation of lower federal courts. In a speech on the repeal of the Judiciary Act of 1801, he asserted that this clause "amounts to a declaration that the *Inferior* Courts *shall* exist" and that "the Congress *shall* ordain and establish them. . . . this is the evident intention, if not the express words, of the Constitution."[79] With respect to the judicial vesting clause, then, Morris was at least a misleading scrivener, if not an outright dishonest one.

Morris made a similar admission regarding the new states and territories clauses in a letter written in December 1803, in the wake of the Louisiana Purchase. To Henry W. Livingston—who was then a New York Congressman, but who had also served as Morris's private secretary during his time in France—he confided: "I always thought that, when we should acquire Canada and Louisiana it would be proper to govern them as provinces, and allow them no voice in our councils. In wording the third section of the fourth article [of the Constitution], I went as far as circumstances would permit to establish the exclusion. Candor obliges me to add my belief, that, had it been more pointedly expressed, a strong opposition would have been made."[80] This time Morris appears to be referring to the Constitution's provisions that "new States may be admitted by the Congress into this Union" and that "Congress shall have power to dispose of and make all needful rules and regulations respecting the territory or other property belonging to the United States."[81] The latter provision was added to the Constitution in late August at Morris's behest, and around the same time he successfully moved to strike out a stipulation in the Committee of Detail's draft constitution that "new States shall be admitted on the same terms with the original States."[82]

As we will see in chapter 5, Morris consistently sought to limit the political power of the western territories out of a combination of an elitist disdain for their backward ways and a progressive worry that they would embrace slavery and tilt the balance of national power in a proslavery direction. His formulation of the new states clause certainly left open the possibility that new states might not be accorded an equal status; all the clause says is that they may be admitted by Congress into the union. Judging from the letter to Livingston, Morris apparently hoped that the stipulation in the territories clause that Congress would have "the power to dispose of and make all needful rules and regulations respecting" the territories would be read in a way that would enable Congress to give these territories less than equal representation even after granting them statehood. Such a reading seems like a stretch, as Morris himself conceded ("I went as far as circumstances would permit ... had it been more pointedly expressed, a strong opposition would have been made"), and of course the states that were carved out of the Louisiana Purchase were eventually admitted on an equal footing despite Morris's objections.[83] Still, we have here a second instance of Morris confessing that he deliberately fudged a constitutional provision in hopes of embedding his own preferences into the nation's fundamental charter, or at least creating sufficient ambiguity to enable multiple interpretations.[84]

Although Morris never admitted having taken liberties with the Constitution's text beyond these two instances, it is almost certain that he did. William Treanor's recent law review article systematically compares Morris's draft of the Constitution with the resolutions that had been previously adopted by the Convention and concludes that Morris made no fewer than fifteen covert but substantive changes to the charter in order to further his own political goals. As Treanor summarizes, Morris

> wrote text that could be read to expand the power of the national government (the Preamble), strengthen the executive (the Vesting Clauses of Articles I and II), mandate the creation of lower federal courts (Article III Vesting Clause), provide a textual basis for judicial review (the law-of-the-land provision), elevate

the constitutional position of both the executive and federal courts (the basic structure of Article I, Article II, and Article III), bar state interference with public contracts (the Contract Clause), block the admission of slave states of Kentucky and Tennessee to the Union while permitting the admission of the free state of Vermont (the New States Clause), include members of Congress in the line of succession to the presidency (the Presidential Succession Clause), expand the ability of the national government to assume state debts (the Engagements Clause), allow Congress to add qualifications to membership (the Qualifications Clause), and broaden the grounds for impeachment (the Impeachment Clause). Morris also removed constitutional text suggesting that slavery was just (the Fugitive Slave Clause).[85]

Treanor further shows that Federalists like Hamilton repeatedly drew on these very passages in the course of fighting for their reading of the Constitution during the republic's early years.

Some of Morris's more important textual changes will be discussed in the succeeding chapters of this book, but it will be impossible to recapitulate all the details of Treanor's painstaking research, as doing so would nearly double the book's length—and perhaps also test the patience of readers who are not themselves experts in constitutional law. Suffice it to say that we now know, thanks to Treanor, that Morris's role as the Constitution's drafter was far more consequential than historians and constitutional lawyers had suspected until just a few years ago.

Morris's draft of the Constitution was read aloud to the delegates on September 12, and they spent the remainder of that day and the following three days discussing it.[86] The changes that they made during this last week were relatively minor. For instance, the delegations voted to lower the threshold for Congress to override a presidential veto from three-fourths to two-thirds of each house, made a few small tweaks to the inspection laws and duties that states could pass, struck a provision stipulating that Congress could appoint a treasurer, added a domestic emoluments clause for the president, included a provision whereby a convention could be called to add amendments, stipulated that no state could be deprived of its equal suffrage in the Senate without its consent, and changed the upper limit on the number of representatives from no more than one for every forty thousand people to no more than one for every thirty thousand.[87] At the close of the session on Saturday, September 15, the state delegations voted unanimously to approve the Constitution with these tweaks.[88] It was thus overwhelmingly the Committee of Style's Constitution—*Morris's* Constitution—that was adopted by the Convention and then ratified by the states, and that remains in effect today.

On the day scheduled for the signing of the Constitution—Monday, September 17—Benjamin Franklin opened the proceedings with a sort of valedictory address, the main aim of which was to convince the delegates who had qualms about the proposed government to make allowances for their own fallibility and to endorse the charter that the group had crafted so painstakingly. It is likely that Morris and James Wilson helped him to write the speech, which was later printed in newspapers across the nation.[89] Upon concluding his speech, Franklin moved that the Constitution be signed by the delegates under the form: "Done in Convention by the unanimous consent of *the States* present, the seventeenth of September, &c. In witness whereof, we have hereunto subscribed our names."[90] The idea was that the delegates would not be signaling their own, personal approval of the Constitution by signing their names to it, only attesting to the fact that the eleven states then present at the Convention had unanimously agreed to it. Madison noted that "this ambiguous form had been drawn up by Mr. Gouverneur Morris, in order to gain the dissenting members, and put in the hands of Doctor Franklin, that it might have the better chance of success."[91] Morris's role in this little scheme was thus doubly Machiavellian: not only did he devise a slightly misleading formulation to try to bring the Convention's recalcitrant members on board and provide the appearance of unanimity, he also had the venerable Franklin introduce it in an attempt to disguise its provenance.[92]

Morris's scheme met with modest, but only modest, success. William Blount of North Carolina announced that he had not intended to sign but that "he was relieved by the form proposed, and would, without committing himself [to support the Constitution], attest the fact that the plan was the unanimous act of the States in Convention"—so Morris and Franklin succeeded in getting at least one extra delegate to add his name to the charter.[93] However, George Mason, Edmund Randolph, and Elbridge Gerry all persisted in their refusal to sign. Randolph declared that he "could not but regard the signing in the proposed form, as the same with signing the Constitution," and Gerry agreed that "the proposed form made no difference with him."[94] Moreover, two South Carolina delegates, Charles Cotesworth Pinckney and Pierce Butler, "thought it best to be candid" and disliked "the ambiguity of the proposed form of signing," so much so that they voted against it: Franklin's motion passed with ten states in favor, none opposed, and South Carolina divided.[95]

In any case, at the close of the session all the delegates present except Mason, Randolph, and Gerry put their names to the document. Although there were thirty-eight signers present that day, the Constitution has thirty-nine signatures, because George Read of Delaware signed on behalf of John Dickinson, who was absent due to illness. Morris's signature appears to be the very last one on the page, but he was not actually the last person to sign it. After Washington signed his name first, the state delegations lined up from north to south. The New Hampshire delegates, followed by those of Massachusetts, Connecticut, New York, New Jersey, and Pennsylvania, signed their names on the righthand side of the page, but at that point they ran out of room, so the delegates from Delaware through Georgia added their names in another column to the left.[96] Morris's abbreviated signature—"Gouvr. Morris"—thus ended up at the bottom right, as the last of the Pennsylvania delegates.

That evening the delegates met for a final dinner at the City Tavern to celebrate all that they had achieved. The next day Morris had an early dinner with Washington and Robert Morris at the latter's house, after which the Morrises accompanied the general as far as Gray's Ferry, on the Schuylkill River just south of Philadelphia. (Washington recorded in his diary in reference to the Morrises, "Took my leave of those families in w[hi]ch I had been most intimate.")[97] Morris soon departed for Morrisania, then Virginia, then Europe. As momentous and action-packed as the remainder of his life would prove to be, none of his other actions or accomplishments would have quite as deep and abiding an impact as his efforts that summer have had.

Before we turn to a more detailed exploration of Morris's positions and arguments at the Convention, a word of caution should be registered. There is, of course, no full or exact transcription of what Morris or anyone else said within the confines of the Pennsylvania State House's Assembly Room. An official journal of the Convention's proceedings was kept by its secretary, William Jackson, but it is mostly a bare-bones record of the votes taken, with almost nothing in the way of detail about what individual figures said.[98] We also have notes from a number of delegates, including Gunning Bedford, Pierce Butler, John Dickinson, Alexander Hamilton, Rufus King, John Lansing, James

Madison, George Mason, James McHenry, William Paterson, William Pierce, James Wilson, and Robert Yates, but most of these notes—all but those of Madison, and in some instances King, Lansing, and Yates—are quite sketchy and fragmentary.[99]

Morris himself took no notes at the Convention, and he later expressed a degree of disdain for those who did:

> While I sat in the Convention, my mind was too much occupied by the interests of our country to keep notes of what we had done. Some gentlemen, I was told, passed their evenings transcribing speeches from shorthand minutes of the day. They can speak positively on matters, of which I have little recollection. My faculties were on the stretch to further our business, remove impediments, obviate objections, and conciliate jarring opinions.[100]

Morris's rather uncharitable implication, of course, is that those delegates (like Madison) who dedicated a great deal of energy and attention to taking and transcribing notes were insufficiently devoted to the Convention's actual work and hence to "the interests of our country." In another letter, Morris remarked that "it is not possible for me to recollect with precision all that passed in the Convention, while we were framing the Constitution; and if I could, it is most probable, that a meaning may have been conceived from incidental expressions, different from that which they were intended to convey, and very different from the fixed opinions of the speaker. This happens daily."[101] Here the obvious insinuation is that no notetaker or other observer could be counted on to accurately represent the views of the other delegates.

Those of us who are interested in Morris—and in what went on at the Convention more generally—must nevertheless remain eternally grateful to Madison, in particular, for having taken on this burdensome chore. After all, it is only because of his notes that we have a real sense of how the Constitution took shape over the course of the summer; they alone enable us to track the flow of the debate and give us insight into the arguments made by individual delegates. Madison's notes are not only far more detailed than those of any other delegate, they are also the only ones that cover every day of the Convention. It should always be remembered, however, that even Madison's notes are a summary of what he understood the various delegates to have said, and which he often pieced together after the fact, rather than a reliable transcription of what they actually said. In the following chapters, then, every claim that

"Morris argued X" should be read as shorthand for "According to Madison (and sometimes also the other recordkeepers), Morris argued X."

It should also be mentioned that Madison later revised his Convention notes at various points, and that some of these revisions appear to have been politically motivated.[102] For instance, after he joined the Jeffersonian Republican camp in the 1790s, Madison may have tried to downplay the depth of his opposition to any remnant of state sovereignty during the Convention. There is little reason to believe, however, that his notes on Morris's speeches were substantially altered.[103] Madison noted at one point that "the correctness of [Morris's] language and the distinctness of his enunciation were particularly favorable to a reporter," perhaps suggesting that his notes on Morris's contributions are among his most reliable.[104] Moreover, if we can believe Madison's later testimony, Morris himself confirmed that Madison had accurately captured one of his most important and audacious speeches, his July 2 discourse on the composition of the Senate. Madison claimed that when he showed his version of the speech to Morris, he "acquiesced in it without even a verbal change."[105] Madison's secretary, Nicholas Trist, also recorded Madison as saying that Morris "was not perhaps himself conscious of how far he went" in the speech, "and when the thing *stared him in the face* . . . as written down by me, it caused him to laugh, while he acknowledged its truth."[106]

So much for overviews and caveats; let us dive into Morris's specific arguments at the Convention, beginning with his views on federalism and the role of the states.

3. A Representative of America: Federalism

When the Constitutional Convention assembled in Philadelphia, the state governments were still the sovereign powers in America. The Articles of Confederation had gone into effect in 1781—three years after Morris signed them on behalf of New York—but this first attempt at a national constitution did not produce a true national government so much as an alliance among the thirteen states—a "firm league of friendship," as the Articles themselves described it.[1] The Confederation Congress scarcely touched on the states' internal affairs, as it was designed to do little more than provide for defense and foreign relations and regulate a few aspects of trade. Moreover, the Congress found it difficult to meet even these minimal objectives. Most of the big decisions that it faced—questions of war and peace, the formation of treaties and alliances, borrowing and spending money—required the concurrence of a supermajority of nine of the thirteen states, which was often hard to come by. And even when the Congress managed to overcome this hurdle, it had no real means of compelling the states to follow its directives, and states routinely refused to pay taxes, supply troops, obey treaties, and respect one another's trading rights. The state legislatures remained the focal point among elected leaders and everyday citizens alike, for this was where the real power resided. The Confederation Congress frequently struggled even to achieve a quorum in order to conduct business.

It is unsurprising that Americans adopted a highly decentralized political system in the midst of the Revolutionary War, for the notion of centralized power ran squarely counter to the intellectual culture that had fueled the revolution in the first place. One of the key principles that the colonists appealed to in order to discredit British rule in America, after all, was that political power should, as far as practicable, be exercised on a local level so as to enable the people to govern themselves rather than be ruled by an elite in a distant capital city over whom they had little influence. Moreover, there was as of yet little sense of collective national identity among the populace; most Americans felt a far deeper sense of loyalty to their state than to the abstract idea of "America."

As the war ended and the 1780s wore on, however, it became more and more evident that the fecklessness of the Confederation was rendering the country weak, poor, and chaotic. That is, of course, why the Philadelphia Convention was called in the first place. This context is important to remember: today many Americans—especially but not exclusively on the political right—assume that the Constitution's primary purpose was to limit the national government through various checks and balances and thereby prevent the tyrannical exercise of power, but in fact the principal impetus for the Convention was less to forestall tyranny than to avoid anarchy. The immediate problem that the framers faced in 1787 was not an overbearing King George but rather an impotent Confederation Congress, so they gathered in Philadelphia in order to make the national government *stronger* and more effective.

The delegates who gathered in Philadelphia were thus almost all "nationalists" in the sense that they appreciated the need to bolster the Confederation's authority, but some were willing to go much further than others in this regard. Some of the delegates—such as those who formulated and supported the New Jersey Plan—thought that the states should retain their basic sovereignty, while others insisted that the states' powers would have to be drastically curtailed.[2] One of the firmest nationalists was Morris's friend Alexander Hamilton, who proclaimed in a marathon speech on June 18 that "we must establish a general and national government, completely sovereign, and annihilate the state distinctions and state operations; and unless we do this, no good purpose can be answered."[3] (Incidentally, Hamilton's son later claimed that Morris pronounced Hamilton's now-infamous speech to be "the most able and impressive he had ever heard," but it seems unlikely that this is entirely accurate, for Morris was off at Morrisania when Hamilton delivered it.)[4] Not to be outdone, George Read of Delaware claimed that "the idea of distinct States ... would be a perpetual source of discord" and that "there can be no cure for this evil but doing away [with the] States altogether, and uniting them all into one great society."[5] Pierce Butler of South Carolina added that he would be content to join with Read "in abolishing the State Legislatures, and becoming one Nation instead of a confed[eratio]n of Republics" as long as the South was given sufficient representation in the legislature on account of its slaves.[6]

Morris was one of the three main leaders of the nationalist camp at the Convention, along with James Madison and James Wilson, but none of these three figures ever went as far as to suggest that the states or state governments should be abolished altogether.[7] While Hamilton, Read, Butler, and perhaps some others were more uncompromising in their nationalism than Morris, he was arguably the Convention's most *passionate* nationalist.[8] Time and again he insisted that "State attachments, and State importance, have been the bane of this country," and time and again he berated his fellow delegates for acting as if they had been "assembled to truck and bargain for our particular States."[9] Whereas most of the delegates regarded themselves as representatives of Virginia or Massachusetts, South Carolina or New Jersey, Morris boldly declared that "he came here as a Representative of America; he flattered himself he came here in some degree as a Representative of the whole human race."[10] "Among the many provisions which had been urged" at the Convention, he complained, "he had seen none for supporting the dignity and splendor of the American Empire. It had been one of our greatest misfortunes that the great objects of the nation had been sacrificed constantly to local views."[11] This stance would not have come as a surprise to anyone who was familiar with Morris's career up to that point.

Morris was effectively a nationalist before there was even an American nation. As early as his 1768 commencement address at King's College, which he delivered when he was just sixteen years old, he expressed pride in being able to "boast the glorious Title of free born American."[12] In his first political post, as a member of the New York provincial congress (1775–1777), Morris advocated both that the state join the independence movement and that the provincial congress draft a new state constitution. In one of his orations, he in fact looked beyond the need for a new state government to the possibility of a new, energetic national government based on the division of the entire country into small districts.[13] At a time when the only national government was the makeshift Second Continental Congress, this was strikingly visionary.

During Morris's time in the Continental Congress itself (1778–1779), we have seen, he proposed numerous reforms—including instituting a more vigorous executive, reorganizing the treasury, consolidating the states' debts, establishing a single national currency, and giving the congress a more effective taxing capability—that would have strengthened the national authority, almost all of which ended up being a decade ahead of their time.[14] One of his reports complained that "the [state] Governments being distinct the Machine is proportionately complex and consequently every Effort will be slow and every System liable to great Derangement."[15] It was also during this time, in his public letters to the Carlisle Commissioners, that Morris first adopted the pseudonym that he would use consistently (if not quite exclusively) for the remainder of his life: "An American."[16] He was still using that continental-minded pen name in 1816, the year of his death.[17]

We have also seen that Morris worked with Robert Morris in the Confederation's finance office (1781–1783) to develop a national financial program—including the issuing of a temporary currency, the implementation of new taxes, and the chartering of a national bank—in an attempt to rescue the nation's sinking credit and thereby to keep the army supplied and in the field. The bane of the Morrises' efforts during these years was the state legislatures, which were forever dilatory in contributing promised funds to the national treasury but all too eager to slap tariffs on commerce from other states in an effort to protect their own industries. The Morrises hoped that their financial policies would eventually give rise to a greater sense of national identity and a more vigorous central government, so much so that when these hopes were frustrated, they sank to the point of encouraging disgruntled army officers to force the Confederation Congress's hand—the so-called Newburgh conspiracy.

After the war's conclusion Morris left politics for several years, partly because he was just as interested in private life as in political matters, but also partly because he felt that there was little use serving in a national government that had insufficient power to govern. As he wrote to John Jay in January 1784, "the general Government wants Energy," and that lack was unlikely to be rectified until "the present Generation" with its stubborn state loyalties "die[s] away, and give[s] Place to a Race of Americans."[18] This may have been one reason why Morris was reluctant to attend the Philadelphia Convention and asked Pennsylvania's General Assembly not to include him in the state's delegation: he was doubtful that the time was yet ripe for creating an effective national government. As he remarked later in life, whatever "national sentiment" had been "generated by fellowship in the revolutionary war," by 1787 that sentiment was "sinking under the pressure of state interest, commercial rivalry, the pursuit of wealth, and those thousand giddy projects, which the intoxication of independence . . . had engendered."[19] Once he agreed to attend the Convention, however, Morris resolved to fight for the centralized power that he had envisioned since the outset of the Revolution.

The fifteen-point Virginia Plan that Morris and Wilson helped Madison and the rest of the Virginia delegation devise prior to the Convention's official opening was not to his liking in every respect, judging from his interventions later in the summer. To take just one glaring example, the plan specified that the executive would be elected by the national legislature, which is an arrangement that Morris went on to fight as vehemently and persistently as anything at the Convention.[20] On the most basic level, however, the Virginia Plan did exactly what Morris thought necessary: it replaced the Confederation Congress and its subservience to the state legislatures with a true, fully empowered, three-branch national government. The fact that this plan ended up serving as the starting point for the Convention's deliberations represented a coup of sorts for the more national-minded delegates, for it established at the outset that they would not limit themselves to proposing amendments to the Articles of Confederation, as they had been charged with doing, but would instead forge an entirely new charter. (One historian has called the lack of a quorum at the Convention's scheduled opening "the delay that produced a revolution.")[21]

As it was presented by Edmund Randolph on May 29, the Virginia Plan's first resolution was somewhat disingenuous. It held that "the Articles of Confederation ought to be so corrected and enlarged as to accomplish the objects proposed by their institution; namely, 'common defence, security of liberty, and general welfare'"—yet the succeeding fourteen resolutions did not correct and enlarge the Articles so much as entirely replace them.[22] When the debate on the plan opened on May 30, Morris immediately sought to clear up the ambiguity, suggesting that the first resolution was dubious "as the subsequent resolutions would not agree with it."[23] At Morris's suggestion, Randolph moved that they postpone consideration of this resolution and instead take up three resolutions that got to the very heart of the matter:

1. That a union of the States merely federal will not accomplish the objects proposed by the Articles of Confederation, namely, common defence, security of liberty, and general welfare.
2. That no treaty or treaties among the whole or part of the States, as individual sovereignties, would be sufficient.
3. That a *national* government ought to be established, consisting of a *supreme* Legislative, Executive and Judiciary.[24]

There they had it: on the first day of substantive debate, less than a week after the Convention's opening, Morris and Randolph had seized control of the agenda and opened the fundamental question of whether to replace the "merely federal" government of the Articles with a new "*national* government."

Some of the delegates, wondering whether the Convention had the authority to propose such a government and whether it would be compatible with the continued existence of the state governments, asked for clarification about what exactly was meant by the terms "national" and "supreme" in the third resolution. Morris did not beat around the bush in his response: he "explained the distinction between a *federal* and a *national, supreme* government; the former being a mere compact resting on the good faith of the parties; the latter having a complete and *compulsive* operation. He contended, that in all communities there must be one supreme power, and one only."[25] The notes of James McHenry have Morris adding that "a federal agreement which each party may violate at pleasure cannot answer the purpose. One government [is] better calculated to prevent wars or render them less expensive or bloody than many [governments]. We had better take a supreme government now, than a despot twenty years hence—for come he must."[26] In order to fulfill the promise of the revolution and ensure that republican government would endure in the United States, in other words, Americans would have to muster the courage to abandon their penchant for decentralization and place the supreme political power squarely in the hands of the national government.

Morris and the nationalists scored an early victory when, after a relatively short debate, the third proposition—the one proposing that they formulate a national government consisting of supreme legislative, executive, and judicial branches—was adopted by a vote of six states in favor, Connecticut opposed, and New York divided.[27] This triumph was not as clear-cut as it might have appeared, however, because the delegations from a number of the smaller states that would later fight to preserve some of the states' sovereignty (New Hampshire, New Jersey, Maryland, and Georgia) had not yet arrived, and New York's vote was sure to switch from divided to opposed once John Lansing showed up later in the week. And, indeed, the nationalists were later forced to back off from this explicit, unequivocal embrace of a supreme national power.

On June 20, when Morris was away at Morrisania, the delegates unanimously agreed to drop the term "national" from the description of the government that they were forming, and it was never reinstated: the word does not appear anywhere in the Constitution itself.[28] The associated term "supreme" survived only in the references to the Supreme Court and in the stipulation in Article VI that the "Constitution, and the laws of the United States which shall be made in pursuance thereof... shall be the supreme law of the land; and the judges in every State shall be bound thereby, any thing in the constitution or laws of any State to the contrary notwithstanding."[29] While the Constitution and federal laws were thus declared to be superior to the state constitutions and state laws, neither the federal government nor its three branches were explicitly described as the supreme political powers, as Morris had proposed to do at the outset of the Convention.

Morris himself, however, never abandoned his commitment to the idea of a supreme national power. The "cover letter" that he and the Committee of Style drafted for submission to the Confederation Congress persisted in using the contentious word "national," along with the even more taboo term "consolidation." The letter began by drawing an analogy between the states joining the union and individuals entering into a Lockean-style social contract: "It is obviously impracticable, in the federal government of these States, to secure all rights of independent sovereignty to each, and yet provide for the interest and safety of all. Individuals entering into society must give up a share of liberty, to preserve the rest." In deciding how much sovereignty the states would have to give up, the letter continued, the delegates had "kept steadily in our view that which appeared to us the great interest of every true American, the consolidation of our union, in which is involved our prosperity, felicity, safety, perhaps our national existence."[30] During the entire Convention the term "consolidation" had been used in a favorable sense only twice—once by George Read and once by Rufus King—and seemingly countless delegates had expressed their horror of it, but Morris and the committee boldly described it as being "the great interest of every true American."[31] This was a rather aggressive move in a document that would be not only submitted to the Confederation Congress but also printed far and wide alongside the Constitution itself.[32] It is puzzling that there were no objections to this language when the letter was read aloud and approved by the Convention on September 12; perhaps the lack of resistance was due to the fact that many of the state-minded delegates had left the Convention by that point, or perhaps it was simply an oversight by a weary group that was eager to turn to Morris's draft of the Constitution.

By the end of the Convention, most of the delegates appear to have regarded their proposed plan as a judicious mixture between a "national" plan and a "federal" one; this is also how Madison went on to sell it in *Federalist* #39. It had been a commonplace of political theory for more than a century—dating back to Jean Bodin and Thomas Hobbes—that sovereignty was necessarily indivisible. In order to prevent a kingdom from being divided against itself, the thinking went, the ultimate political authority had to be vested in a single entity, whether it be monarch or parliament.[33] The framers' response to this purported imperative was to locate the ultimate sovereignty neither in the national government nor in the state governments but rather in the people themselves, who could then allocate the exercise of their sovereign power to a mixture of national and state entities. Morris appears to have accepted this reconceptualization of the issue: later in the Convention, he declared that the president would be more akin to the prime minister than the king in the British system because in America "the people are the King," and in the context of arguing that the Constitution should be ratified by popularly elected conventions rather than by the state legislatures, he described "the people of the United States" as "the supreme authority."[34] As Morris made clear from the outset of the Convention, however, he believed that the people should lodge their sovereign power firmly in the custody of a "supreme" national government and that the hitherto-sovereign state governments should be rendered emphatically subordinate.

Morris spent much of the summer pushing back against what he regarded as his fellow delegates' provincialism. Again, the very fact that these individuals had agreed to attend the Convention indicated that they were among America's more national-minded leaders, but Morris still felt that many of them were too wedded to the state governments in general and to their own states in particular. Any national government that remained "dependent on the States," he insisted on July 2, "will act over again the part which [the Confederation] Congress has acted. A firm government alone can protect our liberties."[35] A few days later he reiterated the point, declaring that "we must have an efficient [national] Government, and if there be an efficiency in the local [i.e., state] Governments, the former is impossible."[36] For corroborating evidence he turned to the examples of Germany, the Dutch Republic, and ancient Greece. In most confederations throughout history, the member-states had constantly encroached on the central authority, leading to conflict and turmoil within the confederacy as well as weakness and humiliation on the international stage. This is why Morris believed that it was so crucial for the American states to be—as the nation's very name implied that they should be—truly united.

Even within a gathering of national-minded leaders, Morris's cosmopolitan outlook stood out. He constantly urged the other delegates to

> extend their views beyond the present moment of time; beyond the narrow limits of place from which they derive their political origin. . . . He wished our ideas to be enlarged to the true interest of man, instead of being circumscribed within the narrow compass of a particular spot. And, after all, how little can be the motive yielded by selfishness for such a policy? Who can say, whether he himself, much less whether his children, will the next year be an inhabitant of this or that state?"[37]

When some of the delegates began to bicker about the relative influence of the northern and southern states within the future Congress, Morris commented that he "regretted the turn of the debate. The States, he found, had many representatives on the floor. Few, he feared, were to be deemed the Representatives of America."[38]

Of course, it was presumably easier for Morris, as a native New Yorker who was currently part of the Pennsylvania delegation, to envision himself as a representative of the entire country than it was for many others. Similarly, Morris may not have known whether he would "next year be an inhabitant of this or that state," given his wealth, far-flung business ventures, and bachelor lifestyle, but most of the delegates knew perfectly well where they would be living for some time to come. Although he proclaimed himself to be a "representative of America," Morris's cosmopolitanism actually made him *un*representative of most Americans, whose orientation tended to be far more local in nature. Moreover, Morris's broad-mindedness rarely extended to the western territories, which he wished to keep permanently subordinate to the original thirteen states—a contradiction that Madison was quick to point out.[39] Still, the Convention surely would have proceeded far more smoothly, and might have also formulated a superior Constitution, if more delegates had heeded Morris's perpetual pleas to rise above local considerations and sectional jealousies.

Like Madison and some of the other nationalist delegates, Morris deemed the state governments to be deeply problematic, both because of their own internal vices—such as their tendency to allow majorities to tyrannize too easily over minorities—and because they so frequently stood in the way of the broader national interest.[40] Morris must have raised more than a few eyebrows when he asked rhetorically, "if all the Charters and Constitutions of the States were thrown into the fire, and all their demagogues into the ocean—what would it be to the happiness of America?"[41] When some delegates worried about how to prevent a national majority "from injuring particular States," Morris responded pointedly that "particular States ought to be injured for the sake of a majority of the people, in case their conduct should deserve it. Suppose they should insist on claims evidently unjust, and pursue them in a manner detrimental to the whole body: suppose they should give themselves up to foreign influence: Ought they to be protected in such cases?"[42]

Perhaps the greatest worry of all, in Morris's eyes, was that divisions among the states would lead to actual military conflict and foreign interference. At one point Gunning Bedford of Delaware warned that if the large states insisted on dissolving the Confederation, then "the small ones will find some foreign ally, of more honor and good faith, who will take them by the hand, and do them justice."[43] Morris's response was ruthlessly blunt: "This country must be united. If persuasion does not unite it, the sword will. . . . The scenes of horror attending civil commotion cannot be described; and the conclusion of them will be worse than the term of their continuance. The stronger party will then make traitors of the weaker; and the gallows and halter will finish the work of the sword."[44] This threat was not exactly well calculated to conciliate the advocates of greater state power, and several delegates quite reasonably protested against Morris's outburst. His emotions had clearly gotten the better of him in this instance. The underlying point that he was trying to make, however, should not be lost: as long as the states remained the dominant political authorities, the potential for a terrible civil war would always loom over them. The states were (and are) often viewed as laboratories of democracy and seminaries of republican virtue, but Morris thought that they were more often repositories of majority faction and engines of national discord.

Morris acknowledged that the states and state governments could not be eliminated, but he did think that they could be rendered less dangerous. As he provocatively put it at one point, "We cannot annihilate, but we may perhaps take out the teeth of, the serpents."[45] In order to achieve that end, Morris was willing to grant the national government as much scope for action as nearly any delegate.

The Virginia Plan had bestowed something close to plenary power on the national government in its sixth resolution, which stipulated that Congress would "enjoy the legislative rights vested in Congress by the Confederation, and moreover to legislate in all cases to which the separate States are incompetent, or in which the harmony of the United States may be interrupted by the exercise of individual [i.e., state] legislation."[46] As the nationalists might have expected, this did not sit well with the more state-minded delegates. When the resolution was taken up for discussion on July 17, Roger Sherman proposed that the national government should be prohibited from interfering in the "internal police" of the individual states; surprisingly, he was seconded in this instance by no less a nationalist than James Wilson.[47] Whereas today the term "police" is typically used to refer to law enforcement, in the eighteenth century it was more often employed to denote the making of policy more generally, and Morris was quick to object that "the internal police, as it would be called and understood by the States, ought to be infringed in many cases, as in the case of paper-money, and other tricks by which citizens of other States may be affected."[48] While Sherman's proposal failed, Morris was the only delegate at the Convention who explicitly advocated giving the national government police power within the states.

The virtually open-ended grant of national power that had been on the table since the Virginia Plan was abandoned by the Committee of Detail, which, apparently on its own initiative, included a list of enumerated congressional powers within its draft constitution.[49] No one objected to this move when it was taken up on August 16, although both Madison and Charles Pinckney submitted a raft of additional powers that they thought should be included in the list.[50] Morris took a slightly different tack, advocating the creation of a Secretary of Domestic Affairs who would, as part of the president's cabinet, "attend to matters of general police, the state of agriculture and manufactures, the opening of roads and navigations, and the facilitating communications through the United States."[51] This proposal was referred to the Committee of Detail and never heard from again. Had it been adopted, it would have served as an alternative means of granting the national government a "general police" power within the states—and handing it to the executive branch rather than the legislature, to boot.

One of the enumerated powers that the Committee of Detail accorded to Congress was the power "to subdue a rebellion in any State, on the application of its Legislature."[52] When this clause was brought before the Convention, Charles Pinckney moved to strike out the part requiring the application of a state's legislature, and Morris seconded him, adding that "the General

Government should enforce obedience in all cases where it may be necessary."⁵³ Several delegates protested that a state ought to give its consent before national forces were brought in, including Elbridge Gerry, who declared himself to be "against letting loose the myrmidons of the United States on a State, without its own consent."⁵⁴ Morris responded that "we are acting a very strange part. We first form a strong man to protect us, and at the same time we wish to tie his hands behind him. The [national] Legislature may surely be trusted with such a power to preserve the public tranquillity."⁵⁵ The language about subduing rebellions was eventually dropped from the Constitution altogether, but the importance of Morris's objection to the Committee of Detail's formulation was made manifest in 1861, when Abraham Lincoln and the Republican Congress would have had a decidedly difficult time obtaining the consent of South Carolina's legislature to set about subduing the rebellion within that state.

There was one means of checking the state governments that Morris opposed. Thanks to Madison, the Virginia Plan gave Congress a "negative" or veto over state laws.⁵⁶ This is something that Madison fought for vigorously and persistently throughout the summer; he felt that "an indefinite power to negative legislative acts of the States [was] absolutely necessary to a perfect system," and in fact "the mildest expedient that could be devised for preventing [the] mischiefs" caused by the state governments.⁵⁷ This provision was, however, rejected time and again by the state delegations, and Morris was among those who argued against it. A federal veto over state laws was, he contended, "likely to be terrible [i.e., objectionable] to the States, and not necessary if sufficient Legislative authority should be given to the General Government."⁵⁸ When Madison continued to advocate for his pet provision, Morris declared himself to be "more and more opposed to the negative. The proposal of it would disgust all the States."⁵⁹

However, Morris went on to suggest that the purpose of the veto could be achieved in a less tendentious way, remarking that "a law that ought to be negatived, will be set aside in the Judiciary department; and if that security should fail, may be repealed by a National law."⁶⁰ In other words, if state laws were subject to judicial review by federal courts, then these courts would have an effective veto over them, and if federal laws were declared to be superior to state laws—as they were in the "supreme law of the land" clause—then Congress could simply pass a law that would supersede any state law that it found problematic. Thus, even in the one prominent instance in which he appeared to break with the other nationalists regarding the scope of national power, Morris revealed that he agreed with their basic aim but simply sought a means of attaining it that would raise fewer hackles.

The debate over the relative power of the national and state governments sometimes—although certainly not always—mapped onto the tensions between the large and small states, with the delegates from the large states generally supporting a stronger national government and those from the small states typically pushing to retain more power within the states.[61] Perhaps the biggest sticking point of the entire summer came in the debate over the basis of representation in the Senate. Most small-state delegates contended that the states should be accorded equal representation in the Senate in order to give the less populous states some protection from the whims of the larger ones, while most large-state delegates insisted that the number of senators should be proportional to each state's population, since equal representation would unfairly grant more political power to individuals who happened to hail from a smaller state. The delegates found this conflict so intractable that at one point David Brearly of New Jersey proposed in exasperation that "a map of the United States be spread out" and "all the existing boundaries be erased, and ... a new partition of the whole be made into thirteen equal parts."[62] It was also in response to this impasse that Benjamin Franklin resorted to suggesting that they open each day's session with a prayer—to which Alexander Hamilton allegedly responded that the Convention did not require any "foreign aid."[63]

Morris, always skeptical of the states and state power, was squarely on the side of proportional representation. Even before the Convention began, as the Pennsylvania and Virginia delegates waited for enough other delegations to arrive to constitute a quorum, he proposed a sort of preemptive strike against state equality. Backed by Robert Morris and some other Pennsylvania delegates, he urged the large states to "unite in firmly refusing the small States an equal vote [within the Convention itself], as unreasonable, and as enabling the small states to negative every good system of government, which must, in the nature of things, be founded on a violation of that equality." As Madison noted, however, the delegates from Virginia "discountenanced and stifled the project" on the grounds that it would be easier to persuade the small states "in the course of the deliberations, to give up their equality" than to require them to "disarm themselves" and "throw themselves on the mercy of the larger States" at the outset.[64] The states were thus given equal votes within the Convention over Morris's objections. It was doubtless prudent to avoid alienating the small states and thereby subverting the Convention before it even began, but Morris was right to assume that this rule would make it much more difficult for the national-minded delegates to get the Constitution that they wanted. William Paterson, the prime architect of the New Jersey Plan, later asked rhetorically, "If a proportional representation be right, why do we not vote so here?"[65]

On May 30, when the delegates began debating the Virginia Plan, George Read threatened to leave the Convention altogether if the states were not given equal representation in the new legislature. While Read was a staunch nationalist, he was also from Delaware, and Delaware's legislature had forbidden its delegates from agreeing to any plan that would surrender the equal vote that the state enjoyed in the Confederation Congress.[66] This was the first flare-up of palpable rancor within the Convention, but Morris refused to back down, asserting that although "the valuable assistance of [the delegates from Delaware] could not be lost without real concern; and . . . so early a proof of discord in the Convention as the secession of a State, would add much to the regret," still the introduction of proportional representation was "so fundamental an article in a national government, that it could not be dispensed with."[67] The standoff was averted by postponing the issue, but it would hover over the deliberations for months to come.

Happily for Morris, he missed much of this futile wrangling, since he was absent from the Convention from May 31 through July 2. On July 5, a committee proposed that the small states get equal representation in the Senate in exchange for proportional representation in the House of Representatives and a provision that all money bills must originate in the House.[68] Morris deemed the proposal thoroughly "objectionable" and "conceived the whole aspect of it to be wrong." If the states were to have equal weight within the Senate, he predicted, "there will be constant disputes and appeals to the States, which will undermine the General Government." Such a system was, in his view, entirely unworkable: "Suppose that the Delegates from Massachusetts and Rhode Island, in the upper house [i.e., Senate], disagree, and that the former are outvoted. What results? They will immediately declare that their State will not abide by the decision, and make such representations as will produce that effect. . . . Of what avail, then, will be what is on paper?"[69] An equality of votes in the Senate would, he added two days later, make the upper house "another [Confederation] Congress, a mere whisp of straw."[70]

The only reason why the states stood on a footing of equality in the

Confederation Congress in the first place, Morris contended, was that the small states, "aware of the necessity of preventing anarchy" in the midst of the war against Britain, had "extorted" an equal vote from the large states when the Articles were drafted. "Standing now on that ground," he went on, "they demand, under the new system, greater rights, as men, than their fellow-citizens of the large States. The proper answer to them is, that the same necessity of which they formerly took advantage does not now exist; and that the large States are at liberty now to consider what is right, rather than what may be expedient."[71] And "what is right," Morris was certain, was to give all citizens an equal say in choosing the nation's leaders, regardless of what state they happen to come from. As Hamilton had put it a week earlier, the states were nothing more than groups of individuals, and "nothing could be more preposterous or absurd" than to privilege these artificial groupings over the people who made them up.[72]

The committee's proposal, complete with equal state representation in the Senate, was narrowly approved by the Convention on July 16, with five states in favor, four opposed, and one divided.[73] Although this agreement would come to be known as the Connecticut Compromise or even the Great Compromise, Morris, Madison, Wilson, and the other nationalists regarded it less as a judicious settlement than as a devastating defeat. Edmund Randolph observed that the vote had "embarrassed the business extremely" and proposed that they adjourn for the day so "that the large States might consider the steps proper to be taken, in the present solemn crisis of the business; and that the small States might also deliberate on the means of conciliation."[74] The small state delegates quickly made it clear that no conciliatory measures would be on offer, but they soon adjourned anyway.

Some of the large state delegates caucused the next morning prior to the opening of that day's debate, but they came to no resolution among themselves. When the Convention came to order, Morris made a last-ditch attempt to overturn the previous day's vote, suggesting that they first decide "in the abstract . . . the powers necessary to be vested in the General Government" and then return to the question of how it would be structured. His motion was not seconded. As Madison commented in his notes, the other opponents of the compromise "probably . . . either despaired of success" using Morris's stratagem "or were apprehensive that the attempt would inflame the jealousies of the smaller States."[75]

A week later, the delegates turned to the question of how the Constitution would be ratified. The debate centered on whether to submit the proposed charter to the state legislatures or to popularly elected conventions in each state, but Morris came up with a third alternative: the Constitution could be submitted "to one General Convention, chosen and authorized by the people, to consider, *amend*, and establish" it.[76] This proposal, too, went without a second: no one else was willing to sideline the states entirely from the ratification process. Morris's suggestion that this national convention could not just approve but also *amend* the Constitution was likely another ploy to overturn the equality of votes in the Senate; while most of the other nationalists had grudgingly accepted the Connecticut Compromise by that point, Morris had not entirely given up hope of dismantling it.[77]

Just moments later, after the delegations had voted overwhelmingly to submit the Constitution to popularly elected ratifying conventions in each state, Morris and Rufus King proposed to have senators vote "per capita," meaning that individual senators would cast their own votes rather than voting together as a state, as the delegations to the Confederation Congress did.[78] (Morris proposed that each state get three senators, but the Convention ended up settling on two.)[79] Luther Martin of Maryland opposed the idea of voting per capita since it marked a departure from "the idea of the *States* being represented in the second branch," but that, of course, was precisely the point.[80] If the senators from a state could potentially disagree with one another and vote differently from one another then the states would have less influence *as states*, even if they had an equal number of representatives. The motion passed with nine states in favor and only Maryland dissenting. Whatever plausible means of minimizing the role of the states that Morris could think up and get accepted, he would take.

At the very end of the Convention, after Morris had drafted the Constitution on behalf of the Committee of Style, the issue of state equality in the Senate arose one final time. On September 15, Roger Sherman voiced a fear that the states' equal votes in the Senate might one day be eliminated via constitutional amendment. In order to avoid this eventuality, he proposed adding a proviso that "no State shall, without its consent, be affected in its internal police, or deprived of its equal suffrage in the Senate."[81] At first his motion was decisively rejected, but Morris, sensing "the circulating murmurs of the small States," proposed to adopt the second part of the proviso—stipulating that "no State, without its consent, shall be deprived of its equal suffrage in the Senate"—which then passed without debate or opposition.[82] Morris managed to discard Sherman's language protecting the states' "internal police" with this move, but in order to appease the small states, the nationalists were forced to agree that it would effectively take the approval of every state legislature, rather than "just" three-quarters of them, to overturn the states' equal votes within the Senate.

Once the new government was up and running, there were no significant political conflicts in which the main divide was between large states and small states; the differences were virtually always between northern states and southern states, or between Federalists and Republicans within all the states. By that point, however, there was no revisiting the structure of the Senate, even had anyone wanted to. Thanks to the last-minute concession that Morris initiated, state equality in the upper house is more deeply entrenched than any other provision in the Constitution.[83] Ironically, then, a key obstacle to reforming the Senate even to this day was the result of a motion by one of the staunchest opponents of state equality.

The states' equal suffrage was not, however, Morris's only reservation about the Senate as it was formulated in the Constitution; his vision of the Senate's very purpose also diverged rather sharply from those of many other delegates.

4. Checking America's Aristocracy: The Senate

There was a general consensus among the framers that the legislature must be the heart of any truly republican government—the first branch among equals, you might say. That was, after all, where the people's elected representatives exercised their lawmaking authority. The legislatures were the dominant branches in the state governments, and the national government under the Articles of Confederation was essentially *just* a legislature. There was also wide—even if not quite complete—agreement that the new Congress should have two houses. While the Confederation Congress was a unicameral body, all the state governments except Georgia and Pennsylvania had bicameral legislatures, and those two states would adopt a second house in 1789 and 1790, respectively. Benjamin Franklin remained partial to Pennsylvania's unicameral model, and the supporters of the New Jersey Plan advocated retaining the single-house Confederation Congress and simply augmenting its powers, but when the question came before the Convention, the state delegations voted firmly in support of a second chamber, with seven states in favor, three opposed, and one divided.[1]

There was less consensus, however, about the precise purpose of the new upper house.[2] There was, of course, no hereditary aristocracy to represent in America, as the House of Lords was designed to do in Britain. Was the Senate simply meant to serve as a check on precipitate legislation—a cooling saucer, as Washington supposedly described it to Jefferson?[3] Was it meant to represent the interests of the states or state legislatures, with the House of Representatives representing the people? Was it meant to be a repository of America's ablest and most educated citizens—the "natural aristocracy"? Was it meant to represent property and wealth? There was also little agreement about how the Senate should be structured. Should its members be chosen by the national legislature's lower house (as was proposed in the Virginia Plan), by the state legislatures, or directly by the people? How long should their terms be?

In what was perhaps his most audacious speech of the entire summer, Morris put forward bold arguments on all these fronts, contending that the Senate should be constructed as an "aristocratic body" that would possess and defend "great personal property" and hence that its members should be appointed by the executive and serve for life without pay.[4] Morris's vision of an aristocratic Senate is often chalked up to his elitism, and not without reason: he was fairly unabashed in his disdain for the common people and in his skepticism about unfettered democracy. Morris's deeper reason for envisioning the Senate in this way, however, was that he distrusted the rich and believed—strangely enough—that this kind of upper house would serve as a means of limiting their power.

Although Morris never wavered in his conviction that the people were the ultimate sovereign—recall his remark that in America "the people are the King"—his elitism was real, and it started early.[5] In a notorious 1774 letter, he described an anti-British protest in New York with piercing patrician disdain: "The mob begin to think and to reason. Poor reptiles! it is with them a vernal morning, they are struggling to cast off their winter's slough, they bask in the sunshine, and ere noon they will bite, depend on it. . . . I see, and see it with fear and trembling, that if the disputes with Britain continue, we shall be under the worst of all possible dominions. We shall be under the domination of a riotous mob."[6] Although Morris was all of twenty-two years old when he wrote these haughty lines, they are among his most frequently quoted remarks and have probably done more to tarnish his reputation among historians than anything else that he said or did. (Note to self: remember not to call people "reptiles.") Even in this letter, however, Morris devoted as much space to criticizing the elites who stirred up and manipulated the common people—the "shepherds" and "belwethers of the flock" who "rouse the mob into an attack upon the bounds of order and decency," as he described them—as he did to belittling the common people themselves.[7]

Morris's reputation as an elitist and a champion of aristocracy has also been propelled by his repeated arguments, in the midst of the French Revolution, that France should retain or restore its nobility. He had little respect for the aristocrats whom he met during his time in Paris, but he also believed that the aristocracy was such an integral part of French history and culture that it would be dangerous to simply do away with it, as the revolutionaries sought to do. In Morris's view, the nobles formed an essential "intermediate order" standing between the king and the people, and their privileged position imbued them with a "constant and regular desire to prevent innovations and change"—a particular blessing in a time of continual turmoil.[8] This is why he included a hereditary senate in the blueprint for an ideal French constitution that he drew up in 1791, even though he never would have dreamed of advocating something like this for the United States.[9]

The nobility were all the more important in France, Morris believed, because of the impoverished, uneducated, beaten-down state of the populace. Without its monarchy and aristocracy, France would be left with "a multitude ungoverned, and very soon ungovernable," which could only lead to "unbridled licentiousness" and then eventually to despotism. The revolutionaries could preach to the rabble all they liked about "the dignity of man, the empire of reason, the majesty of the laws," he declared. "To such fine discourses, you will receive your answer from some decollated victim at the *Place de Grève*."[10] This warning, which Morris made in July 1789, turned out to be astoundingly prescient: the Place de Grève—a plaza in front of the Hôtel de Ville (city hall) in Paris where executions frequently took place—later became the site of the first public use of the guillotine, which decollated its first victim in April 1792.

The horrors that Morris witnessed in France gave him a greater appreciation for the common people of his own country. In August 1792, he wrote to Jefferson, "I verily beleive [sic] that if Mr. de lafayette were to appear just now in Paris unattended by his Army he would be torn to Pieces. Thank God we have no Populace in America and I hope the Education and Manners will long prevent that Evil."[11] Even so, when Morris returned to the United States and entered the Senate, he insisted that one of the primary roles of that body was to check popular whims and those who would prey on them. "Why are we here?" he rhetorically asked his fellow senators at one point. "We are here to save the people from their most dangerous enemy, *to save them from themselves*. What caused the ruin of the Republics of Greece and of Rome? Demagogues, who by flattery prevailed on the populace to establish despotism."[12] Some Republican senators took exception to this jaundiced view of the people, but Morris just doubled down, declaring that this statement "not only fell from my lips, but . . . flowed from my heart" and that the Senate's role was to "guard [the people] against the baneful effects of their own precipitation, their passion, their misguided zeal." During the three decades in which he had served intermittently in public office, he added, "I have frequently been the servant of the people, always their friend; but at no one moment of my life their flatterer, and God forbid that I ever should be."[13]

At the time of the Constitution's drafting and ratification, the idea that the people sometimes err and that majorities sometimes act tyrannically was unremarkable, even trite. This was, for instance, the basic premise of James Madison's *Federalist* #10. By the early nineteenth century, however, many Republicans, taking their cue from President Jefferson, had started to distance themselves from this assumption and to self-consciously cast themselves as apostles of the common man and embodiments of the popular will. The Federalists who continued to be outspoken in their distrust of the people often paid for it at the ballot box, but Morris did not think that that was any reason to disavow an obvious truth. His position was nicely encapsulated in a letter that he wrote to Uriah Tracy, a Federalist senator from Connecticut, in 1804: "The dangerous doctrine, that the public will, expressed by a numerical majority, is in all cases to be obeyed, arises from a perverse confusion of ideas, and leads to horrible results. That numerical majority not only may, but frequently does, will what is unwise and unjust. Those, therefore, who avow the determination strictly to comply with it, acknowledge themselves the willing instruments of folly and vice."[14]

None of this is to say that Morris was a stereotypical conservative in every respect. He welcomed the prospect of a dynamic, commercial society with open arms, and he never hesitated to adopt a radical position when he thought circumstances warranted it, whether it meant standing for American independence at a time when many of his family and friends remained loyal to the crown or advocating the secession of New England and New York from the union in the midst of a foreign war. Morris's wariness of the common people was on full display, however, in his arguments at the Philadelphia Convention about the Senate's structure and purpose.

Morris's main intervention with regard to the Senate came in a lengthy speech that he delivered on July 2, the day that he returned from his prolonged absence from Philadelphia. (The full speech is included in this book's appendix.) That day's session began with a vote on the key question of whether the states would be accorded an equal vote within the Senate, and at this point the delegations remained equally split with five states voting in favor, five against, and Georgia divided.[15] Charles Cotesworth Pinckney proposed that a committee be established to consider the question anew; the committee was duly formed and proposed the so-called Connecticut Compromise on July 5, which was then narrowly adopted on July 16.[16] Although Morris would eventually find the committee's proposal deeply objectionable, on July 2 he deemed the formation of a committee "advisable"—not just because that was the only realistic way to resolve the equal split among the delegations, but also because he saw it as a means by which to entirely reconceive the Senate.[17]

During Morris's absence, the delegates had deliberated about whether senators should be chosen by the House of Representatives, by the state legislatures, or even directly by the people, and in the end the delegations had voted overwhelmingly to have them be appointed by the state legislatures.[18] They had also agreed, after some more wrangling, that senators would serve six-year terms and that they would be paid for their services.[19] Upon resuming his seat Morris promptly and unapologetically called all these settled points into question.

Morris began his oration by declaring that the main "object" of the Senate was "to check the precipitation, changeableness, and excesses" of the House of Representatives. The House was sure to be subject to these ills, he believed, for these problems had always attended governments—and branches of governments—that sprang from and directly represented the people's will. "Every man of observation," Morris noted, "had seen in the democratic branches of the State Legislatures, precipitation—in [the Confederation] Congress, changeableness—in every department, excesses against personal liberty, private property, and personal safety."[20] These, then, were the problems that he thought the Senate should be designed to prevent.

A number of the delegates envisioned the Senate simply as a smaller and thus more select version of the House—a venue for the natural aristocracy—but Morris did not believe that such a Senate would prove sufficient.[21] "*Abilities* and *virtue* are equally necessary in both branches" of Congress, he believed, so "something more" was necessary in the Senate. The senators must not only be capable legislators but also have a "personal interest" in checking the House. Anticipating James Madison's later dictum that "ambition must be made to counteract ambition," Morris argued that "one interest must be opposed to another interest. Vices, as they exist, must be turned against each other."[22] And what would give the senators a personal interest in checking the "precipitation, changeableness, and excesses" of the House, in his view? Two things above all: great wealth and lifetime appointments.

Start with wealth. Morris argued that the senators "must have great personal property," which would give them "the aristocratic spirit" and indeed make them "love to lord it through pride." This spirit would naturally lead them to thwart the inroads on private property to which democratic legislatures had proven so susceptible—"emissions of paper-money, largesses to the people, a remission of debts, and similar measures," as he described them elsewhere.[23] And one way to ensure that senators would be wealthy, Morris suggested, was to refrain from paying them. Once in this high station they might manage to "pay themselves" through covert and illicit means, but few would seek or accept such a position unless they were already rich enough to "do without" formal pay.[24] Whereas Benjamin Franklin opposed the payment of public officers in hopes of ensuring that only disinterested patriots would serve in these positions, then, Morris did so for nearly the opposite reason: to ensure that only the rich could afford to serve.[25] One would have to be quite wealthy indeed to serve in the Senate *for life* without compensation.

Morris argued that lifetime appointments were necessary to give senators the necessary independence from the people and their representatives in the House. "In religion, the creature is apt to forget its Creator," he remarked, but "that it is otherwise in political affairs, the late debates here [i.e., within the Convention] are an unhappy proof." He feared that "the democratic scale will preponderate" in any body that was chosen at regular intervals by the people, or even by the people's representatives in the House or the state legislatures. If the Senate were to remain dependent on the people's will, Morris declared, "we are better off without it. To make it independent, it should be for life." And he suggested that the Senate's independence would be redoubled if the president were to be responsible for selecting senators, filling up vacancies as they occurred, for under this scheme the senators would not be beholden to the people or their representatives for their position.[26]

In addition to conferring greater independence on the senators, lifetime appointments made by the president would have at least three other advantages, as Morris saw it. First, they would give the government greater "permanency" or consistency. "Ask any man if he confides in [the Confederation] Congress—if he confides in the State of Pennsylvania—if he will lend his money, or enter into contract?" Morris suggested. "He will tell you, no. He sees no stability. He can repose no confidence. If Great Britain were to explain her refusal to treat with us, the same reasoning would be employed." One obvious way to avoid changing the laws too often, of course, would be to avoid changing those who make them. Individuals who served for life would have a greater capacity and incentive to plan for the long term; they would have the opportunity to gain more experience in office, and they would not be constantly looking over their shoulder to the next election.[27]

Second, Morris suggested that an "aristocratic" Senate with lifetime appointments might, somewhat ironically, increase the chances of the Constitution being ratified by the people. The people would, after all, be likely to follow their local leaders, and their local leaders would be more apt to support the Constitution if they could expect a grander position under the new government than they had under the Articles of Confederation. Such considerations might be distasteful, Morris conceded, but "he hoped there was strength of mind enough in this House [i.e., the Convention] to look truth in the face. He did not hesitate, therefore, to say that loaves and fishes must bribe the demagogues. . . . A Senate for life will be a noble bait. Without such captivating prospects, the popular leaders will oppose and defeat the plan."[28]

Finally, Morris hoped that lifetime appointments made by the president might help to avoid entirely the question that the delegates had found it so difficult to resolve over the past month, namely whether the states would be equally or proportionally represented in the Senate. If the upper house were to be constructed as he envisioned it, it would not particularly matter how many senators hailed from each state, for "members being independent, and for life, may be taken as well from one place as from another."[29] If the purpose of the Senate was to represent neither the states nor the people but rather wealth, in other words, then the executive could simply choose whomever he wanted to serve in that chamber, irrespective of their place of residence.

The aristocratic body that Morris envisioned was not hereditary, like the one that he would later recommend for France, but the idea that the president would choose among the wealthiest individuals to serve for life in the Senate was still quite bold, and it sprang at least in part from a rather dim view of the people and their elected representatives. In this respect, however, Morris was hardly alone.

Behind the closed doors of the Pennsylvania State House, a number of the delegates expressed a strikingly deep distrust of the people. Because they shock the modern ear, these remarks have become some of the Convention's most frequently quoted lines. Near the outset of the debates, Roger Sherman declared that "the people . . . immediately, should have as little to do as may be about the government. They want information, and are constantly liable to be misled." Elbridge Gerry agreed that "the evils we experience flow from the excess of democracy. The people . . . are daily misled into the most baneful measures and opinions, by the false reports circulated by designing men." Edmund Randolph claimed that "the evils under which the United States labored" stemmed from "the turbulence and follies of democracy." George Mason, too, held that "democracy" was the source of "the oppressions and injustice experienced among us." Alexander Hamilton insisted that "the people are turbulent and changing; they seldom judge or determine right." James Madison lamented that the people were "liable to err . . . from fickleness and passion." John Francis Mercer added that "the people cannot know and judge of the characters of candidates," so that in a popular election "the worst possible choice will be made." One could easily go on in this vein for some time.[30] Indeed, skepticism of the people was so pervasive at the Convention that several state delegations voted against having them directly elect even the *lower house* of Congress—what became the House of Representatives—never mind senators or the president.[31] Morris was far from an outlier, then, in thinking that there must be some kind of check on the popular will.

Nor was Morris the only delegate to argue that the Senate should have some distinctly "aristocratic" features. Charles Cotesworth Pinckney suggested that the Senate "was meant to represent the wealth of the country" and so "ought to be composed of persons of wealth." Abraham Baldwin similarly "thought the second branch ought to be the representation of property." Pierce Butler bluntly proclaimed that "the second branch I consider as the aristocratical part of our government." John Dickinson declared that he "wished the Senate to consist of the most distinguished characters, distinguished for their rank in life and their weight of property, and bearing as strong a likeness to the British House of Lords as possible." Alexander Hamilton described the House of Lords as "a most noble institution" and suggested that they ought to approximate it as closely as they could. Even James Madison claimed (according to the notes of Rufus King) that "the Senate ought to come from, & represent, the Wealth of the nation" and (according to the notes of Robert Yates) that it "ought to be so constituted as to protect the minority of the opulent against the majority."[32]

There were also many delegates who argued for surprisingly long terms—in some cases, lifelong terms—for senators. At the time, the upper houses of the state governments did not have particularly long terms; most state senators served for just one year, and the longest term of any state upper house (Maryland's) was five years.[33] For the new national government, however, the delegates voted overwhelmingly for seven-year terms for senators, eventually switching to six years principally because it made rotation simpler, with one third of the senators going up for reelection every two years.³⁴ And a number of the delegates worried that even six or seven years was not long enough. According to the notes of Robert Yates, Madison argued that the Senate "ought to have permanency and stability" and that "the longer they continue in office, the better will these views be answered." Madison's own notes have him saying that "a considerable duration ought to be given" to the Senate and that a term of nine years would not "threaten any real danger." The idea of nine-year terms received support from several other delegates, including James Wilson, and three state delegations voted in favor of it.³⁵ Charles Pinckney, Alexander Hamilton, George Read, and Robert Morris all supported the idea of senators serving for life.³⁶ (So did Morris's friend John Jay, although he was not at the Convention.)³⁷ Hamilton was most emphatic on the point, insisting that "no temporary Senate will have firmness enough to answer the purpose." Those who "suppose seven years a sufficient period to give the Senate an adequate firmness," he claimed, had not "duly consider[ed] the amazing violence and turbulence of the democratic spirit." Lifetime terms would give the Senate "a permanent will, a weighty interest, which would answer essential purposes."³⁸

Morris's other seemingly outlandish proposals regarding the Senate, too, were supported by other delegates. Charles Cotesworth Pinckney agreed that senators should not be paid since "if no allowance was to be made, the wealthy alone would undertake the service," and Pierce Butler and John Rutledge backed this idea as well. Five states voted in favor of the proposal, though many delegates may have supported it for Benjamin Franklin's high-minded reasons rather than Morris's and Pinckney's more cynical ones.³⁹ One other delegate, George Read, proposed on June 7 that senators be appointed by the executive from a list of nominations by the state legislatures, declaring that "nothing short of this approach towards a proper model of government would answer the purpose, and he thought it best to come directly to the point at once," though his proposal was not seconded, Morris being off at Morrisania at the time.⁴⁰

James Madison later claimed that Morris's speech on the Senate was "very extravagant" and that it contained some of his "most disrelished ideas," and in many respects it was and did.⁴¹ Yet all of Morris's proposals in the speech— that the Senate should be designed as an aristocratic body, that it should represent great wealth, that senators should serve for life, that they should not be paid, and that they should be appointed by the president—were endorsed by at least one other delegate, and in most cases quite a few. Where Morris really stood out was in his motivation. The other delegates supported these proposals because they trusted wealthy elites more than the common people; Morris did so precisely because he did not.

The absence of a hereditary nobility in America led some of the framers to assume that there was little need to institute protections for or against an aristocracy in the Constitution. This case was made most forcefully by Charles Pinckney (Charles Cotesworth's cousin), who argued at length that the United States was "singular" in having "fewer distinctions of fortune, and less of rank, than . . . any other nation"—though this paean to the nation's exceptional egalitarianism must have rung rather hollow to many delegates, coming as it did from a major slaveholder.[42] Morris disagreed vehemently with this line of thinking. "As to the alarm sounded, of an aristocracy," he declared, "his creed was that there never was, nor ever will be, a civilized society without an aristocracy."[43] It was simply not true, Morris thought, that the common people, by virtue of their numbers, would invariably hold most of the effective power within a republican government. Even in the absence of hereditary titles and offices, without some kind of check the propertied elite would find a way to seize power for themselves, either openly or surreptitiously: "Let the rich mix with the poor, and in a commercial country they will establish an oligarchy. . . . Thus it has been all the world over. So it will be among us. Reason tells us we are but men; and we are not to expect any particular interference of Heaven in our favor."[44]

Nor did Morris believe, as some of the other framers did, that the rich would be more trustworthy guardians of the public weal than the common people were, given that they were generally better educated and had a greater stake in maintaining social order. On the contrary, he pointedly told his fellow delegates, many of whom were themselves quite well-to-do, that "wealth tends to corrupt the mind;—to nourish its love of power; and to stimulate it to oppression. History proves this to be the spirit of the opulent."[45] The wealthy may have different vices than the common people, in his view, but they were no less vicious for that. Hence Morris emphasized that "he fears the influence of the rich. They will have the same effect here as elsewhere, if we do not . . . keep them within their proper spheres. . . . The rich will take advantage of [the people's] passions, and make these the instruments for oppressing them. The result of the contest will be a violent aristocracy, or a more violent despotism."[46]

But if these prideful, power-hungry elites were given lifetime appointments in the Senate, as Morris proposed, would they not abuse their authority? His answer was calculated to astound his listeners: "He believed so; he hoped so. The rich will strive to establish their dominion, and enslave the rest. They always did. They always will."[47] The real question, as he saw it, was not whether the wealthy would seek to oppress the people—of course they would—but rather how their attempts at oppression could be resisted, or perhaps even put to good use.

The core of Morris's argument for an aristocratic Senate was that the vices of the rich and the vices of the people could be made to check one another if they were separated into different bodies, with the rich (and only the rich) making up the Senate and the people (and only the people) making up the House of Representatives. For instance, the tendency of the people to subvert property rights would be checked by a Senate made up of individuals who cared a great deal about their own property, and the tendency of the rich to oppress the poor would be checked by a House made up of individuals with a strong interest in combatting this oppression. "By thus combining, and setting apart, the aristocratic interest," Morris argued, "the popular interest will be combined against it. There will be a mutual check and mutual security."[48]

Morris believed that the rich, in particular, would be easier to restrain if they were isolated and confined to a single legislative body, whose actions the people would jealously scrutinize and resist. He explained the point more fully in an essay written two years after the Convention, in which he proposed a similar mechanism for a French constitution. "Leave to the people a corps, which they may consider as the common enemy, and which may, from that circumstance, unite them in a steady and constant support of the rights of mankind," he recommended. If the people were faced with "a body constantly opposed to the popular wish, nay, constantly laboring to oppress," then "they and their representatives will always be as desirous of oppressing the nobility, as that nobility can possibly be of debasing the people. In the legislative struggle, where each having a veto neither can prevail, the good of all must be consulted, to obtain the consent of each."[49] The unmistakable threat that the rich posed to the people, in other words, would ensure that the people would unite against them, and the rich would be easier to unite against if they were concentrated within the Senate. This aristocratic institution would thus help to check aristocratic impulses, as Morris saw it, not just democratic ones.

In many respects Morris's vision of the Senate harkened back to a very old idea, that of the mixed regime. The standard American understanding of the separation of powers, which derived from the French philosopher Montesquieu, was (and is) that the government should be separated into three branches—legislative, executive, and judicial—with checks and balances instituted among them. This idea is different from, though related to, another one that can be traced all the way back to ancient Greece, according to which power should be distributed among the different orders of society, namely the one (i.e., the monarch), the few (i.e., the aristocracy), and the many (i.e., the common people).[50] Although there was of course no monarch or hereditary nobility in America, Morris sought to superimpose an element of the mixed regime onto that of the separation of powers by dividing the legislature between the wealthy and well-born (in the Senate) and the common people (in the House).[51] This element of class conflict would, in his view, both channel and thus mediate that conflict—which was inevitable anyway—and add one more check into the lawmaking process.

Morris was the only delegate in Philadelphia to argue that the influence of the rich could be limited by concentrating them within the Senate, but he was not the only major founder to hold this view. A strikingly similar case was made by none other than John Adams, who was off in London serving as the American minister to Britain. In his magnum opus, *Defence of the Constitutions of Government of the United States*, Adams, too, contended that the wealthy would always manage to prevail within the legislature unless special steps were taken to limit their power: "The rich, the well-born, and the able, acquire an influence among the people that will soon be too much for simple honesty and plain sense, in a house of representatives." And he too contended that the best solution to this problem would be to confine these individuals within a senate, where their ambition, wealth, and guile could be checked by the popular branch. Adams described the establishment of such an upper chamber as being "to all honest and useful intents, an ostracism."[52]

The first volume of Adams's *Defence* had been published earlier in 1787, and excerpts from it appeared in Philadelphia's *Pennsylvania Mercury* every week throughout the duration of the Convention, so it is quite likely that Morris was directly influenced by it. In fact, as one scholar writes, "some of [Morris's] arguments and language seem to have been taken almost verbatim from Adams's *Defence*."[53] That said, there were also important differences between the two. Adams applied his argument principally to the state level rather than the national level, for instance, and he did not go so far as to advocate lifelong terms, appointment by the executive, or denying senators a salary in the way that Morris did. Although some of Morris's analysis followed Adams's, then, his vision of the Senate was still quite novel—and radical.

Even if deliberately fomenting class conflict were desirable in practice—and it is not at all clear to this author that it would be—Morris's vision of the Senate and its role in the new government was not without its problems. First of all, he offered no institutional mechanism to ensure that the House of Representatives would remain truly the "people's branch," made up of common people and representing their interests. As we have seen, Morris thought that refraining from paying senators would ensure that only the rich would serve in that chamber, but he never quite spelled out what would prevent the rich from also infiltrating the House and eventually dominating both parts of the legislature. His assumption seems to have been that the people would be sufficiently suspicious of the wealthy and well-born that they would refuse to vote for them, and perhaps also that the wealthy and well-born would disdain to serve in the lower chamber when a more prestigious and exclusive upper chamber was available to them. Given Morris's own emphasis on the power-hungry nature of the rich and their myriad ways of manipulating and deceiving the people, however, these assumptions seem questionable.

Further, even if the rich and the common people *were* to be confined to separate parts of the legislature, there is little reason to suppose that the two houses would exhibit the kind of unified opposition to one another that Morris appears to have expected. Most of the framers were aghast at the idea of political parties and optimistically assumed that they would not play a major role in the new government, but Morris did not share that assumption. On the contrary, he foresaw the inevitability of partisanship as clearly as anyone at the Convention. A few weeks after his speech on the Senate, in the midst of a debate on the presidency, Morris declared flatly that "in all public bodies there are two parties. The Executive will necessarily be more connected with one than with the other. There will be a personal interest, therefore, in one of the parties, to oppose, as well as in the other to support, him."[54] This was far from a recent realization on his part: as far back as 1779, he had written that "to say there are divisions in [the Continental] Congress is only saying in other words that it is a popular Assembly. Different views of the same subject naturally lead men to differ in sentiments."[55] Nor did Morris think that partisanship was an altogether bad thing; he often described the presence of an opposition party as a kind of "outward conscience" that helped to prevent the ruling party from abusing its power too much.[56] If the House and Senate were to be pervaded by parties, however, then the fellow partisans in each chamber could be expected to work together rather than check one another's vices, at least some of the time.

Finally, Morris's depiction of the wealthy was not entirely consistent. Most of the time he portrayed them as prideful and bent on tyranny, but occasionally he suggested—as other delegates frequently did—that they would be sober and farsighted statesmen.[57] For instance, in the middle of his July 2 speech he hinted that senators might be among "the best, the most able, the most virtuous citizens," and he concluded the speech by describing them as "a select and sagacious body of men, instituted to watch against [encroachments] on all sides."[58] These characterizations, as fleeting and apparently offhand as they were, are difficult to square with Morris's repeated insistence that "wealth tends to corrupt the mind;—to nourish its love of power; and to stimulate it to oppression" and that the vices of the rich must be firmly checked by the people and their representatives in the House.[59] Perhaps his hope was that the senators' lifetime appointments would give them a greater investment in the nation's long-term interests and that the vigilance of the people in overseeing their conduct would force them to pursue the common good. At any rate, something like this seems to be implicit in Robert Yates's version of Morris's speech, which has him declaring: "Give [the rich] the second branch, and you secure their weight for the *public good*. They become responsible for their conduct, and [their] lust for power will ever be checked by the democratic branch, and thus form a stability in your government."[60] If Morris did indeed expect that giving the wealthy lifetime appointments in the Senate would bring out the best in them, then this expectation seems unduly—and uncharacteristically—optimistic on his part.

On the other hand, in Morris's defense, it should be noted that in seeking a way to limit the inordinate influence of the rich on the political process, he was groping for a solution to a problem that *still* has not been adequately solved in the United States. Although his solution may not have been entirely satisfactory, the fact that he recognized the need for one—more clearly than perhaps any other delegate—is a testament to his foresight and his realism.

A wealthy blue-blood himself, Morris frequently looked down on the common people with elitist disdain, but his interventions regarding the Senate revealed that he was also, somewhat ironically, one of the Convention's foremost critics of the rich. There is little evidence, however, that his arguments had any substantive impact on the course of the debate. Immediately after Morris's July 2 monologue, Edmund Randolph opined that "two such opposite bodies as Mr. Morris had planned"—that is, a purely democratic House and a purely aristocratic Senate—"could never long co-exist," and then the delegates turned back to their intractable and seemingly interminable debate over whether the states would be equally or proportionally represented in the Senate.[61]

None of Morris's major proposals regarding the Senate were adopted. Instead of having lifetime appointments, senators would serve six-year terms under the Constitution (although there was no set term limit or requirement for rotation in office, as some delegates had advocated). Instead of being appointed by the executive, they would be chosen by the state legislatures (until the Seventeenth Amendment provided for the direct election of senators in 1913). Instead of being chosen regardless of their place of residence, two senators would be chosen from each state. Instead of receiving no salary, they would be paid from the national treasury. It is thus not surprising that Morris later expressed disappointment in the character of the Senate, even as he served in it. In 1802, he complained to Alexander Hamilton that "our Senate is much too feeble, and indeed when we consider the Manner of it's Composition we cannot expect that it should be a dignified Body," and after leaving office the next year, he told another correspondent that "the complete sovereignty of America is substantially in the House of Representatives. The Senate forms no check."[62] Still later, Morris lamented that the Senate "has not the disposition" to check the House because the members of both branches "are begotten in the same way and by the same sire," so that "they have of course the same temper."[63]

Since Morris did not get anything like what he wanted with respect to the Senate at the Convention, he tried to find an alternative means of achieving some of his broader goals—such as avoiding popular inroads on private property and preventing the tyranny of the rich—through the structure of the House of Representatives.

5. Property and the People's Branch: The House of Representatives

Morris never delivered an extended speech at the Convention laying out his vision of the House of Representatives in the way that he did for the Senate, nor did he contribute as frequently to the debates over the character and structure of the House. By the time of his return from his extended absence on July 2, the other delegates had decided that the members of the House would be elected directly by the people, that they would be paid from the national treasury, that they would serve two-year terms, and that there would not be any kind of term limit or requirement for rotation in office, and Morris took these positions essentially as given from that point forward.[1] The two main issues on which he intervened both related to property—first, the question of whether the number of representatives allocated to each state would be determined solely by its population or whether its property and wealth would be taken into account as well, and second, the question of whether individuals would have to satisfy any kind of property qualification in order to vote for members of the House.

Morris was as deeply committed to the protection of property rights and as firmly convinced of the benefits of commerce as any of the framers. In fact, his basic outlook has been described as one of "aristocratic capitalism."[2] This is not to say that he was by any means a strict libertarian. As we have seen, throughout the Convention he fought for the national government to be as centralized and energetic as possible and contended that it should have a "general police" power within the states. Nor did he have any objection to the government undertaking ambitious internal improvements projects; recall that he spent the last six years of his life as the head of the Erie Canal Commission. But Morris did believe that securing property rights was *the* main object of government, and that commerce was *the* main driver of progress and civilization.

Back in 1776, in one of his few forays into the realm of abstract political theory, Morris drafted a short, unpublished essay titled "Political Enquiries" in which he explored the ultimate ends of government.[3] Of the three great Lockean rights—those to life, liberty, and property—Morris claimed that "the first can be enjoyed as well without the aid of Society as with it" and "the second better," so that property was evidently "the principal Cause & Object of

Society." After briefly tracing humanity's progression from the state of nature to civilized society, he concluded that "where Property is not secure Society cannot advance" and that "the most rapid Advances in the State of Society are produced by Commerce."[4] Not for him, clearly, was the Jeffersonian idea that extensive trade and urbanization were vehicles of corruption and that simple farmers were "the chosen people of God."[5] On the contrary, Morris believed that it was the creators and protectors of property who were truly doing God's work.

Morris further argued that property rights would be insufficiently secure in any society marked by excessive "political liberty," which he defined as "the right of assenting to or dissenting from every Public Act by which a Man is to be bound." In a pure democracy in which the majority always ruled, for instance, "the Laws would be so arbitrary & fluctuating as to destroy Property." Thus, Morris held that progress required limitations on political liberty in the name of "civil liberty," by which he meant the protection of individual rights, especially property rights. This was why a complex government—one in which powers were separated, balanced, and checked—was ultimately necessary, in his view: to create a political and legal environment that would provide security for private property and thereby enable commerce to flourish and society to advance.[6]

These beliefs about the importance of property rights and the benefits of commerce would play a key role in Morris's interventions at the Convention regarding the House of Representatives—but so would his worries about the dangers posed by the rich.

It seems obvious today that the role of the House of Representatives, the "people's branch," is to represent people rather than property, but this was not at all obvious to the framers. The second plank of the Virginia Plan stipulated rather vaguely that "the rights of suffrage in the National Legislature ought to be proportioned to the quotas of contribution, or to the number of free inhabitants, as the one or the other may seem best in different cases."[7] The term "quotas of contribution" was a reference to the states' tax burdens, and it was meant to approximate their levels of wealth. The idea was that wealthier states would both pay more taxes *to* the national government and also require more protection and other services *from* the national government than less wealthy states would, and that their representation in the national legislature should reflect these imbalances. The reference to "free inhabitants" in the resolution just quoted lays bare another difficulty that the framers foresaw with basing representation solely on population, namely that they would have to decide how enslaved people would fit into the calculation. Ultimately, of course, they settled on the notorious three-fifths compromise, according to which three-fifths of the enslaved population would be counted for purposes of representation and taxation—a provision that Morris fiercely opposed. The basis of representation in the House was thus a bone of contention throughout much of the Convention.

Morris was one of the most outspoken proponents of including property in the apportionment of House seats. On July 5, when the committee that formulated the Connecticut Compromise proposed, as part of that compromise, that each state should be allocated no more than one representative for every 40,000 inhabitants, Morris "objected to that scale of apportionment" on the grounds that "property ought to be taken into the estimate as well as the number of inhabitants." Recapitulating his argument from "Political Enquiries," he declared that "life and liberty were generally said to be of more value than property" but that "an accurate view of the matter would, nevertheless, prove that property was the main object of society." After all, "the savage state was more favorable to liberty than the civilized; and sufficiently so to life. It . . . was only renounced for the sake of property which could only be secured by the restraints of regular government." Given that the protection of property was the principal object of government, Morris went on to claim, property "certainly . . . ought to be one measure of the influence due to those who were to be affected by the government."[8] His hope appears to have been that including property in the formula for House apportionment would give the members of that body both the ability and the incentive to refrain from the kinds of inroads on private property to which he thought the popular branches of the state legislatures had proven so susceptible—paper money, debt relief legislation, and the like.

Apparently anticipating objections to his claim that property was the main object of society, Morris added that "these ideas might appear to some new, but they were nevertheless just."[9] In fact, however, several delegates leapt to agree with him. John Rutledge declared that Morris "had spoken some of his sentiments precisely. Property was certainly the principal object of society." The next day, Rufus King agreed that "property was the primary object of society" and Pierce Butler "contended strenuously, that property was the only just measure of representation. This was the great object of government; the great cause of war; the great means of carrying it on."[10] Rutledge and Butler in fact went so far as to argue that representation in the House should be based *entirely* on quotas of contribution, with Rutledge proclaiming that "the justice of this rule ... could not be contested" and Butler adding that "money was power; and ... the States ought to have weight in the government in proportion to their wealth."[11] Morris, however, would not go this far. He felt that "property ought to have its weight, but not all the weight." In a war, for instance, "if the Southern States are to supply money, the Northern States are to spill their blood."[12]

As this last quotation intimates, Morris's motivation—or at least one of his motivations—for proposing that property be used in the formula for House apportionment was virtually the opposite of those of the South Carolinians Rutledge and Butler. When these latter figures suggested that representation should be based entirely on quotas of contribution, they were seeking to give an advantage to the southern states that had amassed great wealth on the backs of—and indeed in the form of—enslaved people. Morris, in contrast, advocated that representation be based on both property *and* population, on the assumption that this would, in effect, force the hands of the southern states. If enslaved people were to count in the apportionment formula as property then presumably they could not *also* be included in the states' population counts, and leaving them out would give an edge to the northern states and their far larger free populations.[13] Enslaved people were one form of "property" that Morris very much did *not* want to protect, and he therefore fought throughout the Convention to minimize the power of the South within the new government.

Morris sought to include property in the House apportionment formula in hopes of curbing the political power of not just the South, but also the West. He predicted that "in time the western people would outnumber the Atlantic States" but that they would not (yet) be as wealthy as the original states when they reached the point of statehood, and he suggested that their influence in the legislature could be limited either by taking property into account when allocating seats or by simply fixing in advance the number or ratio of representatives that new states would be allotted.[14] "This would not be unjust," he insisted, "as the western settlers would previously know the conditions on which they were to possess their lands," and it would also "be politic, as it would recommend the plan [i.e., the Constitution] to the present, as well as future, interest of the States which must decide the fate of it"—that is, the thirteen states that would be asked to ratify the charter.[15]

Morris's arguments for limiting the political power of the West exhibited his usual combination of elitism and progressivism. To begin with, he assumed that "the new States will . . . have an interest in many respects different" from the Atlantic states, particularly those of the northeast.[16] For instance, the land beyond the Appalachians was expected to remain largely agrarian for some time to come, and Morris worried that allocating too much power to these states would "ruin" the commercial and manufacturing interests of the northeastern states.[17] He also predicted that the people of the West "will be little scrupulous of involving the community in wars the burdens and operations of which would fall chiefly on the maritime States," and in particular that if their power were to be joined to that of the (also largely agrarian) South, as he deemed likely, then together they would "inevitably bring on a war with Spain" over navigation rights on the Mississippi River.[18] Although the war with Spain never came, Theodore Roosevelt pointed out that Morris's broader forecast here was borne out during his lifetime: "the South and West brought on the War of 1812, wherein the East was the chief sufferer."[19]

It was not just the different interests of westerners that concerned Morris, but also their different culture and character. His snobbishness was on full display in his remarks on what he regarded as the backwardness of the frontier. "It must be apparent," he opined, that the West "would not be able to furnish men equally enlightened, to share in the administration of our common interests. The busy haunts of men, not the remote wilderness, was the proper school of political talents."[20] In response to this line of argument, James Madison rightly chided Morris for trying to judge "the human character by the points of the compass."[21]

It was not only patrician condescension that moved him, however. Morris also opposed granting too much political power to the western territories because he worried that they would ally themselves with the South and thereby tilt the balance of power in a proslavery direction. This was a particular concern because at that time the population south of the Ohio River—in what became the states of Kentucky and Tennessee—was growing more swiftly than that north of the river, so these territories were expected to join the ranks of statehood sooner. If the South were to join up with "the great interior country," Morris warned, "every thing was to be apprehended from their getting the power into their hands."[22] Here too his fears turned out to be prescient in many respects, at least from his own (Federalist) point of view, as the political dominance of the Republicans in the early nineteenth century was underpinned by support in the slaveholding South and West. Morris's later leadership of the Erie Canal project can also be understood in light of these worries: he knew perfectly well that the population of the West would expand rapidly regardless of what the delegates in Philadelphia decided, and he regarded the canal—situated as it was in New York—as a potential source of northern influence on these burgeoning lands.[23]

Morris was among the floor leaders at the Convention in the search for some way to limit the political power of the western territories, but he was joined by a great many other delegates from both North and South. In fact, far more delegates spoke out against the West than spoke up on behalf of it. When Elbridge Gerry proposed a provision stipulating that the representatives from new states could never outnumber those from the original states, it failed by a razor-thin margin with four states voting in favor, five against, and Morris's Pennsylvania divided.[24] To be fair to Morris and his compatriots, it should be recalled that the idea of granting equal status to new territory was a relative novelty, historically speaking. From ancient Greece and Rome onward, most nations—including most republics—had used territorial expansion as a means of acquiring tribute states from which to extract resources. Still, we may be thankful that the former colonists did not end up choosing, almost immediately after gaining their independence, to relegate a large portion of their own fellow citizens to permanent second-class status solely because of where they lived.

Morris also failed in his broader effort to include property in the formula for apportioning House seats, though it was not for lack of effort on his part. On July 6, at Morris's suggestion, a five-member committee was formed to devise a solution to the apportionment question, and he was chosen to chair the committee.[25] Three days later, he delivered the committee's report, which proposed an initial number of representatives for each state—two for New Hampshire, seven for Massachusetts, one for Rhode Island, four for Connecticut, and so on—and that Congress be given the ability to periodically augment the number of seats, taking into account both population and wealth.[26] Giving

Congress this flexibility with regard to whether, when, and how to reapportion the number of representatives would have solved a number of problems, from Morris's point of view. It would have enabled the Atlantic states to retain their supremacy over the West, if they so chose; it would have enabled the northern states—which would have an initial majority—to retain their supremacy over the South, if they so chose; it would have prevented the House from growing too large and unwieldy, as might happen if the apportionment were tied strictly to the nation's booming population; and it would have made it possible to include property in the apportionment without forcing the delegates to settle on any fixed rule for how to do so.

At first, the proposal to give Congress control of its own future reapportionment passed handily—nine states to two—with no debate, but several delegates pressed for a reconsideration of the matter over the next few days.[27] Should not a periodic census of the states' populations, and perhaps also an estimate of their property, be used to guide future reapportionments according to some fixed standard? Morris opposed this idea "as fettering the Legislature too much."[28] Besides, he asked, "If we cannot agree on a rule that will be just at this time, how can we expect to find one that will be just in all times to come? Surely those who come after us will judge better of things present than we can of things future. . . . The best course that could be taken would be to leave the interests of the people to the representatives of the people."[29] At this point, James Madison expressed surprise that Morris, of all people, would advocate placing so much confidence in the people's representatives, describing him as "a member who, on all occasions, had inculcated so strongly the political depravity of men, and the necessity of checking one vice and interest by opposing them with another vice and interest."[30] Morris, however, saw no contradiction here. In his view, "the Legislature is worthy of unbounded confidence in some respects, and liable to equal distrust in others. When their interest coincides precisely with that of their constituents . . . no abuse of trust is to be apprehended. When a strong personal interest happens to be opposed to the general interest, the Legislature cannot be too much distrusted."[31]

What ultimately sank the committee's proposal, however, was the difficulty that the delegates had in deciding on the initial number of seats that each state would be allocated. When asked how the committee had come up with its proposed numbers, Morris admitted that they were "little more than a guess" based on the committee's sense of the relative populations and wealth of each state.[32] A second, eleven-member committee was then formed on July 9 to reconsider the apportionment, and Morris was once again selected to serve on it.[33] This second committee came back the next day with slightly revised numbers—adding a seat or two to several of the states' allotments and increasing the total number of representatives from fifty-six to sixty-five—but still gave no concrete, specific rationale for why each state was allotted the number of representatives that it was.[34] The delegates continued to wrangle over the apportionment for some time, but the numbers proposed by the second committee were ultimately affirmed, and were duly used to form the first Congress.[35]

However, the protracted squabbling over this issue—and in particular the conflict over how enslaved people should be counted—appears to have soured many of the delegates on both of Morris's pet proposals, namely using property to help determine the apportionment and allowing Congress itself to decide future reapportionments. Contrary to Morris's wish, the Constitution ultimately stipulated that in the future seats in the House would be allotted according to each state's population—including three-fifths of its enslaved population—as determined by a decennial census.

Morris's other main intervention—or rather attempted intervention—with respect to the House of Representatives involved property qualifications for voting. It was only with respect to the House that the scope of the electorate was even an issue in the Constitution, since senators were initially chosen by the state legislatures and the president was chosen by the electoral college rather than directly by the people. This was a question that had not previously been raised on the national stage, since most members of the Confederation Congress, too, were chosen by the state legislatures, and it was made somewhat thorny by the fact that the states had widely divergent requirements to vote for state offices.[36] Free Black men with sufficient property could vote in most states, but not in Virginia, South Carolina, or Georgia, nor could recently manumitted slaves vote in Maryland, and by 1787 only New Jersey granted women the franchise if they met the property requirement. The questions of Black suffrage and women's suffrage were, however, never so much as broached at the Philadelphia Convention; the controversy there revolved around property qualifications. At the time, every state obliged citizens to meet a property requirement of some kind—measured variously by land holdings, net worth, or taxes paid—in order to vote, but some of these requirements were much steeper than others. The most inclusive of the early state constitutions, that of Pennsylvania, enfranchised all adult male taxpayers.

A number of delegates were opposed to including any kind of property requirement for voting within the Constitution. Some, such as James Wilson, stressed that it would be difficult to formulate a uniform rule that all the states would accept; others, such as Oliver Ellsworth, worried that a property requirement would arouse popular opposition to the Constitution and thereby prevent its ratification; while still others, such as Benjamin Franklin, warned that limiting the franchise might "depress the virtue and public spirit of our common people; of which they displayed a great deal during the war."[37] Several delegates, however, felt that the poor could not be trusted with so great a responsibility as choosing the nation's leaders. John Dickinson, for instance, declared that "freeholders"—meaning those who owned land—were "the best guardians of liberty" and that restricting the suffrage to them was "a necessary defence against the dangerous influence of those multitudes without property and without principle, which our country, like all others, will in time abound." James Madison, too, contended that landowners "would be the safest depositories of republican liberty" and that "the rights of property and the public liberty will not be secure" in the hands of those who owned no property.[38]

It was Morris, however, who first proposed limiting the franchise to property owners and who spoke most frequently and at greatest length in favor of the idea.[39] The Committee of Detail's draft constitution stipulated that, essentially, voting qualifications would be left to the states: in order to vote in House elections, the voters in each state would have to meet whatever qualifications they had to meet in order to vote for the larger house of their state legislature.[40] (Many states placed higher property thresholds on voting for governor or for the upper chamber of the state legislature than for the lower chamber.) When this provision came before the Convention on August 7, Morris moved to strike it out and instead to "restrain the right of suffrage to freeholders."[41] This was an idea that he had long favored. Back in 1777, during the New York state constitutional convention, Morris successfully fought to include a £20 freehold requirement for elections to the lower house of the legislature, in addition to the (higher) property requirements for voting for the upper house and the governor that were already included in John Jay's draft constitution.[42]

At the Philadelphia Convention, Morris took it upon himself to answer some of the objections posed by the opponents of property qualifications before laying out his own case in favor of the idea. In response to Wilson's worry that it would be "very hard and disagreeable" for people in states without a freehold requirement—such as his and Morris's own Pennsylvania—to be able to vote for their state legislature but not for the federal House of Representatives, Morris insisted that "such a hardship would be neither great nor novel. The people are accustomed to it, and not dissatisfied with it, in several of the States"—a reference to the fact that it was not at all uncommon for people to be able to vote for some offices but not others. Whereas Ellsworth supposed that "the States are the best judges of the circumstances and temper of their own people" and so should be left to determine what requirements were appropriate, Morris contended that it would be improper to allow voting qualifications for the House to "depend on the will of the States," which would provide an avenue for the states to interfere with—and perhaps even undermine—the national government. As for the claim that a freehold requirement would provoke popular opposition to the Constitution, Morris maintained that the opposite was more likely true: "Nine tenths of the people are at present freeholders, and these will certainly be pleased with it."[43]

When Morris turned to his own argument on behalf of a freehold requirement, it quickly became clear that his motivations were, as was so often the case, both unique and a bit counterintuitive. Much as he had argued back in early July that granting lifetime Senate appointments to the rich would (ironically) be a way to limit their influence, now he contended that a landholding requirement for voting would also (and just as ironically) limit the influence of the rich. His short discourse on the issue was prompted by a comment from Pierce Butler, who claimed that abridgements of the franchise often escalated until they produced a "rank aristocracy."[44] Morris retorted that "he had long learned not to be the dupe of words. The sound of aristocracy, therefore, had no effect upon him. It was the thing, not the name, to which he was opposed; and one of his principal objections to the Constitution, as it is now before us, is, that it threatens the country with an aristocracy. The aristocracy will grow out of the House of Representatives."[45] Morris had *advocated* that the Senate be formed as an aristocratic institution, of course, but he worried that an aristocratic House of Representatives would undermine the government's republican character altogether. Indeed, Rufus King's notes have him declaring that the threat of aristocracy in the House was so great that "I think I shall oppose this Constitution."[46]

Why, then, did Morris fear that an aristocracy would emerge in the House of Representatives, of all places, and why he did believe that this possibility could be forestalled by a landowning requirement for voting, of all things? His basic contention was that if "people who have no property" were enfranchised, then "they will sell [their votes] to the rich, who will be able to buy them." Even if the great majority of American citizens were freeholders at that time, he explained, "we should not confine our attention to the present moment. The time is not distant when this country will abound with mechanics and manufacturers, who will receive their bread from their employers." Those employers, he supposed, would often be able to command the votes of their employees—a special worry in an age when most elections were determined by a public voice vote and few jurisdictions used a secret ballot of the kind that we take for granted today. In Morris's view, "The man who does not give his vote freely, is not represented. It is the man who dictates the vote" who is truly represented. This is why he ultimately believed that the franchise should be restricted to freeholders: because people who possessed their own land were sufficiently independent to think and choose for themselves—to have a "will of their own."[47] Under a system of universal suffrage, by contrast, the votes of the poor would end up going to the favored candidates of the rich, who would then effectively control the branch of the government that was supposed to most closely represent the common people's views and interests.

Whereas the other proponents of property qualifications tended to view the poor as vicious or untrustworthy, then, Morris's main concern was simply that their dependence on the rich opened the door to their being exploited.[48] It was the *rich* whom Morris really distrusted, and he saw a freehold requirement as a means of denying them extra political influence. His motives were thus democratic rather than aristocratic or oligarchic. A decade and a half later, during his time in the Senate, Morris remained convinced that "the strongest aristocratic feature in our political organization is that, which democrats are most attached to, the right of universal suffrage. This takes from men of moderate fortune their proper weight; and will, in process of time, give undue influence to those of great wealth."[49] Nor did he regard a freehold requirement as terribly onerous or exclusionary: again, he estimated at the Convention that "nine tenths of the people are at present freeholders"—although admittedly this was probably an overestimate by perhaps ten or twenty percentage points even within the adult white male population, and Morris himself acknowledged that "the time is not distant when this country will abound with" people who did not own land.[50]

In our age of secret ballots and strict laws against the buying and selling of votes, of course, the suggestion that disenfranchising the poor would actually limit the political power of the rich seems outlandish, if not disingenuous. However, it was common in early America for the wealthy to commandeer the votes of the poor through bribery or bullying, and a freehold requirement may well have curtailed such tactics to some degree. Even today the presence of—and continuing controversy over—campaign finance laws suggests that efforts by the wealthy to buy electoral outcomes are not altogether a relic of the past.

In the end the delegates voted firmly against Morris's proposal to restrict the vote to freeholders, with seven states voting against it, just one in favor, and one divided.[51] Instead, as the Committee of Detail had proposed, the issue of voting qualifications was left to the states. This meant that existing state-level property requirements remained in place for the time being, but most of these requirements were drastically reduced or eliminated altogether over the next few decades. More regrettably, this also meant that states were left free to disenfranchise minorities, particularly Black people—something that many of them did quite explicitly until the Fifteenth Amendment was ratified in 1870, only slightly less openly between then and the passage of the Voting Rights Act in 1965, and more covertly up to the present day.

All told, Morris got little of what he wanted with respect to the legislature at the Philadelphia Convention. The Constitution ultimately provided that each state legislature would choose two senators to serve paid, six-year terms rather than that the president would choose senators irrespective of their place of residence to serve for life without pay. It provided that seats in the House of Representatives would be allotted according to each state's population as determined by a decennial census rather than that Congress would determine its own future apportionments using both population and property as a guide. And, finally, it allowed states to determine their own voting qualifications rather than restricting the suffrage to landowners. The Senate was less aristocratic than Morris wished and the House was more nominally democratic than he wished, and he believed that both of these outcomes would ultimately lead to less stability and consistency within the government, less security for private property, and, ironically, more political power for the rich, who would inevitably use that power to oppress the common people.

These worries were redoubled by Morris's belief that the legislature would always be the most powerful—and hence most dangerous—of the three branches, given that it possessed the lawmaking authority and was the part of the government that was closest to the ultimate sovereign, the people themselves. In this he followed the lead of James Madison, who maintained that the "experience in all the States had evinced a powerful tendency in the Legislature to absorb all power into its vortex."[52] (In *Federalist* #48 he upped the rhetorical ante and made it an "impetuous vortex.")[53] When Elbridge Gerry countered that Congress should be trusted as "the guardians of [the people's] rights and interests," Morris declared that, on the contrary, he "concurred [with Madison] in thinking the public liberty in greater danger from Legislative usurpations, than from any other source."[54] As he saw it, "the Legislature will continually seek to aggrandize and perpetuate themselves; and will seize those critical moments produced by war, invasion, or convulsion, for that purpose."[55]

Many of the delegates assumed that requiring all laws to be passed by both the House of Representatives and the Senate would be sufficient to prevent Congress from acting tyrannically, but Morris regarded this assumption as fatuous, particularly as the two chambers were constructed in the Constitution.[56] "The check provided in the second branch was not meant as a check on legislative usurpations of power," he contended, "but on the abuse of lawful powers, on the propensity of the first branch to legislate too much, to run into projects of paper-money, and similar expedients. It is no check on legislative tyranny. On the contrary it may favor it; and, if the first branch can be seduced, may find the means of success."[57] Even if the Senate managed to prevent the House from pandering continually to the people, in other words, it would not prevent the accumulation of dangerous amounts of power within the legislative branch. Hence Morris insisted that "however the Legislative power may be formed, it will, if disposed, be able to ruin the country."[58]

The need for an effective check on the legislature led Morris to devote a great deal of energy at the Convention to fighting for a powerful executive with a broad popular mandate—and on this score he had far more success.

6. A Reluctant Architect of the Electoral College: Presidential Selection

The framers knew roughly what they were getting into when they set about creating the new Congress, but the presidency was another matter. Even the meticulously prepared James Madison admitted just a month before the Convention's opening that he had "scarcely ventured as yet to form my own opinion either of the manner in which [the executive] ought to be constituted or of the authorities with which it ought to be cloathed."[1] Almost everything about this branch was initially up in the air, including whether there should even *be* an independent executive. The Articles of Confederation did not provide for one, after all, and Roger Sherman contended that the legislature was "the depository of the supreme will of the society" and thus that "an independence of the Executive [from] the supreme Legislature, was, in his opinion, the very essence of tyranny, if there was any such thing."[2]

Sherman was enough of an outlier that the other delegates were able to take the idea of an independent executive for granted—it was never even put up for a formal vote—but there was real disagreement over so basic a question as whether the office should be filled by one person or by several. The New Jersey Plan included a plural executive, and more than a dozen delegates supported the idea at one point or another.[3] Edmund Randolph, for instance, regarded "unity in the executive magistracy . . . as the foetus of monarchy" and avowed that "he felt an opposition to it which he believed he should continue to feel as long as he lived."[4] Although he was far more tentative on the point, even Madison seems to have initially favored a plural executive: Alexander Hamilton recorded him as saying that "if several are admitted [to the executive] as there will be many competitors [i.e., candidates] of equal merit they may be all included—contention prevented—& the republican genius consulted."[5] The initial vote on the creation of a single executive, taken on June 4, was seven states in favor and three against, but the opponents of the idea appear to have become reconciled to it—or at least to have accepted the inevitable—relatively soon afterward, for by July 17 the same proposition carried with no discussion or dissent.[6]

After the unity of the executive was established, there were still myriad questions left to answer, all controversial and devilishly intertwined: How long should the president serve? Should he be eligible to serve more than one term? What powers should he have? Should he have a veto over legislation, and if so, should Congress be able to override it? Should he have a council of advisors, and if so, what should it look like? Should he be liable to impeachment, and if so, by whom and for what offenses? Perhaps the most formidable question of all, however—and the one that produced the most protracted deliberations—was how the president would be chosen. The delegates wrangled over this issue on twenty-one separate days and took more than thirty votes related to it.[7] When the calendar turned to September and they still had not managed to devise a selection method that satisfied a majority of the state delegations, James Wilson stated the obvious: "This subject has greatly divided the House [i.e., the Convention], and it will also divide the people out of doors. It is in truth the most difficult of all on which we have had to decide."[8]

The issue proved so baffling because the two most straightforward methods of choosing the president, namely selection by the legislature and election by the people, both faced a host of strong objections. (Elbridge Gerry repeatedly suggested that the president should be chosen by the state governors, so that the House of Representatives would be chosen by the people of the states, the Senate by the legislatures of the states, and the president by the executives of the states, but the idea never gained any traction.)[9] A great deal was at stake in the conflict over this issue: if the Convention had proposed congressional selection of the president—which for most of the summer seemed to be the likeliest outcome—then that would have gone a long way toward making the American government a parliamentary rather than a presidential system, to use contemporary parlance.

Morris and James Wilson were easily the Convention's foremost advocates of having the people elect the president; without the two of them, it is exceedingly likely that congressional selection would have prevailed.[10] Despite their dogged efforts, however, the other delegates would not agree to a direct popular election, so as an alternative they devised the electoral college that still generates so much controversy and confusion today.[11] They were, in a sense, joint architects of this institution: Wilson first proposed the idea of system of electors, and Morris both helped to refine the idea and did more than anyone else to get it adopted. However, they still regarded it as something of a makeshift, second-best option; both would have preferred a direct vote of the people themselves. (Advocates of a national popular vote, take notice.) Regardless, this is one area in which Morris's impact on the Constitution was pivotal. One scholar even describes "removing the election of the president from the hands of the legislature and placing it in the hands of popular electors" as Morris's "most significant victory at the Convention."[12]

The obvious solution to the conundrum of presidential selection, for most of the delegates, was handing the choice to Congress. Under the great majority of the new state constitutions—eight of the eleven—the governor was chosen by the state legislature. Of the three that provided for popular election of the governor, only the New York constitution that Morris helped to craft stipulated that whichever candidate earned a plurality of the votes would be the winner; in both Massachusetts and New Hampshire, if no candidate received a popular majority then the legislature chose among the top candidates.[13] (The governors of Connecticut and Rhode Island, too, were popularly elected, but neither of these states had drafted a new constitution since declaring independence; both still operated on the basis of their old royal charters.)

Both of the Convention's main early blueprints, the Virginia Plan and the New Jersey Plan, provided that the executive would be chosen by the legislature, and this idea continued to enjoy broad and exceptionally durable support throughout the remainder of the summer.[14] In fact, for the vast majority of the Convention—from May 29, when the Virginia Plan was introduced, until July 19, and then again from July 24 to September 5—the plan on the table included congressional selection of the president.[15] Of the 111 days between the introduction of the Virginia Plan and the close of the Convention, in other words, on only seventeen of them did the framers expect that the president would be chosen by special electors. The idea of direct election by the people never obtained a majority of the state delegations, even for a single day.

Morris fought against congressional selection of the president with all his might. On July 17, the first time that the issue was addressed while he was on the floor, he immediately rose to proclaim that he was "pointedly against" the executive being chosen in this way. Morris gave two main reasons for his opposition. First, he argued that "appointments by numerous bodies are always worse than those made by single responsible individuals or by the people at large." If a large group like the legislature were to select the president, he believed, then partisan infighting would inevitably determine the outcome: "If the Legislature elect, it will be the work of intrigue, of cabal, and of faction;

it will be like the election of a pope by a conclave of cardinals; real merit will rarely be the title to the appointment."[16] As he elaborated the following week, not only would there be constant "intrigues" between parties in Congress and candidates for the presidency "to get into office," there would also be "intrigues to get [the president] out of office. Some leader of a party will always covet his seat, will perplex his administration, will cabal with the Legislature, till he succeeds in supplanting him."[17]

Morris's second, and even more emphatic, grounds for opposing congressional selection was his certainty that the president "will be the mere creature of the Legislature, if appointed and impeachable by that body." In his view, the separation of powers would inevitably be subverted unless they managed to find some other mode of appointment: "If the Executive be chosen by the national Legislature, he will not be independent of it; and if not independent, usurpation and tyranny on the part of the Legislature will be the consequence."[18] How could the president be expected to stand up to the legislators, as he would surely need to do, if he owed his position to them? Morris returned to this point time and again throughout the Convention. On July 24, he reiterated that "of all possible modes of appointment that by the Legislature is the worst. If the Legislature is to appoint, and to impeach, or to influence the impeachment, the Executive will be the mere creature of it."[19] A month later, he once again "dwelt on the danger of rendering the Executive uninterested in maintaining the rights of his station, as leading to legislative tyranny." As he saw it, a congressionally chosen president would be "interested in courting popularity in the Legislature, by sacrificing his Executive rights; and then he can go into that body, after the expiration of his Executive office, and enjoy there the fruits of his policy."[20]

In fact, Morris's opposition to congressional selection ran so deep that he regarded mere chance as preferable. At one point James Wilson suggested in exasperation that if the selection had to be placed in the hands of the legislature, then perhaps a handful or more of legislators ("not more than fifteen") could be chosen by lot and then "retire immediately and make the election without separating." The idea was that by incorporating both randomness and immediacy into the process, "intrigue would be avoided" and "dependence would be diminished."[21] Morris spoke next and declared that while he was "not prepared to decide" on Wilson's suggestion just yet, "he thought it deserved consideration. It would be better that chance should decide than intrigue."[22] The next day, after he had mulled it over a bit more, Morris pronounced that "he could not but favor the idea ... of introducing a mixture of lot" into the scheme if the selection were granted to the legislature: "It will diminish, if not destroy, cabal and dependence."[23] Like Elbridge Gerry's proposal to have the state governors choose the president, this idea never caught on. As George Mason put it when summing up the various alternatives that had been mooted, "Among other expedients, a lottery has been introduced. But as the tickets do not appear to be in much demand, it will probably not be carried on."[24]

Like Wilson, however, Morris ultimately preferred a selection method that was as simple as it was radical: the president "ought to be elected by the people at large."[25]

The idea of allowing the people to choose the nation's chief magistrate seemed so preposterous to so many of the framers that James Wilson felt compelled to disclose, when he first introduced the possibility on June 1, that "he was almost unwilling to declare the mode which he wished to take place, being apprehensive that it might appear chimerical."[26] With Morris having just departed for Morrisania, not a single person supported Wilson's suggestion.[27] On July 17, when the issue of presidential selection was introduced once again, Morris jumped at the chance to propose popular election. He admitted that "difficulties attend this mode," but insisted that "they have been found superable in New York and in Connecticut, and would, he believed, be found so in the case of an Executive for the United States."[28] At this point, Charles Pinckney complained that he "did not expect this question would again have been brought forward; an election by the people being liable to the most obvious and striking objections."[29] The delegates quickly voted down Morris's proposal, nine states to one, with Morris's and Wilson's Pennsylvania alone supporting it.[30]

Morris offered two main arguments in favor of popular election of the president, which were in some senses the flip side of his arguments against congressional selection. Whereas congressional selection would undermine the separation of powers, he contended, popular election would preserve it. One of the main duties of the executive, as he saw it, was to check the legislature and thereby serve as "the great protector of the mass of the people," particularly since he expected Congress to be dominated by the rich: "The Executive magistrate should be the guardian of the people, even of the lower classes, against legislative tyranny; against the great and the wealthy, who, in the course of things will necessarily compose the legislative body." This was a strikingly democratic conception of the president's role—so much for Morris's alleged proclivity for monarchism!—and he believed that it would be best served by choosing the president through democratic election: "If he is to be the guardian of the people, let him be appointed by the people."[31] The president would be more apt to champion the common people's interests, in other words, if his position emanated from their will—and if his reelection chances depended on that will. As a side benefit, Morris noted, "such an ingredient in the plan would render it extremely palatable to the people" and hence might increase the likelihood of the Constitution being ratified.[32]

Given the deep and pervasive distrust of the people at the Convention, Morris's second main argument must have been startling: whereas congressional selection would beget faction and intrigue and hence result in a poor choice being made, he maintained, popular election would result in a far better choice being made. At least at first, few claims could have bewildered the other delegates more. They nearly tripped over each other in the rush to express their incredulity. Roger Sherman scoffed that the people would "never be sufficiently informed of [the candidates'] characters" to choose wisely, and Charles Pinckney insisted that they would just "be led by a few active and designing men." George Mason put the matter most sharply, remarking that "it would be as unnatural to refer the choice of a proper character for Chief Magistrate to the people, as it would, to refer a trial of colors to a blind man. The extent of the country renders it impossible, that the people can have the capacity to judge of the respective pretensions of the candidates."[33]

Curiously, the elitist Morris trusted the common people's judgment in this regard more than almost anyone else at the Convention. One of the first things that he pointed out when introducing the idea of popular election was that "if the people should elect, they will never fail to prefer some man of distinguished character, or services; some man, if he might so speak, of continental reputation."[34] At least for the first few elections, the individual of "distinguished character" and "continental reputation" whom he expected the people to choose was all but self-evident: his hero George Washington. As he saw it, Washington's unparalleled renown throughout the country gave the lie to the claim that the people would be insufficiently informed of—or incapable of judging—the candidates' merits. As Morris put it two days later, if the best candidates were "known to the Legislature, they must have such a notoriety and eminence of character, that they cannot possibly be unknown to the people at large. It cannot be possible that a man shall have sufficiently distinguished himself to merit this high trust, without having his character proclaimed by fame throughout the Empire."[35]

As for the worry that the people would be constantly misled by demagogues or "designing men," Morris insisted that this "might happen in a small district," but "it can never happen throughout the continent." To buttress the point he drew on the other constitution that he had helped to form, which included a popularly elected executive: "In the election of a Governor of New York, it sometimes is the case in particular spots, that the activity and intrigues of little partizans are successful; but the general voice of the State is never influenced by such artifices."[36] There are definite echoes here of the argument that James Madison outlined several times during the Convention, and that he would later make famous in *Federalist* #10, about how a large territory was less susceptible than a small one to majority faction. "An election by the people at large, throughout so great an extent of country," Morris declared, "could not be influenced by those little combinations and those momentary lies, which often decide popular elections within a narrow sphere."[37]

Morris maintained, still further, that the people would be the best judges of whether the president had served them well. Although the delegates had not yet determined exactly what the president's powers would include, he assumed that it would be the president's duty, at the very least, "to appoint the officers, and to command the forces, of the Republic." When it came to the appointment power, he asked, "who will be the best judges whether these appointments be well made?" The answer was obvious: "The people at large, who will know, will see, will feel, the effects of them." As for the president's role as commander-in-chief, "Who can judge so well of the discharge of military duties for the protection and security of the people, as the people themselves, who are to be protected and secured?"[38] Even if the people did not know the arcane details of every political controversy or piece of legislation, Morris thought, surely they would be able to judge whether the nation's chief magistrate had fulfilled his responsibilities.

After Morris laid out his case in a prolonged speech on July 19—one that is included in this book's appendix—some of the other delegates began to come around. Rufus King now remarked that he "was much disposed to think, that . . . the people at large would choose wisely," and James Madison agreed that a popular election "would be as likely as any that could be devised to produce an Executive Magistrate of distinguished character. The people generally could only know and vote for some citizen whose merits had rendered him an object of general attention and esteem." James Wilson, for his part, "perceived with pleasure that the idea [of popular election] was gaining ground."[39]

There were further objections, however, of a more sectional nature. A number of delegates, particularly from the smaller states, pointed out that people would be more likely to vote for presidential candidates from their own state, both because they would trust them more and because they would not be as familiar with candidates who lived far away. The likely result, they claimed, was that it would be difficult for any one candidate to achieve a popular majority, at least once Washington was off the scene, which would in turn open the door for the larger states to collude and thus prevail. As Charles Pinckney put it, "The most populous states, by combining in favor of the same individual, will be able to carry their points."[40] Morris insisted, though, that "the people of such States cannot combine," particularly because their interests were so divergent. If anything, this fear would be more pertinent under a system of congressional selection, where collusion would be far easier: "If there be any combination, it must be among their Representatives in the Legislature."[41] Hugh Williamson of North Carolina, still not convinced, proposed a sort of workaround: if each voter were to select three candidates instead of just one, then one or two of his votes would likely go to candidates from states other than his own. Morris declared that he "liked the idea" but believed that it could be improved upon: he suggested that each voter choose two candidates, with a proviso that at least one of them *had to be* from another state. Madison expressed support for both the general idea and Morris's revision of it, but the delegates narrowly rejected it, six states to five.[42]

Another, even more decisive objection to popular election of the president came not from the small states, but from the slave states. After expressing confidence that the people would choose a president of "distinguished character," Madison noted that there was still "one difficulty . . . of a serious nature, attending an immediate choice by the people": the southern states "could have no influence in the election, on the score of the negroes."[43] Since only free citizens would be able to vote, in other words, in a direct election there would be no way to give the South the kind of advantage that it would enjoy in the House of Representatives thanks to the three-fifths rule. This was one objection to which Morris offered no response, presumably because he saw diminishing the power of the slave states as an *advantage* of direct popular election rather than as a problem to be solved. At any rate, it was the scruples of the small states and (especially) the slave states that ultimately led to the formation of that most befuddling of concoctions, the electoral college.[44]

The idea of having the people choose electors who would in turn choose the president was first proposed by James Wilson on June 2, but after just a couple of brief and unfavorable comments from other delegates, the proposal was defeated, eight states to two, and congressional selection was approved by the same margin.[45] The idea was revived by Rufus King after Morris's long speech in favor of popular election on July 19, and this time it quickly gained momentum. In fact, by the end of the day, a system of electors had gained its first majority, with six states (including Pennsylvania) voting in favor, three opposed, and one divided.[46] As one scholar writes, "In a single day, the delegates had altered the fundamental way they viewed the executive office. If we judge a speech by the votes taken soon afterward, Gouverneur Morris's performance on July 19 was among the most effective of the summer. While he didn't get his exact wish"—since the delegates settled on an indirect election, via a system of electors, rather than a direct popular vote—"he had reversed the thrust of the convention."[47] A number of delegates soon had second thoughts, however, and just five days later they reverted to congressional selection of the president, the arrangement that had been in place since the introduction of the Virginia Plan.[48] Morris tried to revive the idea of using electors on August 24, but was narrowly shot down.[49]

The issue of presidential selection was reassessed yet again in early September by an eleven-member committee that is usually referred to as the Committee on Postponed Parts—"a bureaucratic title of disarming candor," as one commentator remarks.[50] The committee was chaired by David Brearly of New Jersey but also included a number of delegates who had come to support the idea of presidential electors, including Morris, Rufus King, James Madison, and Daniel Carroll of Maryland.[51] On September 4, the committee proposed the system that, with a few added tweaks, has become known as the electoral college, although that term was never used by the delegates, nor does it appear in the Constitution itself.[52]

The committee could not be accused of oversimplifying things. Their proposal was that each state would be allotted a number of electors equal to its number of members of Congress (in both the House and Senate), who would be appointed in a manner chosen by the state legislature. These electors would meet in their own state on a specified date and each vote for two candidates, at least one of whom had to be from a different state. The candidate with the most votes across the nation would become the president, and the candidate with the second most votes would become the vice president (an office that made its first appearance in the committee's proposal)—assuming, that is, that at least one candidate received a majority of the electors' votes. In the event that no candidate received a majority, or that the top vote-getters ended up in a tie, the Senate would choose among the top five candidates or break the tie. It was a hefty paragraph, adding more than three hundred words to the working draft of the constitution.

This was not a self-explanatory system, to say the least, so Edmund Randolph and Charles Pinckney asked for a "particular explanation, and discussion, of the reasons" behind it.[53] Morris responded that "he would give the reasons of the Committee, and his own"—likely suggesting that he was one of the driving forces behind the system within the committee. The idea, he explained, was to find a mode of selection that avoided both "an immediate choice by the people," since many delegates seemed "anxious" about that possibility, and appointment by the legislature, with its twin dangers of having the election decided by "faction and intrigue" and rendering the president dependent on Congress. "As the electors would vote at the same time, throughout the United States, and at so great a distance from each other," Morris pointed out, "the great evil of cabal was avoided. It would be impossible, also, to corrupt them."[54]

Although Morris did not spell it out, allotting to each state a number of electors equal to its number of members of Congress was an attempt to allay the sectional objections that had frustrated the movement for direct popular election. The scheme would balance the influence of the large states and small states, insofar as the large states would get more electors (since they would have more representatives in the House) but the small states would have more than their proportional share (since every state would have two senators, regardless of population). Having each elector vote for two candidates, at least one of whom was from a different state—an idea that had first been proposed by Morris back on July 25 in reference to a direct popular election—was meant to assure the small states that the large states would not always simply elect one of their favorite sons. The scheme would also appease the slave states, since they would have a disproportionate share of representatives in the House, and thus also presidential electors, thanks to the three-fifths clause.

This system of electors seems to have satisfied most of the delegates' misgivings, for it received relatively little pushback. Much more time was spent discussing the designation of the Senate as the adjudicator in the event that no candidate received a majority, or that the top vote-getters ended up in a tie. This became the main focus because almost everyone who expressed an opinion on the matter—including George Mason, Charles Pinckney, Hugh Williamson, James Wilson, Edmund Randolph, John Rutledge, and Alexander Hamilton—assumed that in most elections no candidate would receive a majority of electoral votes, and so the Senate would be left to choose the president. Mason, for instance, remarked that "nineteen times in twenty the President would be chosen by the Senate," and Pinckney agreed that the proposed mode of election "threw the whole appointment in fact, into the hands of the Senate."[55] (Clearly, they did not anticipate the role that political parties would come to play in narrowing the field of candidates.)

If the Senate were to effectively choose the president nearly every time, of course, then that would not only revive all the problems associated with legislative selection but also center those problems in the smaller, more exclusive house of the legislature. Even Wilson was apprehensive that this aspect of the scheme displayed "a dangerous tendency to aristocracy."[56] Yet the small state delegates would not agree to assign the runoff to the House of Representatives, as Wilson proposed, for they worried that this would give the large states the dominant voice in both narrowing the field to five candidates (in the electoral college) *and* making the final selection (in the House).[57]

Morris reported that the committee chose the Senate rather than the House as the backup option because "fewer could then say to the President, 'You owe your appointment to us.'"[58] He emphasized, however, that this whole question was "of less consequence than it was supposed on both sides." Unlike almost everyone else present, Morris thought that it was "probable that a majority of the [electoral] votes will fall on the same man" in most elections and thus that no runoff would be necessary. After all, since each elector would vote for two candidates, including one from a different state, "half the votes will fall on characters eminent and generally known." (Again, think George Washington.) Besides, Morris went on, "if the President shall have given satisfaction, the votes will turn on him of course; and a majority of [the electors] will re-appoint him, without resort to the Senate," while "if he should be disliked, all disliking him would take care to unite their votes, so as to ensure his being supplanted."[59] Thanks to the rise of political parties, which Morris also foresaw, his supposition on this score ended up bearing out: only twice in American history, in 1800 and 1824, have the presidential electors failed to give a majority of their votes to one candidate. As one scholar remarks, "Here as in many other instances, Morris proved to have a better sense of how the politics of the regime would actually work" than most of the other delegates.[60]

After several days of unproductive squabbling, Roger Sherman and Hugh Williamson hit on a solution to the dilemma of where to hold the runoff: the House would choose among the top candidates instead of the Senate, so as to minimize the worries about a potential aristocracy, but the House would vote by state rather than by representative in order to give more weight to the smaller states in the second stage.[61] This fix was quickly approved, ten states to one.[62] The electoral college was born.

The electoral college is a popular target of criticism today for many reasons, but above all for its antimajoritarian features—the fact that the winner of the popular vote does not always win the election, the fact that states with smaller populations (which also tend to be whiter and more conservative) have disproportionate influence, and so on. While there is a good deal of truth to these criticisms, there is no need to rehash them here. It is perhaps worth noting, however, that at the Convention it was the advocates of a direct popular vote such as Morris and James Wilson who led the push for the electoral college, and they did so because it was the closest approximation to a popular vote that the other delegates would accept—in particular, because it placated the small states and slave states, which were accustomed to having outsized clout. In fact, the framers expected the electoral college to approximate a popular vote so closely that at the end of the Convention, after the details of the electoral system had been ironed out, James Madison still described the president as being "elected by the people."[63]

Notably, the framers did *not* conceive of the presidential electors as a body of wise elites whose judgment would be superior to that of the common people. This is how Alexander Hamilton tried to sell the scheme in *Federalist* #68, where he described the electoral college as consisting of some of the nation's "most capable" individuals, who would be "acting under circumstances favourable to deliberation."[64] At the Convention itself, however, not a single delegate described the electors in anything like these terms, at least in the notes that we have.[65] The entire point of having the electors dispersed around the country when they made their decision, recall, was to *prevent* them from acting collectively, as a deliberative body, so as to avoid the danger of "cabal." Moreover, the key architects of the electoral college, Morris and Wilson, were precisely the delegates who trusted the people to be *better* than the elites at choosing a president.

To be sure, the electoral college as it emerged from the Convention did not actually require *any* popular input in the choice of the president. The Constitution stipulated that the presidential electors were to be appointed in a manner chosen by the legislature in each state, and in the first few elections, the majority of the state legislatures picked their state's electors themselves, rather than relying on any kind of popular vote. Clearly, this was not Morris's vision; the state legislatures were among the political institutions that he disdained most fervently. When he proposed a system of electors on his own initiative on August 24, he submitted that the electors would be "chosen by the people of the several States," so it is clear that he would have preferred a binding popular vote in each state.[66] Presumably he was forced to concede the point within the Committee on Postponed Parts, perhaps because the other members felt that it would be too cumbersome to impose a single election method on all the states (much as they had found it impossible to formulate a single set of voting qualifications for the House of Representatives). Within a few decades, however, the states moved closer to Morris's vision. By 1804, a majority of the state legislatures relied on a popular vote to choose their electors, and by 1832, all but one of them did: South Carolina's legislature held out until 1868 before succumbing to the democratic tide. This was not the only modification that the system would undergo in the succeeding decades, however, and Morris disapproved of the other major change.

Despite its somewhat makeshift character and improvised origins within the Convention, the electoral college ended up being widely applauded by the founding generation more broadly. In the midst of the ratification debates, Alexander Hamilton remarked that it was "almost the only part of the [Constitution], of any consequence, which has escaped without severe censure."[67] Within the first few elections, however, it became apparent that a key aspect of the system was not working as planned, thanks to the rise of political parties. The fact that the candidate with the most electoral votes became the president while the candidate with the second most votes became the vice president meant that the two could be partisan rivals, as were President (and Federalist) John Adams and Vice President (and Republican) Thomas Jefferson after the election of 1796—an awkward situation, to say the least. In hopes of bypassing this problem, in 1800 the parties each put forward two candidates for office—Adams and Charles Cotesworth Pinckney for the Federalists and Jefferson and Aaron Burr for the Republicans—and asked the electors to vote for both of them. This expedient, however, produced an electoral tie between Jefferson and Burr when all the Republican electors followed suit and voted for both. The tie was broken by the lame duck (and Federalist-controlled) House of Representatives, which took thirty-six ballots to finally settle on Jefferson for the presidency. Once again, this was far from ideal.

The Twelfth Amendment, which was ratified in 1804, sought to address these issues, thereby making it the first implicit acknowledgment of political parties within the Constitution. The amendment stipulated that electors must indicate on their ballots which candidate they were supporting for president and which for vice president. That small move, its framers hoped, would prevent both the 1796 problem (partisan rivals serving together in an administration) and the 1800 problem (an accidental tie between running mates), and so it did.

Morris, though, opposed the amendment from within the Senate. He did so in part for generic conservative reasons. He was, he declared, "opposed to amendments, on the general ground that changing the articles of a constitutional compact lessens that respect for it, which is a main support of free governments," and he felt that "it is, generally speaking, better to bear an evil, which we know, than hazard those which we are unacquainted with."[68] Morris also, however, disapproved of the change on the merits. One of the great virtues of having the runner-up in the presidential race become the vice president, as he saw it, was that it increased the likelihood that the vice president would be an individual of national stature—someone like John Adams or Thomas Jefferson. If vice presidential candidates were voted for separately, he worried, that would increase the risk that they would be second-rate mediocrities, chosen as running mates in hopes of winning over a certain demographic or geographic region rather than because of their abilities. All too often the winning candidate would be "unfit for those duties, which the death of a President might call on him to perform." In fact, Morris contended that if the electoral system had to be changed, then it might be better to simply "abolish the office of Vice President, and leave to legislative provision the case of a vacancy in the seat of the first magistrate."[69]

In the end, Morris did not get exactly what he wanted when it came to presidential selection—namely a direct popular election—but, unlike with Congress, he did get a great deal of what he wanted. In fact, he arguably did as much to shape the method of choosing the president as any delegate in Philadelphia. By fighting doggedly against congressional selection, which he believed would have fatally undermined the independence of the executive branch, and by helping to devise an alternative that the other delegates would accept, he fundamentally altered the nature of the American presidency. This was, however, far from the only move that Morris made to bolster this part of the government.

7. An Office Fit for Washington: The Presidency

As the delegates debated the structure and powers of the presidency over the course of the Philadelphia Convention, they knew perfectly well who the nation's first president would be. Assuming that he would consent to serve, George Washington's elevation to the executive mansion was a foregone conclusion, no matter what selection method they ended up settling on. As Pierce Butler complained the following year, many of the delegates—and one would have to include Morris here—"cast their eyes towards General Washington as President; and shaped their Ideas of the Powers to be given to a President, by their opinions of his Virtue."[1] Of course, they were well aware that Washington would not be around forever, and that the office would have other occupants. Benjamin Franklin remarked, with an implicit nod in Washington's direction, that "the first man put at the helm will be a good one. Nobody knows what sort may come afterwards."[2] Still, it is unlikely that the framers would have made the position as powerful as they ultimately did had Washington not been waiting in the wings—as well as sitting at the front of the room, presiding over their deliberations.

The executive that was proposed in the Constitution—complete with a renewable four-year term, expansive powers, and a veto over legislation—would have been thoroughly alarming to the vast majority of Americans only a decade earlier. Given their unhappy experiences under the rule of King George III and his colonial governors in the years leading up to the revolution, most Americans at the time looked at executive power with an exceedingly skeptical eye.[3] Hence most of the new state constitutions—all but those of New York and Massachusetts—relegated the executive to a distinctly subordinate role; most governors were appointed by the legislature for a single-year term and had little in the way of independent powers and no legislative veto.[4] On the national level there was virtually no executive at all. There was an officer called the "president" under the Articles of Confederation, but this was simply the member of the Confederation Congress who was chosen to preside over that body, much the way that the vice president presides over the Senate today. It was a largely honorary role that no individual could hold for more than a year in any three-year stretch. Given the fecklessness of the Confederation Congress and most of the state governments over the course of the 1780s, however, by 1787 many Americans had begun to warm to the idea of a leader who would be able to check the legislature more effectively and to carry out the government's will more energetically.

Morris and James Wilson, the Convention's foremost proponents of a popularly elected president, were also the figures most responsible for making the presidency as powerful as it ended up being. There were other delegates who desired an even stronger executive than they did—notably Alexander Hamilton—but no one else promoted the idea of a vigorous chief magistrate as consistently or effectively as Morris and Wilson.[5] Although Wilson began the campaign on his own, while Morris was away from Philadelphia, Morris more than made up for lost time after his return. In fact, he ended up speaking on the presidency more frequently than any other delegate—sixty-five times, with Wilson coming next at fifty-six times.[6] Morris also helped to strengthen the executive in critical ways off the Convention floor, both through committee work and through his role as the Constitution's drafter. Although the honorific "Father of the American Presidency" is more often bestowed upon Wilson, several scholars have contended that, given his myriad contributions, Morris is at least as deserving of the title if anyone is.[7] Indeed, one commentator goes so far as to suggest that "in many respects, our executive is Morris's executive."[8]

The gathering in Philadelphia was not the first constitutional convention at which Morris advocated an energetic executive. The New York state constitution, which he had helped to frame a decade earlier, created what was easily the most powerful executive office among the states.[9] Thanks in part to Morris's efforts, the New York governor was elected by a direct popular vote, which freed him from dependence on the legislature; served a three-year term, which was longer than that of any other governor save Delaware's (who also served for three years); was eligible for immediate and indefinite reelection, which enabled the state's first governor, George Clinton, to serve six straight terms, from 1777 to 1795; and had wide-ranging authority, above all as the commander-in-chief of the state's militia and navy.

Morris was pleased with these features of the office, but there were two respects in which he believed it should have been made still stronger and more independent. At the suggestion of Robert R. Livingston, the New York constitution created a "council of revision" made up of the governor, the chancellor, and the three judges of the state supreme court, which was responsible for considering all proposed legislation. If the council rejected a given bill, then it was sent back to the legislature, which could override its veto with a two-thirds majority of both houses. (This somewhat cumbersome system was the model for the council of revision that James Madison advocated repeatedly but unsuccessfully for the national government at the Philadelphia Convention.) No other governor possessed even a qualified veto over legislation until Massachusetts adopted its new constitution in 1780, but Morris had urged the delegates to go even further by granting the governor an absolute veto—one that he could execute on his own, rather than as part of a council, and that the legislature could not override. He also objected to the limitation put on the governor by the "council of appointment" that was initiated by John Jay. According to this provision, most state officers were appointed by a council made up of the governor and several senators; here, too, Morris would have preferred to lodge the power in the hands of the governor alone.

For all the authority conferred on the New York governor, Morris wrote to Alexander Hamilton soon after the constitution's adoption to lament that the charter was "deficient for the Want of Vigor in the executive" and to blame "the Spirit which now reigns in America," which he deemed overly "Cautious."[10] For anyone who knew this history, Morris's efforts at the Philadelphia Convention would not have come as a surprise. In fact, the New York governorship was one of the most important forerunners of the American presidency, thanks in no small part to the role that Morris played in shaping both.[11]

Morris did not, it should be stressed, believe that the president should have unlimited powers, or even more power than the legislature. On the contrary, he recognized that, as he put it on July 24, "It is the most difficult [thing] of all, rightly to balance the Executive. Make him too weak—the Legislature will usurp his power. Make him too strong—he will usurp on the Legislature."[12] Given the widespread jealousy of executive power in early America, however, he sought to bolster it at nearly every turn in hopes of making the presidency a truly coequal branch. Morris also believed that the size of the country demanded a strong executive. "It has been a maxim in political science, that republican government is not adapted to a large extent of country, because the energy of the executive magistracy cannot reach the extreme parts of it," he remarked. "Our country is an extensive one. We must either then renounce the blessings of the Union, or provide an Executive with sufficient vigor to pervade every part of it."[13] In that sense, he regarded the presidency as "the Key Stone in the great Arche of Empire," as he later described it to George Washington.[14]

Like most of the other delegates, Morris believed that the president should have a good deal of authority—if not the primary authority—over the military and foreign affairs. A single, responsible individual, he believed, would be best placed to "command the forces, of the Republic" and to treat with other nations.[15] (Besides, who could possibly be a better fit than Washington to undertake these responsibilities?) Hence Morris's proposed "Council of State" or cabinet—whose members would, in his vision, be under the firm control of the president—included some strikingly broad job descriptions. The Secretary of Foreign Affairs would "generally . . . attend to the interests of the United States in their connexions with foreign powers"; the Secretary of War would "superintend every thing relating to the War department, such as the raising and equipping of troops, the care of military stores, public fortifications, arsenals, and the like"; and the Secretary of the Marine would likewise "superintend every thing relating to the Marine department, the public ships, dock-yards, naval stores, and arsenals."[16] As a member of the Committee on Postponed Parts, Morris also succeeded in transferring the treaty-making power from the Senate, where it had been lodged by the Committee of Detail, to the president, with the Senate merely adding its "advice and consent."[17]

Morris similarly contended that the president should have expansive, and often unilateral, appointment powers. The cabinet that he envisioned included the three secretaries just mentioned as well as a Secretary of Domestic Affairs, a Secretary of Commerce and Finance, a Secretary of State, and the Chief Justice of the Supreme Court, and he proposed that all but the latter be appointed by the president without any kind of congressional approval and serve during his pleasure, although they would be liable to impeachment.[18] Most state governors, by contrast, were saddled with an executive council whose members were chosen by others. As Morris explained in a letter written two years later, the president must be able to choose and remove his cabinet officers if he is to be held responsible for their actions: "Every subordinate power should be tied to the chief, by those intermediate links of will and pleasure, which, like the elasticity of the arterial system, render sensible the pulsations of the heart at the remotest extremities. For how can the executive be accountable, when its members are not subordinate and obedient to the general volition?"[19] Ultimately, of course, the Constitution stipulated that the principal executive officers would be nominated by the president but would require confirmation by the Senate.

Like the treaty-making power, the power to appoint federal judges—including Supreme Court justices—and foreign ambassadors was transferred from the hands of the Senate to those of the president with the Senate's "advice and consent" by the Committee on Postponed Parts, likely also at Morris's instigation.[20] If he had had his druthers, however, the appointment of judges and justices, at least, would have been lodged in the president's hands alone, for back in July he had seconded a proposal by James Wilson to that effect.[21] And recall that he had also suggested that the executive should be responsible for appointing senators, filling up vacancies as they occurred. All told, then, the appointment powers that Morris would have entrusted to the president were breathtaking. An individual who could appoint cabinet officers, federal judges and justices (for life), and senators (for life), all without congressional approval, would be able to choose much of the national government—essentially all openings except seats in the House of Representatives—with impeachment as the only check on his power in this regard. (Washington was widely known to be an excellent judge of character, after all.)

Morris also enhanced the president's agenda-setting role by initiating a shift in the language surrounding the annual State of the Union address. The Committee of Detail included a provision in its draft constitution stipulating that the president "shall, from time to time, give information to the Legislature, of the state of the Union. He may recommend to their consideration such measures as he shall judge necessary, and expedient."[22] When this section came before the Convention, Morris successfully moved to strike out the phrase "he may" and to combine the two sentences, so that they ultimately read: "He shall, from time to time, give to the Congress information of the State of the union, and recommend to their consideration such measures as he shall judge necessary and expedient." As Morris explained, the idea was "to make it the *duty* of the President to recommend [measures], and thence prevent umbrage or cavil at his doing it."[23] With this small change Morris ensured that the president would be expected to help set the legislative agenda, despite having no authority to formally introduce legislation himself.

One presidential power that was sure to raise red flags was a veto over legislation. Prior to the revolution, the veto that the king and his governors regularly exercised over the laws passed by the colonial assemblies was a major source of discontent among the colonists. In fact, the first three grievances against King George III in the Declaration of Independence all centered on the royal veto power. In reaction, most of the new state constitutions refrained from giving the executive any kind of legislative veto, with the exceptions of Massachusetts, which granted its governor a veto that could be overridden by a two-thirds majority of the legislature, and New York, which included the governor in the council of revision described above.

At the Convention, a number of delegates opposed the idea of a presidential veto. Benjamin Franklin regarded it as "a mischievous sort of check," and Roger Sherman protested against "enabling any one man to stop the will of the whole," given that "no one man could be found so far above all the rest in wisdom." Pierce Butler complained that he never would have supported lodging the executive power in a single set of hands in the first place "could he have entertained the idea" that that individual would be given a legislative veto. George Mason predicted that a president armed with a veto would refuse his "assent to necessary measures" until more and more power was "engrossed . . . into his own hands," so that eventually "the American Executive, like the British, will, by bribery and influence, save himself the trouble and odium of exerting his negative [i.e., veto] afterwards."[24]

In early June, when Morris was away, James Wilson and Alexander Hamilton boldly proposed giving the president an absolute veto over legislation—meaning one that could not be overridden by the legislature—but only Rufus King supported the idea, and the state delegations voted unanimously against it. They settled instead on a conditional veto that could be overridden by a two-thirds majority in both houses of Congress.[25] On August 15, Morris reintroduced the idea of an absolute veto, admitting that such a strong check "might have its inconveniences" but insisting that "the danger on the other side" was much greater. Drawing on various historical examples—the ephors of Sparta, the Council of Censors in Pennsylvania, the British Parliament during the seventeenth-century civil wars—he contended that "encroachments of the popular branch of the Government ought to be guarded against" and that in order to prevent legislative inroads on the president's authority, they must devise "some more effectual check than requiring two thirds only to overrule the negative of the Executive."[26] The other delegates were not convinced that an absolute veto was warranted, but they did narrowly agree to raise the bar for overturning a presidential veto from two-thirds to three-quarters of both houses of Congress, at least for the time being.[27]

After Morris's draft of the Constitution was read aloud on September 12, the issue was brought up once again, with several delegates arguing that the threshold for overriding a veto should be returned to two-thirds. Morris pointed out that the difference between two-thirds and three-quarters was not all that large—only two votes in the Senate and no more than five in the House, as they would initially be constituted—and that, in any case, it was "the excess, rather than the deficiency, of laws" that "was to be dreaded." As Madison recorded, Morris "dwelt on the danger to the public interest from the instability of laws, as the most to be guarded against." A presidential veto could pose "little danger" in the long run, he added, since if a president refused to "consent where he ought, every fourth year another [president] can be substituted."[28] The vote was once again close—six states to four, with one divided—but in the end the delegates chose to revert to the two-thirds threshold.[29]

Although Morris had hoped that the president's check on legislation would be even stronger than it ended up being, it has nonetheless proven to be quite potent. The first override of a presidential veto did not occur until 1845, and throughout American history, less than five percent of vetoes have been overturned by Congress.

Morris also managed to bolster presidential power through his role as the Constitution's drafter. On a symbolic level, the parallel structure of the first three articles—with Article I devoted to the legislature, Article II to the executive, and Article III to the judiciary—suggested that the president was every bit the equal of Congress. As was noted in chapter 2, the state constitutions and the various earlier plans and drafts at the Convention had all devoted many more articles to the legislature than to the other two branches, but Morris's reframing of the document helped to cement the idea of three coequal branches.

More substantively speaking, the vesting clause that opens Article II, which was also Morris's handiwork, became a powerful tool for boosting presidential authority. The Committee of Detail's draft constitution had stated that "the Executive power of the United States shall be vested in a single person."[30] The focus here was on the fact that the executive would be an individual, the president, rather than some kind of council. Morris tweaked the language to state that "the Executive power shall be vested in a President of the United States of

America."³¹ Although the change was subtle, this formulation shifts the focus slightly to the power that was being vested in the president, namely the entirety of "the Executive power." This shift is made more apparent when the clause is read alongside the parallel clause that Morris wrote for Article I, which states that "all Legislative powers *herein granted* shall be vested in a Congress of the United States" (italics added).³² The phrase "herein granted," which had not been included in the Committee of Detail's legislative vesting clause, made clear that Congress's powers were limited to those explicitly granted in the Constitution, but Morris did not repeat the limiting phrase in the executive vesting clause.³³ Soon after the Constitution was ratified, advocates of an energetic presidency, such as Alexander Hamilton, interpreted Morris's Article II vesting clause as a capacious grant of executive power to the president, as he evidently intended it to be read.³⁴

The extent of the president's power would also, of course, be shaped by the length of his term and by whether he would be eligible for reelection. As has been noted, the state governors served very short terms at that time: ten served for only a single year, while South Carolina's served for two years and New York's and Delaware's for three years. In addition, many states either prohibited their governors from serving a second term or limited them to a set number terms (usually three). Of the three states whose governors served for longer than a year, New York's was the only one who was eligible for immediate reelection.

Given this backdrop, the delegates proved unexpectedly amenable to the idea of a long presidential term, although somewhat less so to the idea of perpetual reeligibility. Particularly when they expected the president to be chosen by Congress—as they did for the vast majority of the Convention—the delegates were reluctant to allow him to stand for office in perpetuity precisely because it would make him dependent on the will of the legislature in all the ways that Morris warned about. In fact, the push for a long term was justified on the grounds that it would render reeligibility unnecessary. Thus, the arrangement that the delegates favored at the outset and returned to time and again throughout the summer was to have the president serve a single seven-year term.³⁵

Many delegates, however, were willing to go much further than this. On July 24, after a vote to revert from a system of presidential electors (which had lasted all of five days) back to having the president selected by the legislature, a few of the delegates sought to outdo one another with regard to term length. Luther Martin proposed a term of eleven years, Elbridge Gerry suggested fifteen, and Rufus King opted for twenty, commenting that "this is the medium life of princes."[36] James Wilson then remarked that "the difficulties and perplexities into which the House [i.e., the Convention] is thrown, proceed from the election by the Legislature, which he was sorry had been re-instated. The inconvenience of this mode was such, that he would agree to almost any length of time in order to get rid of the dependence which must result from it."[37]

Nor was Wilson the only one to feel that "almost any length of time" would be acceptable for this purpose. In fact, as unimaginable as it might seem today, many delegates endorsed the idea of the president serving for life, or at least during "good behavior"—meaning, essentially, "unless impeached." The idea was first mooted by Alexander Hamilton, who contended in a long June 18 discourse that an executive who served for only seven years would use a war or some other emergency "to evade or refuse a degradation from his place," whereas "an Executive for life has not this motive for forgetting his fidelity, and would therefore be a safer depository of power."[38] Although Hamilton's speech would later become infamous, he was actually far from an outlier in this particular. On July 17, James McClurg of Virginia proposed that the president serve during good behavior in order to secure his independence from the legislature. Morris seconded the motion—more on this soon—and Jacob Broom of Delaware declared that he "highly approved" of the motion and that "it obviated all his difficulties."[39] A number of delegates spoke out against the idea, of course, but the vote on the motion was surprisingly close. Six states voted against it, but no fewer than four voted in favor—the uncommon combination of New Jersey, Pennsylvania, Delaware, and Virginia.[40] The Virginia delegation's vote for a presidential term of good behavior is particularly notable; since Mason and Edmund Randolph clearly voted against it, both James Madison and George Washington, the presumptive first occupant of the office, must have voted in favor it.[41]

Given that Morris sought to bolster executive power at nearly every turn, it is perhaps predictable that he would second a proposal that the president serve during good behavior. Indeed, he "expressed great pleasure in hearing" McClurg's motion and exclaimed that "this was the way to get a good Government." Morris's "fear that so valuable an ingredient would not be attained," he said, "had led him to take the part he had done"—meaning having opposed congressional selection of the president so strenuously. Morris proclaimed that he was "indifferent how the Executive should be chosen, provided he held his place by this tenure."[42] When George Mason objected to the idea, declaring that from service during good behavior "it would be an easy step to hereditary monarchy," Morris insisted that he "was as little a friend to monarchy as any gentleman." On the contrary, he agreed with Madison that the surest way "to keep out monarchical government was to establish such a Republican government as would make the people happy, and to prevent a desire of change."[43]

To all appearances, however, Morris was unperturbed by the vote against McClurg's motion. In fact, in the long speech that he delivered two days later, he argued that the president should be elected by the people for a "short duration, [so] that he may with propriety be re-eligible" and suggested a term of just two years—shorter than any other delegate had advocated.[44] The following week, he went even further in reversing course on the idea of service during good behavior, declaring that he "preferred a short period, a re-eligibility, but a different mode of election" than the other delegates' perennial favorite, selection by Congress. Adopting his best republican pose, Morris now claimed that a long term for the president "would prevent an adoption of the plan [i.e., the Constitution]. It ought to do so. He should himself be afraid to trust it."[45] That said, in Morris's eyes, the distance between service during good behavior and a short term with perpetual reeligibility was not all that great. He responded to the objection that a two-year term would be too short with assurances that "as long as [the president] should behave himself well he would be continued in his place. The extent of the country would secure his re-election against the factions and discontents of particular States."[46] (Did anyone really believe that George Washington would ever fail to win reelection?)

Ultimately, then, Morris seems to have been relatively indifferent between having the president serve during good behavior (under any selection scheme) and giving him a short term with perpetual reeligibility (as long as he was not appointed by the legislature). He reserved his most vehement opposition for the idea of imposing a set term limit on the presidency.

Every time the other delegates returned to the idea of limiting the president to one fixed term in order to secure his independence from whatever body selected him—which they did with remarkable frequency—Morris fought against it. In fact, he spoke in opposition to a presidential term limit on six separate occasions during the Convention—far more often, and in far greater detail, than anyone else.

Morris's basic argument was that perpetual reeligibility would provide a means of holding the president responsible for his conduct and of discouraging selfish or reckless behavior. Limiting the president to a single term would, he declared, "destroy the great incitement to merit public esteem, by taking away the hope of being rewarded with a re-appointment." More than that, "it may give a dangerous turn to one of the strongest passions in the human breast" by encouraging a president whose term was about to expire to make a last-minute power grab: "Shut the civil road to glory, and he may be compelled to seek it by the sword." As Morris put it on another occasion, a president who was ineligible for reelection "will be unwilling to quit his exaltation; the road to his object through the Constitution will be shut; he will be in possession of the sword; a civil war will ensue, and the commander of the victorious army, on whichever side, will be the despot of America." Alternatively, if more prosaically, Morris worried that a term limit may encourage a president to enrich himself or his associates during his remaining time in office: "It will tempt him to make the most of the short space of time allotted him, to accumulate wealth and provide for his friends." It was like telling him to "make hay while the sun shines."[47]

A president who was eligible for perpetual reappointment would also, Morris maintained, add wisdom and stability to the government. A single fixed term would force the nation to forsake a president's accumulated knowledge and experience, in both the foreign and domestic arenas, whenever his term happened to be up: "The expedient of making [the president] ineligible a second time . . . was as much as to say, we should give him the benefit of experience, and then deprive ourselves of the use of him." The prohibition on reappointment would thereby create "a political school, in which we were always governed by the scholars [i.e., students], and not by the masters." A perpetual reeligibility would likewise give the president an incentive to plan for the long term, Morris added, whereas a president who was limited to one term "will have no interest beyond his period of service." Still further, a required rotation in office would lead to "instability of councils" since "a change of men is ever followed by a change of measures" and new presidents generally "scorn to tread in the paths of their predecessors." In fact, Morris worried that a fixed term limit might undermine the Constitution itself. If the term of a widely admired leader—yet again, think George Washington—were scheduled to end in the midst of a war or some other crisis, he suspected, the constitutional limit would be abandoned: "In moments of pressing danger, the tried abilities and established character of a favorite magistrate will prevail over respect for the forms of the Constitution."[48]

Finally, Morris argued that there was no reason to limit the president to a single term when no other government officers were restricted in this way. George Mason contended that it was "the very palladium of civil liberty, that the great officers of the state, and particularly the Executive, should at fixed periods return to that mass from which they were at first taken, in order that they may feel and respect those rights and interests which are again to be personally valuable to them." Morris objected, however, that "on the same principle the Judiciary ought to be periodically degraded; certain it was, that the Legislature ought, on every principle, yet no one had proposed, or conceived that the members of it should not be re-eligible."[49] Taken together, these arguments closely prefigure the classic case in favor of perpetual reeligibility that Alexander Hamilton set forth in *Federalist* #72 the following year.

Ultimately, of course, Morris's side prevailed on this issue, at least at the Convention. The electoral college system that he and the Committee on Postponed Parts proposed on September 4 included no term limit on the president, nor was one added amid the various tweaks that were made to the system on its way to inclusion in the Constitution. That said, George Washington set a precedent for voluntarily stepping down after two terms that was followed by every president until Franklin Delano Roosevelt, and since 1951 the two-term limit has been constitutionally mandated by the Twenty-Second Amendment. Although the precedent originated with Morris's hero, surely he would not be pleased by this development. (Recall that Morris urged Washington to run for a third term in the election of 1800.)[50]

A final piece of the presidential puzzle, impeachment, is one on which Morris changed his mind during the Convention. In his long speech of July 19, he opposed the inclusion of any provision for impeaching the president. His reasoning was that if the president were selected by Congress, then it would be "dangerous" for Congress to also hold the power of impeachment, for that would just redouble the president's subservience: "It will hold him in such dependence, that he will be no check to the Legislature, will not be a firm guardian of the people and of the public interest. He will be the tool of a faction, of some leading demagogue in the Legislature." On the other hand, if the president were elected by the people for a two-year term, as he was proposing, then a formal impeachment process would be unnecessary. If a president committed some offense, after all, then the people would simply refuse to reelect him, and he would be out of office in a relatively short time. An orderly transfer of power, without the need for a potentially tumultuous impeachment trial, would be built into the system. One great advantage of a short term, in Morris's view, was that it would make it possible to "avoid impeachments, which would be otherwise necessary."[51]

Morris further argued—again, at least at first—that the potential "danger from an unimpeachable magistrate" could not be "formidable" since he presumed that the other officers in the executive branch *would* "be amenable, by impeachment, to the public justice" and that "without these ministers, the Executive can do nothing of consequence."[52] Threats to the cabinet, in effect, could be used as a tool to check the president, much as the royal ministers were often held responsible for the king's misdeeds in Britain. Morris was not the only delegate at the Convention to contend that the president should not be impeachable—a few others, including Charles Pinckney and Rufus King, did so as well—but this was a distinctly minority position.[53] Even Alexander Hamilton thought that the executive should be "liable to impeachment for mal- and corrupt conduct."[54]

Over the course of the following day, however, Morris's position on the issue shifted dramatically. George Mason posed the obvious questions: "Shall any man be above justice? Above all, shall that man be above it who can commit the most extensive injustice?" Benjamin Franklin added a somewhat less obvious point, arguing that the possibility of impeachment was actually "favorable to the Executive," since it provided both an opportunity for an "honorable acquittal, where he should be unjustly accused" and a means of removing an "obnoxious" president without resorting to assassination. At that point Morris started to change his tune, admitting that "corruption, and some few other offences . . . ought to be impeachable."[55] After James Madison, Elbridge Gerry, and Edmund Randolph voiced still more worries about an unimpeachable president, Morris announced that his "opinion had been changed by the arguments used in the discussion. He was now sensible of the necessity of impeachments, if the Executive was to continue for any length of time in office." After all, "no one would say that we ought to expose ourselves to the danger of seeing the First Magistrate in foreign pay, without being able to guard against it by displacing him." And there were other clearly legitimate grounds for impeachment, such as "corrupting his Electors, and incapacity."[56] Later Morris suggested that the members of the president's cabinet should be impeachable for "neglect of duty, malversation [i.e., misbehavior], or corruption."[57]

This was a fairly broad conception of the proper grounds for impeachment, and Morris continued to push in this direction in the final discussion of the topic on September 8.[58] The impeachment clause that emerged from the Committee on Postponed Parts provided that the president could be impeached for "treason and bribery," and George Mason proposed to add "maladministration" to the list. Although James Madison felt that this term was far too "vague," Morris mildly supported it, declaring that it "can do no harm" and anyway "will not be put in force"—a surprisingly breezy response from someone who was generally so worried about rendering the executive overly dependent on the legislature. Mason then altered his proposal to "other high crimes and misdemeanors," which was adopted.[59]

Morris's unexpected casualness on the matter extended into a debate over how an impeached president would be removed from office. James Madison proposed that the Supreme Court rather than the Senate should hold the trial in order to keep the president somewhat more independent of Congress, particularly since the House of Representatives was the body responsible for the first step in the impeachment process. Morris, however, contended that "the Supreme Court were too few in number, and might be warped or corrupted." While he remained "against a dependence of the Executive on the Legislature," he supposed that "there could be no danger that the Senate would say untruly, on their oaths, that the President was guilty of crimes or facts, especially as in four years he can be turned out."[60] Of course, recent years have demonstrated that the real worry is less that the Senate would wrongly convict an innocent president than that it would refuse to convict a plainly guilty one.

In all, Morris came far closer to realizing his vision of the presidency than his vision of Congress. Neither the electoral college system nor the president's four-year term were exactly what he had initially favored, but he did manage to fight off the two arrangements that he found most objectionable, namely congressional selection and a limitation of the president to a single fixed term. Similarly, Morris had hoped that the president's appointment powers would be more unilateral, and his veto more difficult to override, than they ended up being, but on the whole, the president's constitutional authority was remarkably far-reaching, particularly given the wariness that surrounded executive power at the time.

Morris also ended up getting his way, of course, with regard to the first occupant of the office. Over the fifteen months following the Convention's close, he wrote no fewer than four letters imploring George Washington to comply with the nation's seemingly unanimous wish that he become president. The last of these letters made clear what had been fairly obvious all along, namely that Morris had had Washington in mind as he helped to construct the presidency. "I have ever thought, and said," he wrote to the general, "that you *must* be the President. No other Man can *fill* that Office."[61] As will become evident in this book's epilogue, however, Morris did not think as highly of some of Washington's successors.

8. That Fortress of the Constitution: The Judiciary

The delegates devoted far less discussion and scrutiny to the judiciary than to the other two branches over the course of the Philadelphia Convention. Indeed, one historian goes so far as to describe this branch as "the taken-for-granted stepchild of 1787."[1] This was not because the framers had a fleshed-out vision of the judiciary on which they all agreed; on the contrary, they had even less to guide them in the creation of the new court system than they had in forging the presidency. The United States had never had a national judiciary at that point. Under the Articles of Confederation, the vast majority of cases were settled in the state courts, and the Confederation Congress itself adjudicated disputes among the states. The state judiciaries, for their part, varied widely in structure.[2] The judges on the states' highest courts served terms ranging from a single year to good behavior, for instance, and they were appointed by the legislature in five states, by the governor in two states, and by a combination of the two in the remaining six states. By the time of the Convention a handful of state courts had exercised the power of judicial review, striking down laws passed by the state legislature as incompatible with the state constitution, but this move had often proven controversial.[3]

True to his usual form, Morris was an active participant in the handful of discussions that the delegates dedicated to the judiciary. His interventions on this topic, much like those relating to the presidency, were directed at making the judiciary a truly coequal branch. In addition to granting the judiciary its own article in his draft of the Constitution—Article III, paralleling Article I on the legislature and Article II on the executive—Morris sought to secure the independence of judges and justices from Congress, to arm them with the power of judicial review, and to establish a full system of lower federal courts, in addition to the Supreme Court. It is difficult to judge how successful he was in these efforts, as the provisions on the judiciary that emerged from the Convention were fairly vague and open-ended. On such seemingly central questions as whether federal judges and justices would have the power of judicial review, whether lower federal courts would be created, and how many justices would sit on the Supreme Court, the Constitution was either silent or deliberately inconclusive. Many years later, during his time as a senator, Morris sought to further the conception of the judiciary that he had sketched in Philadelphia by opposing the repeal of the Judiciary Act of 1801, but to his great consternation the repeal narrowly passed. In Morris's view, this move marked nothing less than the beginning of the end of the Constitution itself.

At the outset of the Convention, the Virginia Plan stipulated that Congress would select federal judges and justices, although two weeks later, at the insistence of James Madison, this power was lodged in the hands of the Senate alone.[4] James Wilson contended that even the Senate was too large for this purpose and that "intrigue, partiality, and concealment" would inevitably attend their appointments, so in mid-July he proposed that judges and justices be chosen by the president.[5] Morris seconded the motion, but it was defeated, six states to two, with Pennsylvania one of the two states supporting it.[6] Nathaniel Gorham of Massachusetts then proposed that the appointment be made by the president with the "advice and consent" of the Senate—an arrangement modeled on the Massachusetts state constitution—and Morris once again seconded the motion. This time the vote was evenly split, four states to four, but according to the Convention's rules, a majority of the state delegations had to approve a motion in order for it to prevail, so this one, too, was lost, at least for the time being.[7]

On July 21, Morris explained why he preferred judicial appointments to be made by the president rather than the Senate. In addition to the size of the Senate, which Wilson and others had already pointed out would likely give free rein to factional conflict, Morris contended that the Senate's character rendered it ill-suited to choose judges. Given that the states had equal votes in the Senate and that senators were chosen by the state legislatures, the Senate was widely seen as representing the states, but Morris pointed out that "the States, in their corporate capacity, will frequently have an interest staked on the determination of the Judges." In particular, the state legislatures would surely prefer judges who would favor the state governments in potential conflicts with the national government. In view of this bias, Morris contended, "the Judges ought not to be appointed by the Senate." After all, "next to the impropriety of being judge in one's own cause, is the appointment of the Judge."[8]

Many delegates argued that senators would be more familiar with potential judges around the country than the president would be, and thus that they would be in a better position to make an informed choice. To this line of argument, Morris retorted that in fact "the reverse was the truth." Senators, he suggested, would mostly "take the character of candidates from the flattering pictures drawn by their friends," whereas the president, "in the necessary intercourse with every part of the United States required by the nature of his administration, will or may have the best possible information." Other delegates worried that, as Oliver Ellsworth put it, "the Executive will be regarded by the people with a jealous eye. Every power for augmenting unnecessarily his influence will be disliked." Morris, of course, was rarely one to quibble with an increase in presidential power. "If the Executive can be safely trusted with the command of the army," he insisted, then "there cannot surely be any reasonable ground of jealousy" with respect to appointing judges.[9]

Despite Morris's objections, the power of appointing judges and justices remained with the Senate from June 13 all the way until September 7. As noted in the previous chapter, this power was transferred to the president with the Senate's advice and consent—the Massachusetts model—by the Committee on Postponed Parts, with Morris surely pushing for the change within the committee.[10] This time the delegates were so preoccupied with the committee's proposal of the electoral college that the president's newfound appointment powers met with only token questioning. When James Wilson objected that requiring the Senate's advice and consent would make it difficult to hold the president fully accountable for his choices, Morris countered that the committee's proposal combined the best of both worlds: "As the President was to nominate, there would be responsibility; and as the Senate was to concur, there would be security."[11] In truth, of course, Morris agreed with Wilson's position—he too would have preferred to lodge the appointment power in the president's hands alone—but his sales pitch had its intended effect: the committee's proposal was approved without dissent.[12]

Interestingly, Morris not only pushed for the president to choose judges and justices but also envisioned a sort of standing alliance between the executive and judiciary against potential encroachments from the legislature. He suggested, for instance, that the chief justice of the Supreme Court should be a member of the president's cabinet or "Council of State." In fact, Morris appears to have believed that the chief justice should be the *leading* figure of the cabinet, for he proposed that he be "President of the Council, in the absence of the President" as well as first in the line of presidential succession in the event of the president's death, resignation, disability, or impeachment.[13] (This was before the creation of the vice presidency.) In addition to blending the head of the judiciary with the executive branch in this way, Morris expected the chief justice, like the president, to play an important agenda-setting role with respect to the legislature. The job duties of the chief justice, as he described them, included "recommend[ing] such alterations of and additions to the laws of the United States, as may in his opinion be necessary to the due administration of justice; and such as may promote useful learning and inculcate sound morality throughout the Union."[14] None of the other delegates seconded these proposals, however, and they were never even discussed on the Convention floor.

Morris also backed the pet proposal of James Madison and James Wilson that would have combined the president and Supreme Court justices in a "council of revision" modeled on the similar council in the New York state constitution. As this council was outlined in the Virginia Plan, the president and "a convenient number of the national Judiciary" would have been responsible for examining every law passed by Congress. If the council were to "negative" or veto the law, then Congress would have to re-pass it before it would go into effect.[15] The idea was that this conditional preemptive check—a sort of combination of presidential veto and judicial review, but without the finality of either—would encourage Congress to reconsider or reformulate a given law if the council found it to be problematic in some way. As Wilson put it, "Laws may be unjust, may be unwise, may be dangerous, may be destructive" and yet be constitutional, and a council of revision would provide the president and justices with "an opportunity of taking notice of those characters of a law, and of counteracting" them "by the weight of their opinions."[16]

Although he was not quite as obsessed with this provision as Madison and Wilson were, Morris supported it because he believed that the president would be more likely to stand up to Congress if he had the justices standing with him. If the president were to be both appointed and impeachable by Congress—as the delegates assumed he would be for most of the Convention—then "there is the justest grounds to fear his want of firmness in resisting [legislative] encroachments," Morris argued. The "auxiliary firmness and weight of the Judiciary" might help to enhance both the president's authority and his willingness to use it, although he remained "extremely apprehensive" that even this "would not supply the deficiency."[17] Morris further argued that a council of revision would provide a "barrier against the instability of legislative assemblies" and thereby make it easier to avoid legislative inroads on private property—paper money, debt relief legislation, and the like—and to preserve the public credit.[18]

When a number of delegates objected that a council combining the president and the justices would violate the separation of powers, Morris responded that he was "surprised that any defensive provision for securing the effectual separation of the departments should be considered as an improper mixture of them." Given the ever-present danger of congressional intrusions on the authority of the president and the courts, in other words, the latter should be armed with every possible means of resisting them. To suggest that providing the weaker branches with defensive resources "tended to blend and confound powers that ought to be separately exercised," he scoffed, was like saying that "if three neighbors had three distinct farms, a right in each to defend his farm against his neighbours, tended to blend the farms together."[19] Besides, in England the judges were consulted by Parliament in "difficult and doubtful cases" and were sometimes "members of the Privy Council; and can there advise the Executive," and this mixing of the branches appeared to work perfectly well there.[20]

The other delegates, however, remained unconvinced. Although Madison and Wilson campaigned relentlessly for a council of revision over the course of the Convention, it was rejected by a majority of the state delegations every time they brought it up.[21]

The question of judicial review—that is, the question of whether federal judges and Supreme Court justices would have the authority to declare laws passed by Congress and the state legislatures to be unconstitutional and hence null and void—was never discussed in a direct and detailed way at the Convention, as the executive veto, the proposed council of revision, and the proposed congressional veto over state legislation all were. The issue did come up in passing a number of times, however, and eight different delegates—including Madison, Wilson, and Morris—spoke in favor of the practice, while only two—John Francis Mercer and John Dickinson—expressed opposition to it.[22]

Morris has been described as "a leading advocate" of the power of judicial review at the Convention on the grounds that "he expressed his belief that federal courts would be able to hold both state and federal legislation unconstitutional and that judicial review was desirable."[23] It must be admitted, however, that his remarks on the topic were rather casual and cursory.[24] On July 17, in the midst of a debate over the congressional veto over state laws that James Madison championed, Morris commented that such a veto would be unnecessary because "a [state] law that ought to be negatived, will be set aside in the Judiciary department."[25] A month later he stated, once again somewhat offhandedly, that "he could not agree that the Judiciary ... should be bound to say, that a direct violation of the Constitution was law."[26] It is possible, of course, that neither Morris nor any of the other delegates went into much detail on this point because they simply took the existence and desirability of judicial review for granted. Morris himself hinted as much many years later, when he recalled that "it was foreseen" by the delegates that "the judges would ... resist assaults on the Constitution by acts of legislation."[27]

In any case, the question of judicial review was never voted upon by the state delegations, nor was any explicit authorization of this practice included in the Constitution. The firmest textual support for the exercise of judicial review, however, came in a provision that Morris altered in an important way in his draft of the Constitution. Drawing on language from the New Jersey Plan, the Committee of Detail's draft constitution stipulated that the Constitution and the laws made under it "shall be the supreme law of the several States, and of their citizens and inhabitants; and the Judges in the several States shall be bound thereby in their decisions, any thing in the constitutions or laws of the several States to the contrary notwithstanding."[28] In Article VI of the Constitution, Morris changed the language so that it held that the Constitution and the laws made under it "shall be the supreme law of the land; and the judges in every State shall be bound thereby, any thing in the Constitution or laws of any State to the contrary notwithstanding."[29] By declaring that the Constitution was not just "the supreme law of the several States" but "the supreme law of the land," Morris provided a much clearer basis for the idea that federal judges and Supreme Court justices would be responsible for evaluating whether laws passed by Congress were consistent with the Constitution. A decade and a half later, Chief Justice John Marshall duly drew on this clause for this purpose in his famous *Marbury v. Madison* ruling.[30]

Morris never spelled out exactly how he expected or hoped the power of judicial review would be utilized. If his arguments in favor of the council of revision are any indication, however, he seems to have thought that its primary use would be to prevent legislative encroachments on the other two branches and state encroachments on the national government. One might expect that

Morris would also support the idea of judges and justices using this power to protect individual rights, particularly given his longstanding attachment to civil liberty.[31] Indeed, he has been called a "one-man council of civil liberties" in light of his efforts to defend everyone from "Quakers, Catholics, slaves, American Indians, [and] former loyalists" to "the beleaguered king and queen of France" over the course of his career.[32] Morris did advocate the inclusion of several provisions in the Constitution protecting civil liberties, including prohibitions on bills of attainder, religious tests for public office, and the suspension of the writ of habeas corpus except when "in cases of rebellion or invasion, the public safety may require it."[33] He was, in fact, the one who proposed the language of the last of these provisions.

Morris did not, however, support the inclusion of a full bill of rights in the Constitution. He was by no means an outlier in this regard: observers have long marveled at how quickly and casually the delegates dismissed the idea of drawing up a bill of rights—an omission that would come back to haunt them during the ratification struggle. In fact, the state delegations voted *unanimously*—ten states to zero—against forming a committee for this purpose.[34] During the ratification debates, a number of Federalists, perhaps most prominently James Wilson and Alexander Hamilton, argued against the inclusion of a bill of rights in the Constitution, but they appear to have become reconciled to the first ten amendments fairly soon after their passage. More than two decades later, however, Morris still dismissed these amendments as "generally speaking, mere verbiage" whose main purpose had been to "dupe those who clamored against an instrument [i.e., the Constitution], which it had not pleased God should be such as they could understand."[35] (Clearly, old age had not graced him with a sense of generosity toward his opponents.)

Part of Morris's reasoning resembled that of Hamilton in *Federalist* #84. "It is unwise to annex such things [as a bill of rights] to a form of government," Morris suggested, for "if the rights are secured by the Constitution, to detail them is unnecessary; and if they are not, it is worse than useless; for the contradiction between two such instruments becomes a source of dangerous contention." That is, if the Constitution's checks and balances provided adequate protection for individual liberties, then spelling out those liberties was a superfluous exercise, and if they did not, then the tensions between the powers allotted to the government and the rights reserved to the people would be a source of perpetual conflict. Morris himself subscribed to the former alternative. "It would be a tedious work of supererogation to show," he told his correspondent, "that the original Constitution contained those guards, which form the apparent objects of the amendments."[36]

Morris also regarded bills of rights as mere "paper bulwarks" that were incapable of restraining a determined government—a point that he claimed had recently been demonstrated by the very Republicans who had "patronized and matronized" the Bill of Rights. After passing the ill-fated Embargo Act of 1807, President Jefferson and his followers utilized the military to try to prevent smuggling, and Morris argued that their "outrageous" tactics flew in the face of the Fourth Amendment's prohibition on unreasonable searches and seizures. "Considerate men ... never believed that the amendments gave any additional security to life, liberty, or property," he maintained, "but very few in America ... could imagine that the very authors of the [Fourth Amendment] would be the first to violate it, and that in a manner so flagrant and shameless."[37] Clearly, then, Morris had little faith in the ability of judges to protect individual liberties, even armed with a bill of rights and the power of judicial review.

Incidentally, Morris was even more dismissive of the French revolutionaries' Declaration of the Rights of Man and of the Citizen. In a pamphlet published in 1795, he suggested that although it was "a dangerous thing to lay down general Propositions, and therefore unwise to do so when no occasion calls for it," a bill of rights could nevertheless serve one useful purpose: "considering how prone Men are to abuse Power, it might be well, perhaps, that in every free Government, some clear statement were made, by public Authority, of the principal Privileges to which its Citizens are entitled. The World might thereby become acquainted with the Rights of Swiss Men, of Dutchmen, of American Men, and of Frenchmen, as well as of Englishmen." That way "Citizens of the World" like himself, "in their journey through life, might put up at the Inn where the entertainment was most agreeable to them." Yet such national bills of rights, Morris insisted, were a far cry from "those fantastic productions" that have "been pompously proclaimed as the *only* solid foundation for all Government: each purporting to be a Declaration of the natural, indefeasible, imprescriptible, &c. &c. &c. Rights of Man, to doubt of which is a political heresy." These ringing statements of abstract truth, he noted, "differ considerably from each other," so "it is evident, at the first blush, that they cannot all be true." Besides, Morris found it comical to see these visionary idealists, "like the ancient Church Councils, in violent dispute about what other People should be bound to believe."[38]

Another debate at the Convention concerned whether the federal judiciary should consist of a single Supreme Court or whether there should also be a full system of lower courts. The opponents of lower federal courts contended that they would constitute "an unnecessary encroachment on the jurisdiction of the States," as John Rutledge put it, and that "the State tribunals might and ought to be left in all cases to decide in the first instance, the right of appeal to the supreme national tribunal [i.e., Supreme Court] being sufficient to secure the national rights and uniformity of judgments." The more national-minded delegates countered that lower courts were necessary to ensure that the government's authority would be effectively enforced throughout the vast territory that it was charged with governing and that, in the words of Edmund Randolph, "the courts of the States cannot be trusted with the administration of the National Laws."[39]

As might be expected, given his staunch nationalism, Morris supported the creation of lower federal courts, although James Madison's notes do not give any sense of the specific arguments that he made on this score.[40] In the end, the framers essentially punted on this issue, as they did on so many others relating to the judiciary: they voted to leave the door open for Congress to create lower courts, but not to mandate their creation.[41] As we saw in chapter 2, however, Morris deliberately tweaked the judicial vesting clause in his draft of the Constitution so as to insinuate that Congress was required to establish lower federal courts, or at the very least that it could do so at its own discretion and not just when it found such courts to be "necessary," as the Committee of Detail's draft of the clause had suggested.[42]

This issue resurfaced during Morris's time in the Senate, in the debate over the Judiciary Act of 1801. This act reorganized the federal judiciary in a variety of ways.[43] For instance, it specified that the Supreme Court would hold two sessions per year but that the justices would no longer be required to "ride circuit," attending sessions at the outlying circuit courts. It provided that the number of Supreme Court justices would be reduced from six to five the next time there was a vacancy so that there would be an odd number of justices and tie votes would be avoided. And it created six new circuits and sixteen new federal judgeships so as to extend the reach of the federal court system. The act was passed in the waning days of the Adams administration by the lame-duck Federalist-controlled Congress, and the Republicans regarded it as a shameless partisan move, since had it stood it would have both wiped out incoming President Jefferson's first chance at a Supreme Court pick and allowed outgoing

President Adams to stack the rest of the federal judiciary with Federalists (the so-called "midnight judges"). While the act certainly had these partisan effects, the reforms were ones that many Federalists had long desired. The bill was first introduced in the Senate back in March 1798, so clearly it was not prompted by the Republicans' electoral victory in 1800—although that victory surely hastened its passage.

Morris "heartily and cordially" supported the act at the time of its enactment, remarking that it "answers the double purpose of bringing justice near to men's doors, and of giving additional fibres to the root of government." He acknowledged that the Federalists would likely "use this opportunity to provide for friends and adherents" and that "if they were my enemies I should condemn them for it." Still, given that the Federalists were "about to experience a heavy gale of adverse wind," he did not think that they could be inordinately blamed for "casting many anchors to hold their ship through the storm."[44]

Unsurprisingly, the Republicans felt differently. Jefferson complained that the Federalists had "retired into the Judiciary as a strong hold" and "multiplied useless judges merely to strengthen their phalanx."[45] In January 1802, the Republicans set about repealing the Judiciary Act, which spurred a protracted, rancorous debate in the Senate. After the Senate narrowly voted in favor of the repeal, sixteen to fifteen, the House of Representatives quickly passed it, and Jefferson just as quickly signed it. Morris was aghast for a number of reasons, one of them being that the repeal reduced the number of lower federal courts and federal judges and thereby made it more difficult for the national government to enforce its own laws.[46] As he contended on the Senate floor, the framers presumed that "the State Courts would not always make a cool and calm investigation, a fair and just decision" regarding national laws, and they empowered Congress to create a system of lower federal courts precisely "to try causes, by the wrongful decision of which the Union might be endangered, or domestic tranquillity be disturbed." If the reach of the federal courts was reduced, he worried, "the great security of our Union, that necessary guard of our tranquillity" would "be completely paralyzed, if not destroyed."[47]

Morris was even more disturbed, however, by another feature of the repeal of the Judiciary Act: it effectively revoked the promised lifetime appointments of federal judges—the only time in American history that Congress has done this.

The idea that federal judges and Supreme Court justices would hold their offices during good behavior—meaning, again, for life unless impeached—was included in the Virginia Plan and never seriously challenged during the Convention.[48] Such a tenure was necessary, the framers believed, in order to give judges the requisite independence from the other two branches as well as from the people themselves. After all, two of the judiciary's key functions, as they saw it, were to combat violations of the separation of powers, particularly by the legislature, and to protect the rights of individuals and minorities from the whims of the majority.

Neither Morris nor any of the other delegates were called upon to explain the benefits of life tenure in any detail since no one explicitly opposed it, but we do have one fleeting comment from Morris on this topic. In late August, John Dickinson proposed that federal judges and justices serve during good behavior "provided that they may be removed by the Executive on the application by the Senate and House of Representatives." If the president and both houses of Congress agreed, in other words, a judge could be dismissed without going through a formal impeachment process. (This was known as "removal by address," and derived from England's 1701 Act of Settlement.) Morris objected that it was "a contradiction in terms, to say, that the Judges should hold their offices during good behaviour, and yet be removeable without a trial. Besides, it was fundamentally wrong to subject judges to so arbitrary an authority." After a brief discussion, Dickinson's proposal was handily rejected, seven states to one.[49]

The importance that Morris attached to judicial independence was also on display in his later writings on France. In a speech that he drafted for King Louis XVI (but which the king never actually delivered), Morris wrote that "those who are charged with the important duties of administering justice, should, if possible, depend only on God. Their impartiality is of the last importance to every member of society, but principally to the most numerous class, who by that [impartiality] alone can be shielded from oppression."[50] Similarly, in a blueprint for a new French constitution that he drew up in 1791, Morris emphasized that "the interpreters of the law ought to enjoy an independence proportioned to the extent and importance of their functions," which meant that "judges ought to be as immovable as the law which they interpret."[51]

It comes as no surprise, then, that when the Republicans rescinded the positions of the judges who had been appointed under the Judiciary Act of 1801, Morris considered the move to be a dangerous precedent and a flagrant violation of the Constitution. The Republicans' justification was that they were eliminating the judgeships that these individuals occupied rather than removing the judges themselves from office, but Morris regarded this as the flimsiest of pretexts. To say that "you shall not take the man from the office, but you may take the office from the man" was, in his view, like saying that "you shall not throw him overboard, but you may sink his boat under him."[52] It had been Congress's prerogative whether or not to create the positions in the first place, he acknowledged, but he insisted that once they were created their duration was irrevocably fixed by the Constitution, and future Congresses were not free to eliminate them.

Even more damning, in Morris's eyes, was the effect that the repeal would have on the remaining federal judges. As he saw it, the judges still on the bench were being told, in effect, "that they hold their offices subject to your [i.e., Congress's] will, and during your pleasure." Such a message threatened to turn the judiciary into a partisan tool of the legislature and to destroy "the independent spirit essential to a due exercise of [judicial] authority." The ultimate effect of the repeal, Morris predicted, was that "the check established by the Constitution, desired by the people, and necessary in every contemplation of common sense, will be destroyed."[53]

The perorations of Morris's two great speeches on the repeal of the Judiciary Act revealed the tremendous importance that he attached to this issue. He concluded his first speech with a warning that "we are now about to violate our Constitution. Once touch it with unhallowed hands, sacrifice one of its important provisions, and we are gone. We commit the fate of America to the mercy of time and chance.... Surely, Sir, the contract with a judge is, of all others, the most solemn. It is sanctioned by the highest of all authority. Can you then violate it? If you can, you may throw this Constitution into the flames. It is gone—It is dead."[54] The finale of the speech that he delivered the following week reached, if anything, even greater rhetorical heights: "The judicial power, that fortress of the Constitution, is now to be overturned.... Cast not away this only anchor of our safety [i.e., the Constitution]. I have seen its progress. I know the difficulties through which it was obtained. I stand in the presence of Almighty God and of the world. I declare to you, that if you lose this charter, never, no never, will you get another. We are now perhaps arrived at the parting point. Here, even here, we stand on the brink of fate. Pause, then—Pause. For Heaven's sake—Pause."[55]

When the Republicans refused to pause and the repeal went through,

Morris's faith in America's constitutional order was severely weakened. This was, in fact, the first important step on the path to his late-life disillusionment. Before we turn to an exploration of that disillusionment, however, two of Morris's most noteworthy contributions to the Convention remain to be examined.

9. The Curse of Heaven: Slavery

Morris's finest hour at the Philadelphia Convention, from today's vantage point, came in the debates over slavery. No one spoke more passionately, more graphically, or at greater length about the evils of this institution than him. His extended speech of August 8, which is included in this book's appendix, has been described as "the most powerful antislavery speech of the entire convention"; "the Convention's most eloquent and stinging denunciation of slavery"; "perhaps the most eloquent speech heard that summer in the Convention"; "the closest thing to an abolitionist sermon to be heard at the convention"; "the first abolitionist speech in American political life"; "one of the most eloquent condemnations of slavery ever written"; and "a prime example of what we mean when we say someone was on the right side of history."[1] Although Morris's campaign against slavery at the Convention has largely vanished from the public consciousness, Abraham Lincoln remembered him as one of "the most noted anti-slavery men" among the framers.[2] Also in the nineteenth century, Henry Cabot Lodge remarked that "nothing shows the breadth of view, the far-reaching vision, and the generous spirit of the man better than his relentless and outspoken resistance to the malignant system which was destined to bring the country so near to utter ruin and dissolution."[3]

Admittedly, Morris did not have all that much success in combatting protections for slavery within the Constitution. This was an issue on which the delegates from the Deep South simply refused to budge. At times Morris was so exasperated by their intransigence that he seemed to be ready to give up on the union and the Constitution altogether. He exclaimed at one point that if the southerners were unwilling to make any concessions, then the North and South might as well "at once take a friendly leave of each other," and he concluded his August 8 speech by declaring that "he would sooner submit himself to a tax for paying for all the negroes in the United States, than saddle posterity with . . . a Constitution" that rewarded the southern states for holding people in bondage by according them extra representation.[4] Ultimately, however, he was forced to give in. In fact, we will see that Morris was the one who suggested linking the basis of representation to the basis of taxation and the overseas slave trade to navigation laws, thereby paving the way toward two of the key compromises that the delegates forged on this issue—compromises that, ironically, he ended up opposing.

Some scholars have actually criticized Morris for speaking out so forcefully against slavery in the first place, given the furious reaction that he provoked among defenders of the institution. One maintains that "Morris's speeches—rousing as they were—did not affect the final outcome and . . . threatened a break-up of the Convention in the process," while another says of one of his statements that "Morris's outburst may have been good for his psyche, but it only served to fan the fires among the more extreme proslavery delegates."[5] It is, however, difficult not to admire Morris's moral clarity, regardless of how off-putting the other delegates may have found it. The debates about this issue would have been much flatter, and in retrospect much more shameful, if Morris had not spoken out as he did. Historians frequently remind us that it is unfair to judge figures of the past on the basis of today's values, which is true, but Morris's ringing denunciations of slavery make it harder to accept the idea that the framers, as creatures of their times, simply did not know any better. Morris knew better, and he told them so. When it came to slavery, Morris served as the framers' conscience—even if that conscience was all too often ignored.

Morris was intimately familiar with slavery's evils, for he came from a slaveholding family. His father bequeathed forty-six enslaved people to his heirs when he died in 1762, including one—"a Negroe boy called George"—to ten-year-old Morris. George was granted his freedom at some point; it is unclear exactly when, but at all events by the time Morris reached adulthood.[6] Morris's mother still "owned" three people when she died in 1786, who were passed on to Morris's sisters. It should also be noted that Morris himself purchased two slaves after his return from Europe, one in 1799 and one in 1803. In each case, he immediately freed the individual in question and engaged him as an indentured servant for a number of years; he paid them regular wages, which are recorded in his account books.[7] Morris also periodically hired free Black men to work for him at Morrisania.

As we saw in chapter 1, Morris's antislavery efforts began early. At the New York state constitutional convention in 1777, when he was only twenty-five, he proposed a provision urging the state's future legislatures to abolish slavery whenever it could be done "consistent with the public safety." Given that "a regard to the rights of human nature and the principles of our holy religion, loudly call upon us to dispense the blessings of freedom to all mankind," he urged, they should do everything that they could at the new government's outset to ensure that "in future ages, every human being who breathes the air of this State, shall enjoy the privileges of a freeman."[8] It took remarkable foresight to introduce this proposal in the midst of the fight for independence, at a time when slavery was still legal and practiced in all thirteen states. Although the proposal received support from John Jay and a few others, Robert R. Livingston managed to orchestrate its defeat by a vote of thirty-one to five.[9]

Morris's home state was deeply entangled with slavery and the slave trade. In the 1790 census, New York counted 21,324 enslaved people—more than the rest of the northern states combined—and a sizable chunk of New York City's economy revolved around the shipment of human chattel and the goods that they produced. New York did not pass a gradual abolition law until 1799, which made it one of the last of the northern states to do so, and slavery persisted within its borders until 1827.[10] Morris's adopted state, by contrast, had one of the best records on this issue, thanks in part to its large population of antislavery Quakers. Philadelphia's Society for the Relief of Free Negroes Unlawfully Held in Bondage—better known as the Pennsylvania Abolition Society—was founded in 1775 and was the first organization in the world dedicated to the eradication of slavery. Pennsylvania was also the first state to move toward abolition when it adopted a gradual emancipation scheme in 1780.[11]

Pennsylvania was soon joined by the New England states, all of which either passed a gradual emancipation law or banned slavery outright in the years leading up to the Philadelphia Convention. By the time of the 1790 census, there were some 694,280 enslaved people in the United States, 645,023 of whom were held in the five states from Maryland southward. However, the debates over this issue at the Convention did not always split neatly along North-South lines. The Connecticut delegates often seemed positively eager to introduce protections for slavery, for instance, and even the Pennsylvania delegation was frequently divided between Morris's firm antislavery stance and James Wilson's more accommodationist impulses.[12] Conversely, some of the strongest denunciations of slavery, next to Morris's, came from Luther Martin of Maryland, who insisted that the slave trade was "inconsistent with the principles of the Revolution, and dishonorable to the American character," and George Mason of Virginia, who portrayed slavery as a national sin that would "bring the judgment of Heaven on [the] country"—slaveholders both.[13]

No one at the Convention defended slavery as a positive moral good, as John C. Calhoun and his ilk would do beginning in the late 1830s. The closest thing to a proslavery speech that was recorded that summer came from Charles Pinckney of South Carolina, who declared that "if slavery be wrong, it is justified by the example of all the world. . . . In all ages one half of mankind have been slaves." For the most part, however, the southern delegates appealed less to moral principles than to the political and economic interests of their states, and to the fact that the people of these states would never ratify a charter that interfered with their peculiar institution. As John Rutledge put it, "Religion and humanity had nothing to do with this question. Interest alone is the governing principle with nations. The true question at present is, whether the Southern States shall or shall not be parties to the Union." Yet another South Carolinian, Charles Cotesworth Pinckney, put the bottom line as bluntly as possible: "South Carolina and Georgia cannot do without slaves."[14]

Whereas the delegates from the Deep South were sent to the Convention with explicit instructions from their state legislatures to fight for safeguards for slavery within the new Constitution, none of the northern delegates were charged with resisting such safeguards.[15] Even the individuals who abhorred the institution tended to regard it as at best a secondary (or tertiary) consideration, one whose importance paled in comparison to the central issue of the powers and structure of the government itself. Particularly given the widespread—and not entirely unreasonable—fears that pushing too hard on this issue would destroy the fledgling republic in its infancy, combatting slavery was simply never a top or immediate priority for almost any of them.

Scholars, students, and citizens will debate until the end of time whether the compromises that the delegates reached were an unfortunate but unavoidable concession to reality or a "covenant with death, and an agreement with Hell," as William Lloyd Garrison later put it.[16] Morris tended toward the latter view, even as he helped to forge the compromises.

The single biggest controversy connected to slavery at the Convention centered on whether and how enslaved people would be counted toward the apportionment of the House of Representatives. In 1787 there was no precedent for allotting extra representation to states for the people that they held in bondage. While some of the state legislatures used property more generally in their apportionment, none of them singled out human chattel for special treatment.

Nor, of course, did the Confederation Congress. The southern states worried, however, that they would be severely outnumbered in the new Congress if enslaved people—who made up around forty percent of their population—were not counted.

As most of the delegates saw it, the country was split between either eight northern states and five southern ones or seven northern states and six southern ones, depending on how Delaware was categorized. Either way, with two senators for each state, the new Senate would have a northern majority. The populations of the northern and southern states were nearly identical if enslaved people were counted, but if they were excluded, then the northern states would have a decided advantage in a population-based House of Representatives as well. On the other hand, most people at the time believed—wrongly, as it turned out—that the population of the South would grow much more rapidly than that of the North. As Morris noted, it was a common belief that "North Carolina, South Carolina, and Georgia only, will in a little time have a majority of the people of America."[17] The two sides were thus set up for a struggle over this issue.

Tensions over the inclusion of enslaved people in the apportionment of the House emerged as early as May 30, the day after the Virginia Plan was introduced, but the issue was tabled after a short and inconclusive discussion. On June 11, when Morris was away, James Wilson suggested that three-fifths of the enslaved population should be counted for purposes of representation. This ratio came from an amendment that had been proposed to the Articles of Confederation in 1783 in the context of tax assessment. The amendment had never achieved the unanimous support among the state legislatures that was needed to send it into effect, and it did not, in any case, pertain to representation, since the states were equally represented in the Confederation Congress. Wilson's application of the three-fifths ratio to representation in the House was therefore something of a novelty, but it was quickly approved for the time being, nine states to two.[18] The majority of the delegates seemed to view the three-fifths clause as a reasonable compromise, but Morris most decidedly did not.

Upon his return from Morrisania, Morris began by approaching the issue somewhat gingerly rather than immediately launching into a bold moral case against slavery, presumably because he hoped to avoid antagonizing the delegates from the slaveholding states. As we saw in chapter 5, Morris advocated that Congress itself be given the ability to periodically augment the number of

House seats, taking into account each state's population and property. His assumption seems to have been that enslaved people would be counted as property but not included in the states' population counts, which would give a clear edge to the North. On July 11, the idea of the three-fifths ratio was brought up once again, although Pierce Butler and Charles Cotesworth Pinckney went even further, insisting that the enslaved should be counted *equally* with the free population. Evidently biting his tongue, Morris said only that "the people of Pennsylvania would revolt at the idea of being put on a footing with slaves. They would reject any plan that was to have such an effect."[19] At this point he was merely reporting the attitude of the people whom he was representing rather than offering his own views, and he was suggesting—to put the point bluntly—that the voters were racist enough that they would balk at the idea of enslaved people being counted equally with them. This, surely, was speaking in a language that the southern delegates could understand.

During the ensuing debate, most of the northern delegates who addressed the issue—including Roger Sherman, Nathaniel Gorham, and James Wilson, though not Rufus King—seemed inclined to accept the three-fifths ratio. Toward the end of the session, Morris spoke up somewhat more forcefully, declaring that he felt "reduced to the dilemma of doing injustice to the Southern States, or to human nature; and he must therefore do it to the former. For he could never agree to give such encouragement to the slave trade, as would be given by allowing them a representation for their negroes; and he did not believe those States would ever confederate on terms that would deprive them of that trade."[20] Measured by the standards of Morris's August 8 speech, this was still quite restrained. Although he spoke of an "injustice to ... human nature," he was referring to the slave trade rather than to slavery itself, and even most southerners acknowledged the iniquity of the Middle Passage. Moreover, he expressed regret at the idea of doing "injustice to the Southern States" by denying them "representation for their negroes."

It quickly became apparent, however, that Morris's restraint would not mollify the hardline southerners. The next morning, Charles Cotesworth Pinckney remarked that he was "alarmed by what was said [by Morris] yesterday, concerning the negroes." The normally quiet William R. Davie—the future founder of the University of North Carolina—exploded, declaring that "it was high time now to speak out." It appeared, Davie said, that "it was meant by some gentlemen to deprive the Southern States of any share of representation for their blacks," and if that was their intent then "the business [i.e., the

Convention] was at an end."[21] Pinckney and Davie were being unduly sensitive here, for by all appearances there were very few northerners who actually wanted to exclude enslaved people from the House apportionment altogether. They were right, however, to assume that Morris was one of them. He shot back at Davie: "It had been said that it is high time to speak out. As one member, he would candidly do so." He had come to the Convention, he said, "to form a compact for the good of America," and he "hoped and believed that all [the states] would enter into such a compact," but "if they would not, he was ready to join with any States that would." It was true, he admitted, that "it is in vain for the Eastern States to insist on what the Southern States will never agree to," but he insisted that it was "equally vain for the [South] to require what the other States can never admit; and he verily believed the people of Pennsylvania will never agree to a representation of negroes."[22] At this point, then, Morris seemed to be ready to give up on the union altogether over this issue—or at the very least to try to call the hardliners' bluff.

Over the next few days Morris pursued a twofold strategy. On the one hand, he sought to stiffen the backs of his fellow antislavery northerners by suggesting that the southerners were seeking to gain "a majority in the public councils" and by painting in vivid colors what would happen if they did. First, he noted that "a transfer of power from the maritime to the interior and landed interest" in the House would result in "such an oppression to commerce, that he shall be obliged to vote for the vicious principle of equality in the second branch [i.e., the Senate], in order to provide some defence for the Northern States against it." In addition, he predicted that "if the Southern States get the power into their hands, and be joined, as they will be, with the interior country [i.e., the West], they will inevitably bring on a war with Spain for the Mississippi"—that is, navigation rights on the Mississippi River. Still further, Morris pointed out that the more populous North would have to supply the bulk of the troops for such a war, as well as for putting down slave insurrections in the South: they would be forced to "march their militia for the defence of the Southern States . . . against those very slaves of whom they complain," whereas the southerners would not "be restrained from importing fresh supplies of wretched Africans, at once to increase the danger of attack, and the difficulty of defence; nay, they are to be encouraged to it, by an assurance of having their votes in the National Government increased in proportion." In short, Morris warned that "every thing was to be apprehended from [the South] getting the power into their hands."[23]

The second prong of Morris's strategy was directed at the southern delegates. In the contest over the three-fifths ratio back in 1783, under the Articles of Confederation, the southern states had argued that the ratio was too high, since they had wanted to reduce their tax burden. Now Morris proposed a proviso that under the Constitution "taxation shall be in proportion to representation."[24] His hope, clearly, was that linking the basis of taxation to the basis of representation would diminish the southerners' ardor for counting enslaved people toward the House apportionment, since it would increase their taxes at the same time. That hope quickly proved to be unfounded. Without a moment's hesitation, Pierce Butler supported Morris's proposal and went right back to arguing that enslaved people should be counted fully toward both representation and taxation.[25] Plainly the southern delegates placed far greater value on increasing the South's political power in the new Congress than on decreasing its tax bill. This was particularly true because Morris's proposal was restricted to direct taxes—as opposed to excise taxes and taxes on imports and exports—and the delegates were well aware that direct taxes would make up only a small fraction of the taxes that Congress would impose.[26]

Although Morris's proposal laid the groundwork for the compromise that the delegates ultimately reached on this issue, he himself soon came to regret it. On July 24, just twelve days after proposing the link between representation and taxation, he expressed a hope that the Committee of Detail would eliminate this link when it formulated its draft constitution, remarking that "he had only meant it as a bridge to assist us over a certain gulf; having passed the gulf, the bridge may be removed."[27] Clearly, Morris was still hoping that there was some chance of avoiding extra representation for the slave states. As it turned out, however, the committee kept the link between representation and direct taxation that he had suggested, and applied the three-fifths ratio to both.[28] At this point Morris was no longer willing to hold back.

On August 8, the delegates reached the part of the Committee of Detail's report that addressed the apportionment of the House of Representatives. Seemingly out of nowhere, Morris launched into a tirade the likes of which the Convention had not yet seen, nor would see again. He moved that representation should be based entirely on each state's number of free inhabitants, with no representation at all for enslaved people, declaring that "much . . . would depend on this point. He never would concur in upholding domestic slavery."

Looking around at his fellow delegates, twenty-five of whom were themselves slaveholders, he proclaimed that slavery "was a nefarious institution" and "the curse of Heaven on the States where it prevailed." He then took his colleagues on a virtual tour of the nation to prove the point:

> Compare the free regions of the Middle States, where a rich and noble cultivation marks the prosperity and happiness of the people, with the misery and poverty which overspread the barren wastes of Virginia, Maryland, and the other States having slaves. Travel through the whole continent, and you behold the prospect continually varying with the appearance and disappearance of slavery. The moment you leave the Eastern States, and enter New York, the effects of the institution become visible. Passing through the Jerseys and entering Pennsylvania, every criterion of superior improvement witnesses the change. Proceed southwardly, and every step you take, through the great regions of slaves, presents a desert increasing with the increasing population of these wretched beings.[29]

Morris insisted that there was no good reason why enslaved people should count toward the House apportionment at all, according to any ratio: "Are they men? Then make them citizens, and let them vote. Are they property? Why, then, is no other property included?" These questions were unanswerable, which is why the southern delegates scarcely even attempted to do so.

Morris then got to the true crux of the matter:

> The admission of slaves into the representation, when fairly explained, comes to this,—that the inhabitant of Georgia and South Carolina who goes to the coast of Africa, and, in defiance of the most sacred laws of humanity, tears away his fellow creatures from their dearest connexions, and damns them to the most cruel bondage, shall have more votes in a government instituted for protection of the rights of mankind, than the citizen of Pennsylvania or New Jersey, who views with a laudable horror so nefarious a practice.

Giving the South extra representation on behalf of the people whom they had enslaved, he declared, would require "a sacrifice of every principle of right, of every impulse of humanity."[30] This was Morris at his courageous and farsighted best. No speech that summer was more graphic in describing slavery's evils, or more pointed about its utter incompatibility with the nation's ideals.[31]

Alas, it was all but ignored. Jonathan Dayton, the Convention's youngest delegate, seconded Morris's motion simply so that "his sentiments on the subject might appear, whatever might be the fate of the amendment." As Dayton evidently anticipated, the motion quickly went down to a decisive defeat. Roger Sherman, ever eager to compromise, declared that the inclusion of enslaved people in the apportionment did not seem to him to be "liable to such insuperable objections," and even Morris's colleague James Wilson deemed the motion "premature." Charles Pinckney, realizing that the motion had no chance of passing, merely remarked that he would respond to Morris's charges more fully "if the occasion were a proper one." The motion then lost by a vote of ten states to one, with Dayton's New Jersey alone supporting it.[32] The three-fifths clause would not be seriously challenged again at the Convention.

This clause gave the southern states thirteen extra representatives in the first Congress, thereby achieving its intended aim of bringing them close to parity with the North. It also, of course, gave the South an extra thirteen votes in the electoral college, since each state was allotted a number of electors equal to its number of members of Congress (in both the House and Senate). For the southern states, this was a gift that kept on giving. For the next seven decades, they would be rewarded with more political power for every human being whom they kept in bondage. As the number of enslaved people ballooned to around four million over this period, so did the South's extra clout. It is therefore appropriate that a recent book on the "slave power thesis"—that is, the idea that slaveholding southerners effectively controlled the reins of the federal government in antebellum America—contains a chapter titled "Morris's Prophecy."[33]

―――――

Another major source of controversy concerned the overseas slave trade, which the framers discussed in the latter half of August. Although several of the Virginia delegates spoke against the continued importation of enslaved people, the delegates from the Deep South insisted on it. As Charles Pinckney put it, "South Carolina can never receive the plan [i.e., the Constitution] if it prohibits the slave-trade. In every proposed extension of the powers of Congress, that State has expressly and watchfully excepted that of meddling with the importation of negroes."[34] The Committee of Detail's draft constitution accordingly stipulated that the overseas slave trade could not be prohibited, or even taxed, by Congress. Nor was this the only notably pro-southern feature of this draft constitution. It also prohibited export taxes, a provision that southern states favored since their economies revolved around the exportation of staple crops like tobacco, rice, and indigo. (Cotton only became a major export item after the development of the cotton gin in 1793.) By contrast, the northern states, whose economies relied more on manufacturing and shipping, favored navigation acts to protect American shipping interests, and the Committee of Detail's draft constitution required a two-thirds majority in both houses of Congress in order to pass such acts.[35]

During the initial debate over these topics, Morris spoke out forcefully against the prohibition on export taxes, which he predicted would force the North to provide far more than its fair share of government revenue, but he said nothing about the slave trade.[36] Presumably he deemed it prudent, after having attacked slavery so boldly in his August 8 speech, to let the Virginians fight this battle, which they did with laudable vigor. (Of course, as the South Carolina delegates were quick to point out, Virginia would benefit economically from a ban on the overseas slave trade, since it already had more than enough enslaved people to supply its needs, and the value of its human chattel would increase if further importations were prohibited.)[37]

Just as in the debate over how enslaved people would be counted toward the House apportionment, Morris pointed toward the grounds on which a compromise was eventually built. On August 22, he proposed that a committee should be formed to address the slave trade, export taxes, and navigation acts, suggesting that "these things may form a bargain among the Northern and Southern States."[38] The committee was duly formed, and two days later it proposed what has been called the Convention's "dirty compromise": the overseas slave trade would be protected from a congressional ban until at least 1800, the prohibition on export taxes would remain in place, and in exchange the southern delegates would drop the requirement for a congressional supermajority to pass navigation acts.[39]

Here, too, however, Morris ultimately opposed the compromise that the committee forged. When these clauses came up for discussion, Charles Cotesworth Pinckney proposed that the constitutional protection for the overseas slave trade be extended another eight years, to 1808. Although James Madison protested that such a provision would be "dishonorable to the American character," it passed by a vote of seven states to four, with Pennsylvania in the minority.[40] Once again Morris was unable to contain himself. The clause as it then stood was worded in an extremely convoluted manner so as to avoid explicitly naming what it was really about: "The migration or importation of such persons as the several States, now existing, shall think proper to admit, shall not be prohibited by the Legislature prior to the year 1800 [now 1808]." Morris proposed that they stop beating around the bush and change the provision "at once" so that it would instead read: "The importation of slaves into North Carolina, South Carolina, and Georgia, shall not be prohibited, &c." Not only would this wording avoid "ambiguity," he suggested, it would also be "most fair" because it would make clear that "this part of the Constitution was a compliance with those States." He cheekily added that if the change "should be objected to, by the members from those states, he should not urge it."[41]

Obviously, the aim of Morris's deliberately impolitic suggestion was to shame the advocates of the slave trade. George Mason, who had opposed that trade as fiercely as anyone, ingenuously objected that "naming North Carolina, South Carolina, and Georgia" within the clause might "give offence to the people of those States"—but of course that was the whole point.[42] After a few other delegates protested, Morris withdrew his motion. He had underscored the fact that the overseas slave trade was so heinous that even its proponents were reluctant to admit what they were advocating, but he was ultimately powerless to prevent the inclusion of the clause within the Constitution. To his horror, the Deep South would have another two decades to continue kidnapping Africans with the full protection of the national government—a window, we now know, in which more enslaved people were imported into the United States than in any prior twenty-year period.[43]

A final major provision relating to slavery was tacked onto the Constitution almost at the last minute, with next to no debate. On August 29, Pierce Butler proposed the addition of a clause guaranteeing that people seeking to escape slavery by fleeing to a free state must be returned to their legal owners. There had been no fugitive slave clause included in the Articles of Confederation, although the Northwest Ordinance that had just recently been passed by the Confederation Congress did contain one. Butler's motion passed without opposition; apparently the antislavery delegates were too tired to commence yet another contest over slavery at this late date, or perhaps—even more disgracefully—they welcomed the idea of a fugitive slave clause because it would prevent an influx of runaways from inundating the North.[44]

There is no record of Morris saying anything about this provision when it came to the Convention floor, but he did alter it in two small but important ways during the drafting process. First, Butler's version of the clause had described enslaved people as being "bound to service or labor," but Morris tweaked it so that it referred to them as "legally held to service or labor." The addition of the term "legally" was likely meant to avoid giving any kind of sanction to the then-common (though illegal) practice of capturing free Black people and enslaving them on the pretense that they were in fact runaways. Second, Butler's version of the clause had stipulated that escaped slaves "shall be delivered up to the person justly claiming their service or labor." Morris changed this concluding phrase to read that escapees "shall be delivered up, on claim of the party to whom such service or labor may be due." With this shift in wording, he was able to dispose of the word "justly," thereby eliminating any implication that holding a person in bondage could be just.[45] As the historian Sean Wilentz notes, by taking this small but deliberate step, Morris and the Committee of Style ensured that "the fugitive slave clause did not acknowledge [the validity of] property in man, let alone slaveholders' rights to such property."[46]

The final version of the clause stipulated that "no person held to service or labor in one State, under the laws thereof, escaping into another, shall, in consequence of any law or regulation therein, be discharged from such service or labor; but shall be delivered up, on claim of the party to whom such service or labor may be due."[47] Like the other major constitutional provisions relating to slavery, this one pointedly avoided the use of the words "slave" and "slavery." Luther Martin later explained that the framers "anxiously sought to avoid the admission of expressions which might be odious in the ears of Americans, although they were willing to admit into their system those *things* which the *expressions* signified."[48] As one scholar has noted, however, in the fugitive slave clause "harsh reality bled through the words 'held' and 'escaping': This was a clause about humans in bondage seeking liberation."[49]

As valiantly as Morris fought against slavery at the Convention, in the end he failed to make any real headway against it. Nor, alas, did he continue to fight it in the succeeding years in any meaningful way. Throughout the remainder of Morris's life, slavery only appeared as an occasional blip on his radar screen. Soon after he entered the Senate in May 1800, for instance, he voted with the Federalist majority against a bill that would have permitted the importation of enslaved people into the Mississippi Territory (an area that also included present-day Alabama), though we have no record of him speaking on the subject.[50] Toward the end of his time in the Senate, in contrast, Morris advanced a rather reprehensible argument in the context of advocating the use of force against France to keep the Mississippi River open to American shipping. In an attempt to goad southerners into supporting the seizure of New Orleans, he suggested that control of that crucial port would allow the United States to help put down slave insurrections in the Caribbean. And that, he told his fellow senators from the South, "will give to your slaves the conviction, that it is impossible for them to become free. Men in their unhappy condition must be impelled by fear and discouraged by despair."[51] If any proof were necessary that there were no unsullied moral heroes when it came to slavery in the early republic, this glib suggestion of Morris's would provide it.[52]

Still later, during the War of 1812, Morris wielded slavery as a moral cudgel against southern Republicans. "If peace be not immediately made with England," he predicted at the outset of the war, "the question on negro votes"—that is, the disproportionate power accorded to the South by the three-fifths clause—"must divide this Union." The North could then leave it to the slaveholding states, he declared, to "exercise the privilege of strangling commerce, whipping Negroes, and bawling about the inborn inalienable rights of man."[53] The remark about "strangling commerce" was a reference to the Republicans' trade policies, starting with the Non-Importation Act of 1806 and the disastrous Embargo Act of 1807, that did severe damage to northern commercial interests. As Morris saw it, these policies were one more piece of evidence of just how irreconcilable the divide between North and South had become. "I cannot blame Southern gentlemen for striving to put down commerce," he told another correspondent, "because commerce, if it survives, will, I think, put them down." In his view, "commerce and domestic slavery are mortal foes; and, bound together, one must destroy the other."[54]

By this point Morris regarded the nation in rather Manichean terms, divided between the forces of light (a commercial order in the North based on free labor) and darkness (an agricultural order in the South based on slavery)—and it was the latter that was prevailing, as he saw it, thanks to the protections for slavery that were written into the Constitution. His darkest fears from the Philadelphia Convention were being realized. It is no wonder, then, that Morris gave up hope for the union.

10. A Declaration of Motives: The Preamble

Surely Morris's most famous contribution to the creation of the Constitution was his authorship of the charter's preamble. Even if few Americans realize that the preamble was written by him, its majestic language is familiar to almost everyone: "We, the people of the United States, in order to form a more perfect union, establish justice, insure domestic tranquility, provide for the common defence, promote the general welfare, and secure the blessings of liberty to ourselves and our posterity, do ordain and establish this Constitution for the United States of America."[1] This grand opening is the most memorable and inspiring part of the Constitution, and it is also the part that, by all appearances, Morris composed most nearly from scratch. There is something of an irony, of course, in the fact that one of the most celebrated sentences in the annals of democracy was written by a man of rather elitist inclinations who is all but forgotten today.

Although American schoolchildren still occasionally memorize the preamble as part of a civics lesson, within the legal community it is often regarded as a mere rhetorical flourish without any substantive import. The Supreme Court rarely cites the preamble in its rulings and, as one legal scholar notes, "Modern law students . . . skate past this text with Olympic speed."[2] This is regrettable, as another expert remarks, "for it is *the single most important part* of the Constitution. The reason is simple: It announces the *point* of the entire enterprise."[3] Morris himself later described the preamble in similar terms, calling it "a declaration of the motives, which induced the American people to bind themselves by this compact."[4] On this reading, the preamble describes the broad ends that the Constitution was meant to achieve, and the rest of the charter—the seven articles laying out the institutional structure of the three branches and the rest—is simply a means to those ends. Moreover, for all its brevity, the preamble not only summarizes the Constitution's purposes but also indicates the ultimate source of its authority—it is ordained and established by "the people of the United States," as opposed to the states themselves—and specifies who it was designed to govern, namely "ourselves and our posterity." The preamble has thus been aptly characterized as "the Founders' foundation."[5]

The closest analogue to the preamble among the early state constitutions came in the Massachusetts constitution that was drafted by John Adams in 1779 and ratified by the people of that state in 1780. After a few sentences about the end of government being the securing of people's natural rights, this document declared:

> We, therefore, the people of Massachusetts, acknowledging, with grateful hearts, the goodness of the great Legislator of the universe, in affording us, in the course of His providence, an opportunity, deliberately and peaceably, without fraud, violence or surprise, of entering into an original, explicit, and solemn compact with each other; and of forming a new constitution of civil government, for ourselves and posterity; and devoutly imploring His direction in so interesting a design, do agree upon, ordain and establish the following Declaration of Rights, and Frame of Government, as the Constitution of the Commonwealth of Massachusetts.[6]

Several of the phrases in this rather unwieldy sentence were precursors to Morris's more economical preamble, including "we . . . the people," "ourselves and our posterity," and "ordain and establish." The most notable difference, of course, is that the Massachusetts preamble is littered with references to "the great Legislator of the universe," "His providence," and "His direction." In fact, the great majority of the early state constitutions invoked God in their opening or closing passages or both, as did the Articles of Confederation ("the Great Governor of the World"). It is therefore notable that Morris's preamble contains no appeals or even allusions to the divine—a conspicuous absence if ever there was one. The purposes of the Constitution, as Morris laid them out, were entirely secular in nature.

The first crack at a preamble at the Philadelphia Convention came in the Committee of Detail's draft constitution. Until that committee was convened in late July, there had been no discussion among the delegates about the need for a preamble or what one might contain. We have a set of notes from Edmund Randolph, who was one of the five members of the committee, that represent the first comments on this issue. Randolph maintained that the preamble should *not* be dedicated to "designating the ends of government and human polities." Such a "display of theory," he thought, "howsoever proper in the first formation of state governments, is unfit here; since we are not working on the natural rights of men not yet gathered into society, but upon those rights, modified by society, and interwoven with what we call the rights of states."[7] Morris's preamble, of course, *did* announce the ends that the new government was expected to serve, although it did not consist of the kind of abstract declaration of rights that Randolph cautioned against.

Randolph's notes go on to suggest that the preamble should "declare, that the present foederal government [i.e., the Confederation Congress] is insufficient to the general happiness, that the conviction of this fact gave birth to this convention; and that the only effectual means which they could devise, for curing this insufficiency, is the establishment of a supreme legislative executive and judiciary."[8] (The language about "a supreme legislative executive and judiciary" was drawn straight from a proposal that Randolph and Morris had made together at the outset of the Convention.)[9] Although Morris's preamble gestures toward the insufficiency of the Articles of Confederation by declaring the framers' ambition "to form a more perfect union" and the rest, it does not make the kind of explicit statement to that effect that Randolph seems to have had in mind. In many respects, the "cover letter" that Morris and the Committee of Style drafted for submission to the Confederation Congress was a closer approximation to the preamble that Randolph envisioned than Morris's preamble itself was.[10]

The preamble that was actually included in the Committee of Detail's draft constitution was written not by Randolph but rather by James Wilson, and it does not bear much resemblance to what Randolph had apparently advocated within the committee. Wilson's preamble says nothing at all about the problems of the Articles of Confederation or the purposes of the Constitution, but instead just lists the states and declares that the people of those states were authorizing the Constitution: "We the people of the States of New Hampshire, Massachusetts, Rhode Island and Providence Plantations, Connecticut, New York, New Jersey, Pennsylvania, Delaware, Maryland, Virginia, North Carolina, South Carolina, and Georgia, do ordain, declare, and establish, the following Constitution for the government of ourselves and our posterity."[11] One would be hard pressed to write a more spare opening than this. The delegates seem to have approved of it, however, for on August 7 they agreed to it unanimously, without any discussion.[12]

After that there was no more mention of the preamble until Morris wrote a new draft of the Constitution on behalf of the Committee of Style between September 8 and 12. We have no drafts of Morris's preamble or recorded comments about his drafting process. All we know is that sometime during this period he transformed Wilson's colorless opening into the stirring recital of the Constitution's fundamental aims that is so familiar today—"fifty-two words of political poetry," as one scholar puts it.[13] Actually, Morris's version of the preamble contained fifty-three words. He had written, "We, the people of the United States, in order to form a more perfect union, to establish justice, insure domestic tranquility," and the rest; the one change that the delegates made was to eliminate the second "to" (before "establish justice"), presumably because they deemed it redundant.[14] Aside from that tiny verbal alteration, there is no record of any discussion of the preamble on the Convention floor. It was approved along with the rest of the Constitution on September 15, and from there it was sent on to the state ratifying conventions, and ultimately to the "posterity" that the preamble invoked.

One major change that Morris made to the Committee of Detail's preamble was to replace the roll call of the states—"We the people of the States of New Hampshire, Massachusetts, Rhode Island and Providence Plantations," and so on down the eastern seaboard—with "We, the people of the United States." Morris's version is, of course, much tighter stylistically, which was all the more important because he followed it with a list of the Constitution's substantive aims that was absent from the Committee of Detail's version. Morris's version also smoothly addressed the possibility that one or more of the thirteen states might not ratify the Constitution. Rhode Island had refused to send a delegation to the Convention, after all, and the framers were well aware that ratification would be an uphill battle in a number of states, including Morris's New York. If they did not ratify, would their names have to be removed from the list? (As it happened, neither North Carolina nor Rhode Island ended up ratifying until after the new government had been up and running for a number of months.) Morris's version likewise eliminated any complications that would arise from future states joining the union; there would be no need to amend the preamble when Vermont, Kentucky, or any other territory was ready for statehood.

Morris's invocation of "the people of the United States" also had larger philosophical implications, however. The Committee of Detail's preamble had stated that the Constitution would be ordained and established by "the people of the States of New Hampshire" and the rest, which left some ambiguity as to whether the people or the states would be primary. Morris's version makes crystal clear that the ultimate sovereign in the new government would be the people of the nation as a whole. Joseph Ellis goes so far as to say that this seemingly small change "was probably the most consequential editorial act in American history."[15] Whereas the Articles of Confederation had rested on the authority of "the Delegates of the United States of America in Congress assembled" and operated on the populace through the intermediary of the state governments, the Constitution would be authorized by and act directly on the American people. As one scholar notes, the fact that the people themselves—not the states or state governments, and not the people's elected representatives—were the ones to "ordain and establish" the Constitution was extraordinary: "In the late 1780s, this was the most democratic deed the world had ever seen."[16]

Although the nationalist implications of the preamble's opening words have sometimes been downplayed, particularly by individuals who favor a greater role for the states within America's constitutional order, they are difficult to miss. These were, after all, the first and most prominent words of the entire document; they were often put in large font and capital letters in early printings of the Constitution.[17] The implications were clear, at any rate, to Patrick Henry, who protested at the Virginia ratifying convention in Richmond: "Who authorised them to speak the language of, *We, the people*, instead of, *We, the states*? States are the characteristics, and the soul of a confederation. If the States be not the agents of this compact, it must be one great consolidated National Government of the people of all the States."[18] Up in Massachusetts, Samuel Adams had the same reaction: "I confess, as I enter the Building I stumble at the Threshold. I meet with a National Government, instead of a Federal Union of Sovereign States."[19] Of course, a consolidated national government is exactly what Morris wanted.

Morris began his list of the Constitution's substantive aims with the overarching one of forming "a more perfect union." Several of the aims on his list had been included in the Articles of Confederation and the Virginia Plan, as we will see, but this one was not. There was a reference to the union in the New Jersey Plan, the declared goal of which was to "render the Federal Constitution adequate to the exigencies of government, and the preservation of the Union," but of course this plan had sought to do little more than add a few tweaks to the Articles of Confederation—to preserve the union more or less as it stood in 1787, rather than rendering it "more perfect" with an entirely new constitution.[20] Morris's formulation may have borrowed, consciously or not, from the Act of Union of 1707 that combined the English and Scottish Parliaments, which promised to render "the union of the two kingdoms more intire and compleat," or Queen Anne's 1706 letter to the Scottish Parliament, which referred to "an entire and perfect union" between the two.[21]

The idea that the Constitution sought to form "a more perfect union" suggests, of course, that in the framers' minds the union already existed. They were not creating a new nation from scratch, but rather making the existing union "more perfect" than it had been under the Articles of Confederation. This was a point that Abraham Lincoln stressed in his First Inaugural Address in the process of contesting the legitimacy of southern secession. In Lincoln's view, the idea that "the Union is perpetual" was supported by the fact that it was "much older than the Constitution"—indeed, at least as old as the Articles of Association that were adopted by the First Continental Congress in 1774. Hence, he noted, "one of the declared objects for ordaining and establishing the Constitution was '*to form a more perfect Union.*'"[22]

While Morris and the framers believed that the union already existed, they also believed that it required perfecting. The word "perfect" has at least two meanings here: it suggests both that under the Constitution the states would be tied together more closely than they had been under the Articles and that the form of government itself would be superior. Of course, the framers had no illusions that the new government that they were forming would be *perfect*, if such a thing could even be imagined, only *more* perfect than it had been up to that point. Progress is possible, but never complete. Presumably the constitutional order would require continual perfecting, using either of the amendment processes laid out in Article V, if the framers' "posterity" were to enjoy all of the "blessings" that the Constitution sought to secure.

Morris then went on to list five slightly more specific ways in which the union would be made more perfect: the Constitution would "establish justice, insure domestic tranquility, provide for the common defence, promote the general welfare, and secure the blessings of liberty to ourselves and our posterity." The recurring verbs—establish, insure, provide, promote, secure—inject energy into what could have been a dry list; Catherine Drinker Bowen writes in her classic work on the Convention that "one might challenge the centuries to better these verbs."[23] As for the nouns, it is noteworthy that the preamble lists a variety of ends that the new government was meant to achieve—justice, domestic tranquility, the common defense, the general welfare, and liberty—without ranking them or singling out any of them as preeminent. As value pluralists like Isaiah Berlin would later suggest, there are a variety of goods or values that governments generally aim to achieve, and they cannot all be reduced to one "supervalue" that should be prized and pursued above all others.[24]

The proximate source for the last three aims on Morris's list—the common defense, the general welfare, and liberty—is fairly clear. The Articles of Confederation had declared that the states were entering into "a firm league of friendship with each other, for their common defence, the security of their Liberties, and their mutual and general welfare." Although the Articles were concerned primarily with the defense, liberty, and general welfare of the *states* rather than the people themselves, this language was carried into the first plank of the Virginia Plan, which maintained that the Articles "ought to be so corrected and enlarged as to accomplish the objects proposed by their institution; namely 'common defence, security of liberty, and general welfare.'"[25] Two of these aims were also included in a constitutional provision that had been proposed by the Committee on Postponed Parts (of which Morris was a member) and unanimously approved by the delegates just days before Morris took up his pen, namely the clause granting Congress the power to "lay and collect taxes, duties, imposts, and excises, to pay the debts and provide for the common defence and general welfare of the United States."[26] The phrase "the blessings of liberty," for its part, was included in the Pennsylvania state constitution of 1776 as well as Morris's own oration before the New York provincial congress in which he urged the state to join the independence movement.[27]

There is no similar precursor or direct constitutional analogue to "establish justice" or "insure domestic tranquility." The former is, however, at least implicit in the formation of the federal judiciary in Article III, as Morris himself noted many years later in a speech in the Senate. The preamble indicated that "the people intended *to establish justice*," he argued in 1802, and the "provision . . . they made to fulfil that intention" was the establishment of the court system.[28] Perhaps the closest counterpart to the preamble's aim of ensuring domestic tranquility within the body of the Constitution is the clause in Article IV that promises the states protection against "domestic violence." This clause had first been proposed by James Wilson back in mid-July, and the context of the proposal made clear that its main purpose was to enable the suppression of a rebellion within a state's borders, such as Shays's Rebellion in Massachusetts.[29]

In all, Morris's preamble nicely sums up what the framers were trying to achieve in the Constitution, much as Thomas Jefferson's list of inalienable rights summed up what the colonists tried to achieve by declaring their independence from Britain. Also like the Declaration's opening paragraph, the preamble would come to be regarded as a sort of political scripture for succeeding generations of Americans.

In the immediate wake of the Convention, leading figures on both sides of the battle over ratification regarded the preamble as being of central importance. We have already seen Patrick Henry's objection to its invocation of "We, the people" rather than "We, the states." James Monroe, who moderately opposed the adoption of the Constitution at the Virginia ratifying convention, described the preamble as "the Key of the Constitution."[30] Arguably the most formidable Anti-Federalist author of all, who wrote in New York under the pen name Brutus, remarked that "to discover the spirit of the constitution, it is of the first importance to attend to the principal ends and designs it has in view," which were, as he saw it, "expressed in the preamble." Judging from the preamble's wide-ranging aims, he lamented, the Constitution was designed "to subvert and abolish all the powers of the state government, and to embrace every object to which any government extends."[31] On the other side of the contest, James Wilson proclaimed at the Pennsylvania ratifying convention that the "single sentence in the preamble is tantamount to a volume, and contains the essence of all the bills of rights that have been or can be devised."[32] Alexander Hamilton likewise insisted in *Federalist* #84 that the preamble constituted "a better recognition of popular rights, than volumes of those aphorisms, which make the principal figure in several of our state bills of rights, and which would sound much better in a treatise of ethics than in a constitution of government."[33]

In the early republic, many figures—mostly Federalists—invoked the preamble as a substantive grant of power. In the debates over whether the president could remove executive officers without congressional approval (1789), over whether Congress could establish a national bank (1791), over the Alien and Sedition Acts (1798), and over the repeal of the Judiciary Act of 1801, among others, members of Congress relied on Morris's list of aims in the preamble to make their case. Benjamin Franklin even appealed to the language about securing "the blessings of liberty" in urging Congress to combat slavery.[34] Many Republicans, however, resisted the idea that the preamble should have independent legal force. James Madison, for one, insisted in 1791 that "the preamble only states the objects of the confederation," whereas the clauses in the body of the Constitution "designate the express powers by which those objects are to be obtained."[35] Much later, he expressed regret that the preamble had become "a source of so much constructive ingenuity."[36]

The Supreme Court has generally refrained from relying directly on the preamble in its rulings. To be sure, in some of the early important cases on questions of federalism—including *Chisholm v. Georgia* (1793), *Martin v. Hunter's Lessee* (1816), and *McCulloch v. Maryland* (1819)—the Court made use of the preamble's claim that the Constitution was ordained and established in the name of the people rather than the states.[37] It has also had intermittent recourse to the preamble in a variety of cases since then.[38] Especially in recent years, however, the Court has generally followed the holding of *Jacobson v. Massachusetts* (1905) that "although [the] Preamble indicates the general purposes for which the people ordained and established the Constitution, it has never been regarded as the source of any substantive power conferred on the Government of the United States or on any of its Departments. Such powers embrace only those expressly granted in the body of the Constitution."[39]

In reaching its decision in *Jacobson*, the Court relied on Justice Joseph Story's venerable *Commentaries on the Constitution of the United States* (1833), which emphasized that "the preamble never can be resorted to, to enlarge the powers confided to the general government. . . . Its true office is to expound the nature, and extent, and application of the powers actually conferred by the constitution, and not substantively to create them."[40] While Story denied that the preamble had any independent legal weight, he was fulsome in his acknowledgement of its importance more broadly, describing it as the "key to open the mind of the makers [of the Constitution], as to the mischiefs, which are to be remedied, and the objects, which are to be accomplished" by the charter.[41]

Over the course of American history, then, the preamble's chief impact has been inspirational rather than legal. Each generation has revisited and drawn encouragement from its lofty ambitions as it has sought to perfect the union still further.[42] Frederick Douglass and other abolitionists, for instance, appealed to the "noble purposes avowed in [the] preamble" in their fight against slavery.[43] Among other champions of women's suffrage, Susan B. Anthony insisted that the preamble buttressed their cause: "It was we, the people, not we, the white male citizens, nor yet we, the male citizens, but we, the whole people who formed this Union. And we formed it, not to give the blessings of liberty, but to secure them; not to the half of ourselves and the half of our posterity, but to the whole people—women as well as men."[44] In making the case for the New Deal, Franklin D. Roosevelt invited his fellow citizens to "read and reread the preamble of the Constitution," which he believed demonstrated that the nation's basic charter should "be used as an instrument of progress, and not as a device for prevention of action."[45] Civil rights activists, too, invoked the preamble as they urged the country to live up to its ideals, such as when Martin Luther King, Jr., looked forward to "the resumption of that noble journey toward the goals reflected in the Preamble to the Constitution."[46]

Although the preamble has more often been used for progressive purposes, conservatives too have found sustenance in its words. Ronald Reagan, for instance, saw it as enshrining "the genius, the hope, and the promise of America forever and for all mankind."[47] Americans of all political persuasions can thus be grateful that Morris chose, at the end of a long summer and in the middle of an intensive drafting process, to convert a bland opening into a stirring statement of purpose.

Epilogue:
From Constitution-Maker to Aspiring Constitution-Breaker

In some respects it is surprising—even shocking—that the individual who played such a dominant role at the Philadelphia Convention eventually advocated the dismemberment of the "more perfect union" that the framers had created. Given everything that we have seen about Morris's constitutional vision in this book, however, perhaps this reversal is not quite as inexplicable as it might seem at first glance.

As great as Morris's impact on the Constitution was, the charter teemed with provisions that he deemed objectionable. The structure of the new Congress diverged particularly sharply from his vision. The states were represented equally rather than proportionally in the Senate. Senators were appointed by the state legislatures rather than by the president. They served six-year terms rather than for life. They were paid from the national treasury rather than receiving no salary. Seats in the House of Representatives were allotted by population according to a decennial census rather than by Congress using both population and property as a guide. And there was no restriction of the suffrage to landowners. Morris believed that all these provisions would undermine the national character and the stability of the government, render property rights less secure, and open the door for the rich to oppress the common people.

The presidency that emerged from the Convention was much closer to Morris's liking, but even here he did not get his way entirely. Morris certainly preferred the electoral college to legislative selection of the president, but he believed that a direct election by the people would have been still better. He also favored giving the president even greater powers than the Constitution did, including an absolute veto over legislation and the ability to unilaterally appoint Cabinet officers, federal judges (including Supreme Court justices), and senators. The constitutional provisions relating to the judiciary were fairly open-ended; Morris would have preferred to spell out explicitly that judges and justices would have the power of judicial review and that there would be a full system of lower federal courts, in addition to the Supreme Court. Finally, to his great disgust, the states were allotted extra seats in the House of

Representatives and extra votes in the electoral college for every human being who was held in bondage within their borders, and the abominable overseas slave trade was protected from a congressional ban for twenty years.

Morris's ambivalence about the charter that he and his fellow delegates were devising was apparent during the Convention itself. Like James Madison, George Washington, James Wilson, and the other leaders of the nationalist camp, he was thoroughly convinced that almost anything would be an improvement on the Articles of Confederation. Yet, as we have already seen, Morris sometimes seemed to be ready to give up on the Convention during the debates over slavery, such as when he suggested on July 13 that the North and South might be forced to "take a friendly leave of each other," or when he declared on August 8 that "he would sooner submit himself to a tax for paying for all the negroes in the United States, than saddle posterity with . . . a Constitution" that protected slavery in the ways that the southerners demanded.[1] Morris was also frustrated by the other delegates' unwillingness to go as far as he wanted in consolidating the federal government's power and ensuring its supremacy over the state governments. On August 31, when George Mason proclaimed that "he would sooner chop off his right hand, than put it to the Constitution as it now stands," Morris immediately chimed in that he was "ready for a postponement" of their deliberations and that "he had long wished for another Convention, that will have the firmness to provide a vigorous government, which we are afraid to do."[2]

Ultimately, however, Morris concluded that he could not abandon everything that they had achieved over the course of the summer. On the Convention's final day, when Edmund Randolph announced his refusal to sign the Constitution, Morris declared that "he too had objections, but considering the present plan as the best that was to be attained, he should take it with all its faults." The "great question" that the nation faced, as he saw it, was "shall there be a National Government, or not?" And without a national government, he was certain, "general anarchy will be the alternative."[3]

When asked, near the end of his life, why he had supported the Constitution as it emerged from the Convention, Morris recalled thinking that "nothing human can be perfect," that "the obstacles to a less imperfect system were insurmountable," and that "the Old Confederation was worse. . . . Surrounded by difficulties, we did the best we could; leaving it with those who should come after us to take counsel from experience, and exercise prudently the power of amendment, which we had provided."[4] To another correspondent, he wrote with typical puckishness that "in adopting a republican form of government, I not only took it as a man does his wife, for better or for worse, but what few men do with their wives, I took it knowing all its bad qualities."[5] Given that Morris's assessment of the Constitution was so mixed from the very outset, it would have been somewhat surprising if he *had* been entirely pleased with the new government. The real question is why his dissatisfaction grew so deep that he longed for a divorce.

After the Convention's close, a number of the delegates who had similarly strong reservations about the Constitution, such as James Madison and Alexander Hamilton, nevertheless jumped into the fight for ratification with both feet, reckoning that a partial solution to the nation's woes was better than none at all. Morris, however, did not. His letters from this period indicate that he hoped the charter would be ratified, but he did not speak publicly or publish anything on its behalf, he did not participate in the ratifying conventions in either Pennsylvania or New York, and he did not contribute to *The Federalist* despite being "warmly pressed" by Hamilton to do so.[6] Morris's disengagement from the ratification process was surely due in large part to his desire to focus on his business affairs and on making improvements to his recently acquired Morrisania estate. He had not wanted to attend the Convention in the first place and had absented himself from Philadelphia for the entire month of June, so clearly he had other matters on his mind. One of Morris's recent biographers suggests that perhaps he also "did not wish to become involved as an advocate for a charter he had such a great share in bringing to fruition" because he "felt that in both style and content the Constitution's merit was self-evident and would be recognized."[7] It seems just as likely, however, that his qualms about the charter left him less inclined to campaign on its behalf.

Judging from his letters over the next decade, Morris's view of the Constitution actually grew more favorable during his time in Europe. There are several plausible explanations for his increased optimism in this period. First, he was pleased by the direction that the government took under the guidance of President Washington, Secretary of the Treasury Hamilton, and the Federalist-controlled Congress. As early as the summer of 1789, Morris told one correspondent that "the pulse of our government . . . is vigorous beyond my hopes, far beyond my expectations, and comes up to my wishes."[8] Moreover, particularly after he took up his post as the minister to France, Morris was generally given fairly glowing reports of America's domestic affairs by his principal correspondents within the government—Washington, Hamilton, and Secretary of State Jefferson—since these figures were eager to put a good face on things for a European audience. Finally, America's new Constitution could not help but look better when viewed in comparison to the upheavals that Morris witnessed in France, ranging from the failed constitution of 1791 to the Terror.

Morris's confidence in America's constitutional order remained intact for several years after his return to the United States, even after the Republicans swept to power in the election of 1800. He wrote to Rufus King, his old comrade from the Convention who was now in London serving as the nation's minister to Britain, that although "our legislature is anti-federal, and . . . our present system is somewhat wild," still "*nil desperandum de Republica* [never despair of the republic], is a sound principle."[9] During the debate in the Senate over the repeal of the Judiciary Act of 1801, Morris continued to appeal to the Constitution as the rock of their salvation, declaring that "I . . . wish to support this Constitution, because I love it. And I love it, because I consider it as the bond of our union; because, in my soul, I believe, that on it depends our harmony and our peace; that without it, we should soon be plunged in all the horrors of civil war."[10] If the Constitution were to be abandoned and a new convention were to be called, he warned, "my life for it . . . they will part without doing anything. Never in the flow of time was there a moment so propitious, as that in which the [Philadelphia] Convention assembled."[11]

As we saw in chapter 8, the repeal of the Judiciary Act over Morris's fierce objections was the first critical step on the path to his disillusionment. This move was, in his view, a flagrant violation of the Constitution that both reduced the reach of the federal courts and fatally undermined the independence of the judiciary. Soon after the repeal went through, he wrote matter-of-factly to Robert R. Livingston, who was then serving as minister to France, that "we have here as yet done nothing of importance, except destroying the Constitution by repealing the judiciary law of last session."[12] The next year, he declared to another correspondent that "the Judiciary has been overthrown. The Constitution is, therefore, in my opinion gone. The complete sovereignty of America is substantially in the House of Representatives." Yet he added that he had not completely lost heart:

You may, from what I have said, be perhaps inclined to set me down as a croaker, but in this you would be deceived. There is always a counter current in human affairs, which opposes alike both good and evil. Thus the good we hope is seldom obtained, and the evil we fear is rarely realized. The leaders of faction must, for their own sakes, avoid errors of enormous magnitude; so that, while the Republican form lasts, we shall be tolerably well governed.[13]

Although Morris regarded the repeal of the Judiciary Act as a great blow to the nation's prospects, then, his deepest despair would not emerge until James Madison's presidency.

Several of the factors that led to Morris's late-life disillusionment were already mentioned in chapter 9, including the disproportionate share of political power that the South claimed on behalf of the people whom they enslaved and the way that Republicans used that power, beginning with the Non-Importation Act of 1806 and the Embargo Act of 1807, to devastate the commercial interests of the North—all very much in line with what Morris predicted back at the Philadelphia Convention. As Morris put it in 1810, the Republicans had not only "assailed the Constitution" with the repeal of the Judiciary Act but also "impoverished the Citizens, dried up the Revenue, squandered the Treasure, hazarded the Peace and surrendered the Independence of the united States."[14] The latter items on this list of grievances referred to the events leading up to the War of 1812, a conflict that Morris regarded as an almost unmitigated disaster.

The nation was distinctly unprepared for this three-year war with Britain, particularly since the Republicans had spent the previous twelve years shrinking the army and navy, slashing taxes, and allowing the charter for the national bank to lapse.[15] Opposition to the war was widespread in the North, which bore the brunt of the hostilities in terms of blood, treasure, and forgone trading opportunities. Morris thought that "this unjust, unwise, mismanaged war," as he described it, was in fact "waged as much against New England as against Old England."[16] He was also far from alone in judging the Madison administration to be rather bungling in its conduct of the war. Morris's opinion of his erstwhile ally at the Philadelphia Convention was astonishingly uncharitable by this point. A few years earlier he had described Madison as "a man of feeble mind" and as exhibiting "a deep decline of character, for which we fear there is no remedy."[17] In 1813, he gossiped that he had "been told that [Madison] never goes sober to bed. Whether intoxicated by opium or wine was not said, but I learned last winter that pains in his teeth had driven him to use the former too freely."[18]

Morris's flirtation with the idea of secession began even before the war did. In April 1812, he wrote to Harrison Gray Otis of Massachusetts, who was emerging as one of the leaders of the separatist movement, that "in framing our national Constitution, we were not at all blind to its defects, but none of us, I believe, expected they would bear fruit so soon and so bitter." Although Morris still believed that "the union, being the means of preserving freedom, should be prized as such," he felt compelled to add that "the end should not be sacrificed to the means." The war would not officially commence for another two months, but he was already speculating that a convention of northern states—"the friends of peace and commerce"—would soon be necessary.[19] When Congress declared war in mid-June, every Federalist voted against it. Later that month Morris forecast "a storm gathering in the East which may blow our Union flag from the mast-head."[20]

In August Morris published an address—under his usual pen name, "An American," no less—in which he declared that although "few men in the United States are more bound than he by sentiment and by interest to the preservation of our National Union," he feared that "the general current of events, for some years past, drives us rapidly towards a condition in which no human power can prevent these States from separating into two, or more sections, independent of each other."[21] Most of Morris's tirades over the next few years would appear within the confines of private letters; this address was the closest that he ever came to publicly advocating disunion.[22]

By 1814, the war was grinding toward a stalemate, and Morris had had more than enough. He wrote histrionically to Rufus King, who was by this point a senator from New York:

> Where, in God's name is all this to End? Men without Talents ... exercise a Tyranny which would drive the Slaves of Asia to Despair, and no Man is hardy enough to raise a finger. Am I awake or do I dream? Is this the People that resisted a mere Claim of arbitrary Power? It seems to me I was once a Member of Congress during a revolutionary War; but is it certain there was such a thing as a Congress? Was there a revolutionary War? ... We once had Hearts—Hearts that beat high with the Love of Liberty—But tis over, Adieu.[23]

In addition to invoking the revolutionary spirit of his youth, Morris now insisted that the Constitution that he had penned in his middle age would need to be repaired if not revamped. As he told another correspondent, "The present form [of government] was good, but has been so much perverted that it can hardly be restored to what it was." If America's "posterity" was to "inherit freedom," as the preamble had promised, then the people must be persuaded "not merely to permit, but to effect a change."[24]

By the end of the year, however, even constitutional reform would not have been enough to satisfy Morris. He now believed that nothing less than secession would do. "A union of the commercial States to take care of themselves, leaving the war, its expense, and its debt to those choice spirits, so ready to declare and so eager to carry it on, seems to be now the only rational course," he told Rufus King.[25] The real question for Morris, by this point, was not whether disunion was desirable or necessary, but rather where the border should be drawn. Should the northern confederacy end at the Delaware River (which separates New Jersey from Pennsylvania), the Susquehanna (which would have also included Pennsylvania within the North), or the Potomac (which would have put the border south of Maryland)? Morris tended toward the middle option.[26] To those who cried that this would mean civil war, he did not mince words: "Unquestionably it is civil war. And what of it?"[27]

For a time, Morris placed his hopes in the Hartford Convention, a gathering of disaffected representatives from the New England states that met between December 15, 1814, and January 5, 1815.[28] In the months leading up to the convention, Morris told Harrison Gray Otis, one of its leading organizers, that he "felt as an American some little selfrespect, when I perceived a glimmering from the lamp of public spirit in Massachusetts," which had glowed so "bright in 1775." He predicted that New York would go along with the convention's measures as long as they were not too "feeble": "We know from experience, that public confidence adheres to those, who adopt bold measures, for when the general trembles the soldier must quake."[29] To Timothy Pickering, who was even more of a hardliner, Morris wrote that his eyes were "fixed on a star in the east," which he regarded as "the day-spring of freedom and glory." While the gathering in Hartford might be regarded by some of their contemporaries as a set of "madmen and traitors," Morris was convinced that they would "if not too tame and timid, be hailed hereafter as patriots and sages of their day and generation."[30]

While some of the delegates to the Hartford Convention hoped for a declaration of independence and a separate peace with Britain, in the end the moderates prevailed. The convention proposed a series of amendments to the Constitution, including a requirement for a two-thirds supermajority in Congress to declare war, institute an embargo, or admit a new state to the union; a one-term limit on the presidency; a prohibition on consecutive presidents from the same state (read: Virginia); and the elimination of the three-fifths clause. In a futile attempt to give its recommendations some bite, the convention warned that if they were rejected then a second convention would be held in Boston that summer to consider secession. There was, however, virtually no chance that any of these measures would be ratified, given the overwhelming majorities that the Republicans enjoyed in Congress and in most of the state legislatures.

As Richard Brookhiser has noted, "the Gouverneur Morris of 1787 would have scoffed at most of the Hartford Convention's proposals" beyond the elimination of the three-fifths clause and perhaps the higher hurdle for the admission of new states.[31] The Morris who served in Philadelphia had wanted to *empower* the national government, particularly the presidency, not to put fetters on it. The Morris of 1815, however, lamented that the Hartford Convention's resolutions had not gone far enough. At the very least, he believed, they should have declared that the New England states would provide no more money or troops for the war effort and that "honorable Conditions of Peace shall if proposed on the Part of Great Britain, be immediately accepted." As it was, he told Rufus King, the convention had "fallen short" and "will be laughed at by many."[32] To another correspondent he wrote that the Republicans "will doubtless make themselves merry, at the mildness of Yankee measures."[33]

Morris's hopes for a separation were dashed for good a few weeks later when news arrived of both the Treaty of Ghent, which officially ended the war, and a smashing victory at the Battle of New Orleans under the leadership of Andrew Jackson. At that point, the Federalist party's little remaining clout vanished almost entirely, and those who had supported the Hartford Convention fell into disgrace. Morris grumbled that the peace treaty "surrendered to England every contested point" and thus "tacitly acknowledged the injustice of a war rashly declared, prodigally maintained, weakly conducted, and meanly concluded."[34] The best that they could hope for, he told his nephew, was that "the peace may prevent a separation of the States, patch up our tattered Constitution, and perpetuate the blessings of a Jacobin administration."[35]

Morris felt that his advocacy of northern secession was perfectly consistent with the views that he had held while helping to frame the Constitution. In fact, in the letter to Timothy Pickering in which he looked to the Hartford Convention as "the day-spring of freedom and glory," he insisted that his "sentiments and opinions" had "undergone no essential change in forty years."[36] It is true that even in 1787 Morris had not regarded the union as sacrosanct. During the debate over slavery, recall, he insisted that he had come to Philadelphia "to form a compact for the good of America," and if some of the states refused to join such a compact then "he was ready to join with any States that would."[37] The ends laid out in the preamble—justice, domestic tranquility, the common defense, the general welfare, and liberty—were always more important to him than the means to those ends. Morris had also, however, been arguably the Convention's most passionate nationalist—"a Representative of America" rather than of a particular state or region, as he had proudly put it. The bitter, short-fused, elderly Morris appeared to most objective observers to embody the kind of narrow parochialism that he had decried in Philadelphia. In any case, the willingness—indeed, apparent eagerness—of the Constitution's penman to give up on the foremost accomplishment of his life is heartbreaking, even if not altogether incomprehensible.

Given all that Morris did to shape the Constitution and lay the foundation for the government under which Americans still live, it seems like a shame to leave him on this sour note. Happily, in his final year he performed one last turnaround. Once it became clear that the Federalists' political fortunes would not be revived any time soon, if ever, Morris managed to make peace with that fact. In August 1816, he advised a Federalist Committee of Correspondence to "forget party, and think of our country." After all, "men of sense, experience, and integrity . . . may, I trust, be found in both parties; and, if our country be delivered, what does it signify whether those who operate her salvation wear a federal or a democratic cloak?" He ended the letter with a bit of apt self-characterization, writing that "perhaps the expression of these sentiments may be imprudent; but, when it appears proper to speak truth, I know not concealment."[38]

That autumn, Morris became the second president of the New-York Historical Society, a group that was—and is—dedicated to preserving and exhibiting the history of his city, his state, and his nation (and that now houses Morris's peg leg). In his inaugural discourse, which he delivered just two months before his death, he exclaimed: "America has shown examples of heroic ardour not excelled by Rome, in her brightest day of glory, and blended with milder virtue than the Romans ever knew. These examples will be handed down, by your care, for the instruction and imitation of our children's children; make them acquainted with their fathers; and grant, Oh God! that a long and late posterity, enjoying freedom in the bosom of peace, may look, with grateful exultation, at the day-dawn of our empire."[39] This seems like a more appropriate place to leave our amiable companion on this tour of the creation of America's Constitution. Morris was certainly not without his faults, any more than the other founders were, but anyone who has spent significant time with him will agree that he left us, his posterity, a rather large shoe to fill.

Appendix: Morris's Great Convention Speeches

This appendix contains the text of three of Morris's longest and most important speeches at the Philadelphia Convention as recorded by James Madison. The notes that Madison took on longer speeches, such as these, often begin in the third person and switch to the first person. Although there are no paragraph breaks in Madison's notes, I have inserted them into all three speeches in order to facilitate reading.

JULY 2 SPEECH ON THE SENATE

When Morris returned from an extended absence from the Convention on July 2, the delegates were deadlocked on the question of whether representation in the Senate would be equal for each state or proportional to the states' populations. Morris suggested that they step back and consider the broader purpose of the Senate within the government.

Mr. Gouverneur Morris thought a Committee [to consider the basis of representation in the Senate] advisable, as the Convention had been equally divided. He had a stronger reason also. The mode of appointing the second branch [i.e., by the state legislatures] tended, he was sure, to defeat the object of it. What is this object? To check the precipitation, changeableness, and excesses, of the first branch. Every man of observation had seen in the democratic branches of the State Legislatures, precipitation—in [the Confederation] Congress, changeableness—in every department, excesses against personal liberty, private property, and personal safety.

What qualities are necessary to constitute a check in this case? *Abilities* and *virtue* are equally necessary in both branches. Something more, then, is now wanted. In the first place, the checking branch must have a personal interest in checking the other branch. One interest must be opposed to another interest. Vices, as they exist, must be turned against each other. In the second place, it must have great personal property; it must have the aristocratic spirit; it must love to lord it through pride. Pride is, indeed, the great principle that actuates both the poor and the rich. It is this principle which in the former resists, in the latter abuses, authority. In the third place, it should be independent. In religion, the creature is apt to forget its Creator. That it is otherwise in political affairs, the late debates here are an unhappy proof. The aristocratic body should be as independent, and as firm, as the democratic. If the members of it are to revert to a dependence on the democratic choice, the democratic scale will preponderate. All the guards contrived by America have not restrained the Senatorial branches of the [state] Legislatures from a servile complaisance to the democratic. If the second branch is to be dependent, we are better without it.

To make it independent, it should be for life. It will then do wrong, it will be said. He believed so; he hoped so. The rich will strive to establish their dominion, and enslave the rest. They always did. They always will. The proper security against them is to form them into a separate interest. The two forces will then control each other. Let the rich mix with the poor, and in a commercial country they will establish an oligarchy. Take away commerce, and the democracy will triumph. Thus it has been all the world over. So it will be among us. Reason tells us we are but men; and we are not to expect any particular interference of Heaven in our favor. By thus combining, and setting apart, the aristocratic interest, the popular interest will be combined against it. There will be a mutual check and mutual security.

In the fourth place, an independence for life involves the necessary permanency. If we change measures nobody will trust us,—and how avoid a change of measures, but by avoiding a change of men? Ask any man if he confides in [the Confederation] Congress—if he confides in the State of Pennsylvania—if he will lend his money, or enter into contract? He will tell you, no. He sees no stability. He can repose no confidence. If Great Britain were to explain her refusal to treat with us, the same reasoning would be employed.

He disliked the exclusion of the second branch from holding offices. It is dangerous. It is like the imprudent exclusion of the military officers, during the war, from civil appointments. It deprives the Executive of the principal source of influence. If danger be apprehended from the Executive, what a left-handed way is this of obviating it! If the son, the brother, or the friend can be appointed, the danger may be even increased, as the disqualified father, &c. can then boast of a disinterestedness which he does not possess. Besides, shall the best, the most able, the most virtuous citizens not be permitted to hold offices? Who then are to hold them?

He was also against paying the Senators. They will pay themselves, if they can. If they cannot, they will be rich, and can do without it. Of such the second branch ought to consist; and none but such can compose it, if they are not to be paid.

He contended, that the Executive should appoint the Senate, and fill up vacancies. This gets rid of the difficulty in the present question [i.e., whether representation in the Senate would be equal for each state or proportional to the states' populations]. You may begin with any ratio you please, it will come to the same thing. The members being independent, and for life, may be taken as well from one place as from another.

It should be considered, too, how the scheme could be carried through [i.e., ratified by] the States. He hoped there was strength of mind enough in this House to look truth in the face. He did not hesitate, therefore, to say that loaves and fishes must bribe the demagogues. They must be made to expect higher offices under the General than the State Governments. A Senate for life will be a noble bait. Without such captivating prospects, the popular leaders will oppose and defeat the plan.

He perceived that the first branch was to be chosen by the people of the States, the second by those chosen by the people. Is not here a government by the States—a government by compact between Virginia in the first and second branch, Massachusetts in the first and second branch, &c.? This is going back to mere treaty. It is no government at all. It is altogether dependent on the States, and will act over again the part which [the Confederation] Congress has acted. A firm government alone can protect our liberties.

He fears the influence of the rich. They will have the same effect here as elsewhere, if we do not, by such a government, keep them within their proper spheres. We should remember that the people never act from reason alone. The rich will take advantage of their passions, and make these the instruments for oppressing them. The result of the contest will be a violent aristocracy, or a more violent despotism. The schemes of the rich will be favored by the extent of the country. The people in such distant parts cannot communicate and act in concert. They will be the dupes of those who have more knowledge and intercourse. The only security against encroachments, will be a select and sagacious body of men, instituted to watch against them on all sides. He meant only to hint these observations, without grounding any motion on them.[1]

JULY 19 SPEECH ON THE PRESIDENCY

Morris's longest speech of the summer, which he delivered on July 19, was a comprehensive look at the presidency. He later changed his mind regarding some of the proposals that he made in the speech, particularly the suggestion that the president should not be impeachable, but this was his initial vision of how the various pieces of the presidential puzzle could be made to fit together.

Mr. Gouverneur Morris. It is necessary to take into one view all that relates to the establishment of the Executive; on the due formation of which must depend the efficacy and utility of the union among the present and future States. It has been a maxim in political science, that republican government is not adapted to a large extent of country, because the energy of the executive magistracy cannot reach the extreme parts of it. Our country is an extensive one. We must either then renounce the blessings of the Union, or provide an Executive with sufficient vigor to pervade every part of it. This subject was of so much importance that he hoped to be indulged in an extensive view of it.

One great object of the Executive is, to control the Legislature. The Legislature will continually seek to aggrandize and perpetuate themselves; and will seize those critical moments produced by war, invasion, or convulsion, for that purpose. It is necessary, then, that the Executive magistrate should be the guardian of the people, even of the lower classes, against legislative tyranny; against the great and the wealthy, who, in the course of things will necessarily compose the legislative body. Wealth tends to corrupt the mind;—to nourish its love of power; and to stimulate it to oppression. History proves this to be the spirit of the opulent. The check provided in the second branch was not meant as a check on legislative usurpations of power, but on the abuse of lawful powers, on the propensity of the first branch to legislate too much, to run into projects of paper-money, and similar expedients. It is no check on legislative tyranny. On the contrary it may favor it; and, if the first branch can be seduced, may find the means of success. The Executive, therefore, ought to be so constituted as to be the great protector of the mass of the people.

It is the duty of the Executive to appoint the officers, and to command the forces, of the Republic; to appoint, first, ministerial officers for the administration of public affairs; secondly, officers for the dispensation of justice. Who will be the best judges whether these appointments be well made? The people at large, who will know, will see, will feel, the effects of them. Again, who can judge so well of the discharge of military duties for the protection and security of the people, as the people themselves, who are to be protected and secured?

He finds, too, that the Executive is not to be re-eligible. What effect will this have? In the first place, it will destroy the great incitement to merit, public esteem, by taking away the hope of being rewarded with a re-appointment. It may give a dangerous turn to one of the strongest passions in the human breast. The love of fame is the great spring to noble and illustrious actions. Shut the civil road to glory, and he may be compelled to seek it by the sword. In the second place, it will tempt him to make the most of the short space of time allotted him, to accumulate wealth and provide for his friends. In the third place, it will produce violations of the very Constitution it is meant to secure. In moments of pressing danger, the tried abilities and established character of a favorite magistrate will prevail over respect for the forms of the Constitution.

The Executive is also to be impeachable. This is a dangerous part of the plan. It will hold him in such dependence, that he will be no check to the Legislature, will not be a firm guardian of the people and of the public interest. He will be the tool of a faction, of some leading demagogue in the Legislature.

These, then, are the faults of the Executive establishment, as now proposed. Can no better establishment be devised? If he is to be the guardian of the people, let him be appointed by the people. If he is to be a check on the Legislature, let him not be impeachable. Let him be of short duration, that he may with propriety be re-eligible. It has been said that the candidates for this office will not be known to the people. If they be known to the Legislature, they must have such a notoriety and eminence of character, that they cannot possibly be unknown to the people at large. It cannot be possible that a man shall have sufficiently distinguished himself to merit this high trust, without having his character proclaimed by fame throughout the Empire. As to the danger from an unimpeachable magistrate, he could not regard it as formidable. There must be certain great officers of state, a minister of finance, of war, of foreign affairs, &c. These, he presumes, will exercise their functions in subordination to the Executive, and will be amenable, by impeachment, to the public justice. Without these ministers, the Executive can do nothing of consequence.

He suggested a biennial election of the Executive, at the time of electing the first branch; and the Executive to hold over, so as to prevent any interregnum in the administration. An election by the people at large, throughout so great an extent of country, could not be influenced by those little combinations and those momentary lies, which often decide popular elections within a narrow sphere.

It will probably be objected, that the election will be influenced by the members of the Legislature, particularly of the first branch; and that it will be nearly the same thing with an election by the Legislature itself. It could not be denied that such an influence would exist. But it might be answered, that, as the Legislature or the candidates for it, would be divided the enmity of one part would counteract the friendship of another; that if the administration of the Executive were good, it would be unpopular to oppose his re-election; if bad, it ought to be opposed, and a re-appointment prevented; and lastly, that in every view this indirect dependence on the favor of the Legislature could not be so mischievous as a direct dependence for his appointment. He saw no alternative for making the Executive independent of the Legislature, but either to give him his office for life, or make him eligible by the people.

Again, it might be objected, that two years would be too short a duration. But he believes that as long as he should behave himself well he would be continued in his place. The extent of the country would secure his re-election against the factions and discontents of particular States. It deserved consideration, also, that such an ingredient in the plan would render it extremely palatable to the people. These were the general ideas which occurred to him on the subject, and which led him to wish and move that the whole constitution of the Executive might undergo reconsideration.[2]

AUGUST 8 SPEECH ON SLAVERY

On August 8, Morris delivered one of the most eloquent and biting speeches of the entire Convention in the context of a debate over the inclusion of enslaved people in the apportionment of the House of Representatives using a three-fifths ratio.

Mr. Gouverneur Morris moved to insert "free" before the word "inhabitants" [in the representation clause of the Committee of Detail's draft constitution, which stipulated that "the legislature shall ... regulate the number of Representatives by the number of inhabitants, according to the provisions hereinafter made, at the rate of one for every forty thousand"; the "provisions hereinafter made" included the three-fifths clause]. Much, he said, would depend on this point. He never would concur in upholding domestic slavery. It was a nefarious institution. It was the curse of Heaven on the States where it prevailed.

Compare the free regions of the Middle States, where a rich and noble cultivation marks the prosperity and happiness of the people, with the misery and poverty which overspread the barren wastes of Virginia, Maryland, and the other States having slaves. Travel through the whole continent, and you behold the prospect continually varying with the appearance and disappearance of slavery. The moment you leave the Eastern States, and enter New York, the effects of the institution become visible. Passing through the Jerseys and entering Pennsylvania, every criterion of superior improvement witnesses the change. Proceed southwardly, and every step you take, through the great regions of slaves, presents a desert increasing with the increasing population of these wretched beings.

Upon what principle is it that the slaves shall be computed in the representation? Are they men? Then make them citizens, and let them vote. Are they property? Why, then, is no other property included? The houses in this city (Philadelphia) are worth more than all the wretched slaves who cover the rice swaps of South Carolina.

The admission of slaves into the representation, when fairly explained, comes to this,—that the inhabitant of Georgia and South Carolina who goes to the coast of Africa, and, in defiance of the most sacred laws of humanity, tears away his fellow creatures from their dearest connexions, and damns them to the most cruel bondage, shall have more votes in a government instituted for protection of the rights of mankind, than the citizen of Pennsylvania or New Jersey, who views with a laudable horror so nefarious a practice.

He would add, that domestic slavery is the most prominent feature in the aristocratic countenance of the proposed Constitution. The vassalage of the poor has ever been the favorite offspring of aristocracy.

And what is the proposed compensation to the Northern States, for a sacrifice of every principle of right, of every impulse of humanity? They are to bind themselves to march their militia for the defence of the Southern States, for their defence against those very slaves of whom they complain. They must supply vessels and seamen, in case of foreign attack. The Legislature will have indefinite power to tax them by excises, and duties on imports; both of which will fall heavier on them than on the Southern inhabitants; for the Bohea tea used by a Northern freeman will pay more tax than the whole consumption of the miserable slave, which consists of nothing more than his physical subsistence and the rag that covers his nakedness.

On the other side, the Southern States are not to be restrained from importing fresh supplies of wretched Africans, at once to increase the danger of attack, and the difficulty of defence; nay, they are to be encouraged to it, by an assurance of having their votes in the National Government increased in proportion: and are, at the same time, to have their exports and their slaves exempt from all contributions for the public service. Let it not be said, that direct taxation is to be proportioned to representation. It is idle to suppose that the General Government can stretch its hand directly into the pockets of the people, scattered over so vast a country. They can only do it through the medium of exports, imports, and excises. For what, then, are all the sacrifices to be made? He would sooner submit himself to a tax for paying for all the negroes in the United States, than saddle posterity with such a Constitution.[3]

Notes

The standard source for the debates at the Constitutional Convention is the four-volume *Records of the Federal Convention of 1787*, ed. Max Farrand (New Haven, CT: Yale University Press, [1911] 1966). These volumes, together with the *Supplement to Max Farrand's Records of the Federal Convention of 1787*, ed. James H. Hutson (New Haven, CT: Yale University Press, 1987), contain the notes taken at the Convention by the various delegates as well as many letters and other contemporaneous writings that comment on the Convention's actions. However, when quoting James Madison's notes—by far the fullest set that we have—in the text, I have used *Debates in the Federal Convention of 1787 by James Madison, a Member*, ed. Gordon Lloyd (Ashland, OH: Ashbrook Center, 2014), which incorporates the revisions that Madison made to his notes from the close of the Convention all the way through the 1830s. Because Madison later spelled out his abbreviations and corrected spelling and punctuation, this version tends to be far more readable than the version contained in Farrand's *Records*. (On the reliability of Madison's more substantive revisions, see the last section of chapter 2.) Since most students and scholars of the period rely on Farrand's *Records*, when citing Lloyd's *Debates* I have also indicated the corresponding page(s) in Farrand's volumes, as well as the date on which the particular speech, motion, or vote was made (for example: Gouverneur Morris, 30 May: *Debates*, 11; *Records* 1:34). The notes use the following abbreviations for some of the more frequently cited texts.

Debates *Debates in the Federal Convention of 1787 by James Madison, a Member*, ed. Gordon Lloyd (Ashland, OH: Ashbrook Center, 2014).
FO Founders Online, http://founders.archives.gov.
Records *The Records of the Federal Convention of 1787*, ed. Max Farrand, 4 vols. (New Haven, CT: Yale University Press, [1911] 1966).
Sparks Jared Sparks, *The Life of Gouverneur Morris, with Selections from His Correspondence and Miscellaneous Papers*, 3 vols. (Boston: Gray and Bowen, 1832).
Writings *To Secure the Blessings of Liberty: Selected Writings of Gouverneur Morris*, ed. J. Jackson Barlow (Indianapolis: Liberty Fund, 2012).

INTRODUCTION: FORGOTTEN YET UNFORGETTABLE

1. The earliest use of this now-common sobriquet that I have been able find came in an 1887 issue of the journal *Forest and Stream* in an article about George Washington as an angler, of all places. The author refers to Morris, Washington's sometime fishing buddy, as "the inspired penman of the Federal Constitution." See George H. Moore, "Washington an Angler," *Forest and Stream*, August 11, 1887, 48.

2. See, for instance, Danielle Allen, *Our Declaration: A Reading of the Declaration of*

Independence in Defense of Equality (New York: W. W. Norton, 2014), part 2; and Pauline Maier, *American Scripture: Making the Declaration of Independence* (New York: Alfred A. Knopf, 1997), chap. 3.

3. See John Adams, *Autobiography*, in *The Diary and Autobiography of John Adams*, ed. L. H. Butterfield (Cambridge, MA: Harvard University Press, 1961), 3:336; John Adams to Timothy Pickering, 6 August 1822, in *FO*; and Thomas Jefferson to James Madison, 20 August 1823, in *FO*.

4. The version of the Virginia Declaration of Rights that appeared in the *Pennsylvania Gazette* on June 12, 1776—which Jefferson would have had access to—proclaimed that "all men are born equally free and independent, and have certain inherent natural rights . . . among which are, the enjoyment of life and liberty, with the means of acquiring and possessing property, and pursuing and obtaining happiness and safety"; that "power is vested in, and consequently derived from, the people"; and that "whenever any government shall be found inadequate or contrary to these purposes, a majority of the community hath an indubitable, unalienable, indefeasible right, to reform, alter, or abolish it, in such manner as shall be judged most conducive to the publick Weal." "Committee Draft of the Virginia Declaration of Rights," 27 May 1776, in *The Papers of George Mason*, ed. Robert A. Rutland (Chapel Hill: University of North Carolina Press, 1970), 1:283. Jefferson's first full draft of the Declaration held "that all men are created equal & independant, that from that equal creation they derive rights inherent & inalienable, among which are the preservation of life, & liberty, & the pursuit of happiness; that to secure these ends, governments are instituted among men, deriving their just powers from the consent of the governed; that whenever any form of government shall become destructive of these ends, it is the right of the people to alter or to abolish it, & to institute new government, laying it's foundation on such principles & organising it's powers in such form, as to them shall seem most likely to effect their safety & happiness." Thomas Jefferson, "'Original Rough Draught' of the Declaration of Independence," 11 June–4 July 1776, in *The Papers of Thomas Jefferson*, ed. Julian P. Boyd et al. (Princeton, NJ: Princeton University Press, 1950–2017), 1:423–424.

5. Thomas Jefferson to Henry Lee, 8 May 1825, in *FO*.

6. David Nichols writes that "Morris deserves to be called the author of the Constitution in two senses: first, he shaped the language of the final draft; and second, he played a major role in the debates over its drafting." David K. Nichols, "Gouverneur Morris and the Creation of American Constitutionalism," in *Natural Right and Political Philosophy: Essays in Honor of Catherine Zuckert and Michael Zuckert*, ed. Ann Ward and Lee Ward (Notre Dame, IN: University of Notre Dame Press, 2013), 253–254.

7. Gouverneur Morris, 8 August: *Debates*, 331; *Records* 2:221.

8. In support of this claim, Ellis writes that "Madison's major contributions were made before the convention, in setting the agenda, then after, in orchestrating the ratification process as Publius alongside Hamilton in the Federalist Papers. During the convention, Morris rose to speak more often than any other delegate, offered some of the sharpest criticisms of slavery as a cancer that must be removed before it spread, and garnered more favorable commentary from fellow delegates for his oratorical prowess. (The

same delegates frequently reported that Madison spoke so softly they could not hear what he said.) Most persuasively, Morris actually wrote the version of the Constitution in the iconic form that has come down to us now." Joseph J. Ellis, *American Dialogue: The Founders and Us* (New York: Alfred A. Knopf, 2018), 239. For similar statements, see Joseph J. Ellis, *The Quartet: Orchestrating the Second American Revolution, 1783–1789* (New York: Alfred A. Knopf, 2015), 150, 206.

9. Richard Brookhiser, *Gentleman Revolutionary: Gouverneur Morris, the Rake Who Wrote the Constitution* (New York: Free Press, 2003), xiv–xv.

10. By one scholar's count, forty of the seventy-one proposals that Madison moved, seconded, or unequivocally supported at the Convention ended up losing. See Forrest McDonald, *Novus Ordo Seclorum: The Intellectual Origins of the Constitution* (Lawrence: University Press of Kansas, 1985), 208–209. The most serious of these losses, in Madison's eyes, included the defeat of his proposed congressional veto over state legislation, the defeat of his proposed council of revision, and the fact that the states were granted equal (rather than proportional) representation in the Senate. Given these losses, many historians have recently cast doubt on whether Madison deserves his traditional moniker. For instance, Christopher Collier and James Lincoln Collier maintain that "in the end, the Convention fought off too many of Madison's basic ideas for him to be called [the Constitution's] father." Christopher Collier and James Lincoln Collier, *Decision in Philadelphia: The Constitutional Convention of 1787* (New York: Random House, 1986), 33. Similarly, Andrew Burstein and Nancy Isenberg write that "Madison was not particularly successful at the Constitutional Convention, certainly not in the way Americans have been taught and certainly not enough to warrant the title 'Father of the Constitution.'" Andrew Burstein and Nancy Isenberg, *Madison and Jefferson* (New York: Random House, 2010), xix. Greg Weiner likewise argues that "Madison is miscast as the father of the Constitution" and that he would be "better understood as the attending physician at its birth—and, later, as its tutor." Greg Weiner, *Madison's Metronome: The Constitution, Majority Rule, and the Tempo of American Politics* (Lawrence: University Press of Kansas, 2012), xi. Late in life, Madison himself all but disavowed the moniker, writing to a correspondent, "You give me a credit to which I have no claim, in calling me '*The* writer of the Constitution of the U.S.' This was not, like the fabled Goddess of Wisdom, the offspring of a single brain. It ought to be regarded as the work of many heads & many hands." James Madison to William Cogswell, 10 March 1834, in *FO*.

11. James Madison to Thomas Jefferson, 6 September 1787, in *The Papers of James Madison*, ed. William T. Hutchinson et al. (Chicago: University of Chicago Press and Charlottesville: University Press of Virginia, 1962–1991), 10:163–164; see also James Madison to Thomas Jefferson, 24 October 1787, in *Papers of James Madison*, 10:205–220. Jack Rakove writes that "save for the handful of delegates who later opposed its ratification, few members left Philadelphia in September more disappointed with the Constitution than the man history has called its 'Father.'" Jack N. Rakove, *James Madison and the Creation of the American Republic*, 3rd ed. (New York: Pearson Longman, 2006), 61.

12. Eric Nelson writes that "Madison's influence in the convention, and the degree to which he shaped the Constitution itself, have been exaggerated. It is beyond question that

he played a decisive role in the political maneuvering that led to the calling of the convention and that his 'Virginia Plan' set the broad parameters for its agenda. But [James] Wilson and Morris came a good deal closer to getting their way in Philadelphia than did Madison." Eric Nelson, *The Royalist Revolution: Monarchy and the American Founding* (Cambridge, MA: Belknap Press of Harvard University Press, 2014), 202.

13. Noah Feldman, *The Three Lives of James Madison: Genius, Partisan, President* (New York: Random House, 2017), 110.

14. Alan Taylor, "Foundering Father," *Washington Post Book Review*, June 29, 2003, 3–4.

15. George Washington, "Comments on James Monroe's *A View of the Conduct of the Executive of the United States*," March 1798, in *The Papers of George Washington: Retirement Series*, ed. W. W. Abbot (Charlottesville: University Press of Virginia, 1998–1999), 2:171.

16. Alexander Hamilton, "Conversation with George Beckwith," 25–30 September 1790, in *The Papers of Alexander Hamilton*, ed. Harold C. Syrett and Jacob Cooke (New York: Columbia University Press, 1961–1987), 7:72.

17. James Madison to Jared Sparks, 8 April 1831, in *FO*.

18. Thomas Jefferson, "Memoranda of Consultations with the President," 12 March 1792, in *Papers of Thomas Jefferson*, 23:260; and Thomas Jefferson to DeWitt Clinton, 24 November 1816, in *The Papers of Thomas Jefferson: Retirement Series*, ed. J. Jefferson Looney (Princeton, NJ: Princeton University Press, 2004–2017), 10:546. John Adams, on the other hand, called Morris "a Man of Wit . . . but of a Character trés legere"—though this was when Morris was only twenty-seven years old. John Adams, diary entry of 22 June 1779, in *Diary and Autobiography of John Adams*, 2:390.

19. Roosevelt does register one common note of criticism, remarking that "had [Morris] possessed but a little more steadiness and self-control he would have stood among the two or three very foremost" of American statesmen. Theodore Roosevelt, *Gouverneur Morris* (Boston: Houghton, Mifflin, 1890), 363–364.

20. William Michael Treanor, "The Case of the Dishonest Scrivener: Gouverneur Morris and the Creation of the Federalist Constitution," *Michigan Law Review* 120, no. 1 (2021), 10.

21. See William Howard Adams, *Gouverneur Morris: An Independent Life* (New Haven, CT: Yale University Press, 2003); Brookhiser, *Gentleman Revolutionary*; James J. Kirschke, *Gouverneur Morris: Author, Statesman, and Man of the World* (New York: St. Martin's Press, 2005); Melanie Randolph Miller, *An Incautious Man: The Life of Gouverneur Morris* (Wilmington, DE: Intercollegiate Studies Institute, 2008); *To Secure the Blessings of Liberty: Selected Writings of Gouverneur Morris*, ed. J. Jackson Barlow (Indianapolis: Liberty Fund, 2012); *The Diaries of Gouverneur Morris: European Travels, 1794–1798*, ed. Melanie Randolph Miller (Charlottesville: University of Virginia Press, 2011); and *The Diaries of Gouverneur Morris: New York, 1799–1816*, ed. Melanie Randolph Miller (Charlottesville: University of Virginia Press, 2018).

22. See Gary L. Gregg II and Mark David Hall, eds., *America's Forgotten Founders*, 2nd ed. (Wilmington, DE: Intercollegiate Studies Institute, 2012), 167.

23. See, for instance, Adams, *Gouverneur Morris*, xi–xvi; Richard Brookhiser, "The Forgotten Founding Father," *City Journal* (Spring 2002), 74–83; Melanie Randolph Miller, *Envoy to the Terror: Gouverneur Morris and the French Revolution* (Dulles, VA: Potomac Books, 2005), 239–243; and Miller, *An Incautious Man*, xii–xvi.

24. See Barlow, ed., *To Secure the Blessings of Liberty*.

25. Nichols, "Gouverneur Morris and the Creation of American Constitutionalism," 254.

26. Miller, *An Incautious Man*, xv.

27. Dennis C. Rasmussen, *Fears of a Setting Sun: The Disillusionment of America's Founders* (Princeton, NJ: Princeton University Press, 2021).

28. See, for instance, Thomas Jefferson, "Solemn Declaration and Protest of the Commonwealth of Virginia," 24 December 1825, in *FO*; Thomas Jefferson to William Branch Giles, 26 December 1825, in *FO*; and Thomas Jefferson to William Gordon, 1 January 1826, in *FO*. For discussion, see Rasmussen, *Fears of a Setting Sun*, 189–191.

29. This pattern began with the first biography of Morris, published in 1832 by Jared Sparks, which devoted a mere ten pages out of three full volumes to Morris's role at the Philadelphia Convention. Sparks's volumes were published before Madison's records of the Convention, and as a result he had very little material to draw on: "As there is not a note or memorandum among his papers, indicating his acts in the Convention," Sparks lamented, "very little can be said on that subject." Sparks 1:282. See also Jared Sparks to James Madison, 14 November 1831, in *FO*; and Jared Sparks to James Madison, 17 January 1832, in *FO*. For the fullest account of Morris's actions in Philadelphia among the modern biographies, see Kirschke, *Gouverneur Morris*, chap. 5.

30. See Arthur Paul Kaufman, "The Constitutional Views of Gouverneur Morris" (PhD diss., Georgetown University, 1992); Christopher Bissex, "Institutionalizing Class Conflict: Gouverneur Morris on Mediating Class Warfare through Separation of Powers" (PhD diss., Baylor University, 2014); and Treanor, "Dishonest Scrivener." Even Kaufman's "The Constitutional Views of Gouverneur Morris," despite its title, devotes only one of its five parts to Morris's contributions to the framing of the US Constitution, with the other four devoted to one of Morris's early unpublished essays, his views on the necessity of American independence, his contributions to the framing of the New York state constitution, and his assessment of the Articles of Confederation. Two excellent shorter studies are John Patrick Coby, "America's Machiavellian: Gouverneur Morris at the Constitutional Convention," *Review of Politics* 79, no. 4 (Fall 2017), 621–648; and Nichols, "Gouverneur Morris and the Creation of American Constitutionalism."

31. Treanor describes Morris's constitutional vision as "an almost unexamined topic" that "has received almost no scholarly attention." Treanor, "Dishonest Scrivener," 6, 27.

32. Will Wilkinson, "The Fun-Loving Founding Father: Gouverneur Morris, the First Modern American," *Reason* (July 2004), 59–63. David Nichols writes that "in his later years Morris despaired that the Jeffersonians were undermining his handiwork, but after more than two hundred years it is his vision much more than Jefferson's that is reflected in the contemporary United States." Nichols, "Gouverneur Morris and the Creation of American Constitutionalism," 258.

CHAPTER 1. THE PENMAN'S STORY: A BRIEF BIOGRAPHY

1. On the uncertainty over Morris's birthdate, see Melanie Randolph Miller, editor's note in *The Diaries of Gouverneur Morris: New York, 1799–1816* (Charlottesville: University of Virginia Press, 2018), lxxi.

2. J. Jackson Barlow, editor's introduction, *Writings*, ix.

3. See William Howard Adams, *Gouverneur Morris: An Independent Life* (New Haven, CT: Yale University Press, 2003), 298n21; and Abigail Adams to Mary Smith Cranch, 8 June 1798, in *FO*.

4. For a fuller description of Morrisania and its whereabouts, see Max M. Mintz, *Gouverneur Morris and the American Revolution* (Norman: University of Oklahoma Press, 1970), 6–7.

5. See Adams, *Gouverneur Morris*, 11–12, 75–76.

6. On the (mostly Greek and Latin) texts that Morris would have read at King's, see James J. Kirschke, *Gouverneur Morris: Author, Statesman, and Man of the World* (New York: St. Martin's Press, 2005), 7–10.

7. On Jay, see Walter Stahr, *John Jay: Founding Father* (New York: Diversion Books, 2012). On Livingston, see George Dangerfield, *Chancellor Robert R. Livingston of New York, 1746–1813* (New York: Harcourt, Brace, and Company, 1960).

8. See Gouverneur Morris, "To the Inhabitants of the Colony of New-York" (1769), in *Writings*, 1–4.

9. Mintz, *Gouverneur Morris and the American Revolution*, vii.

10. Morris recorded in his diary: "Go to Mr. Hudon's. . . . I stand for his Statue of Genl. Washington, being the humble Employment of a Manakin. This is literally taking the Advice of St. Paul to be all Things to all Men." Gouverneur Morris, diary entry of 5 June 1789, in Beatrix Cary Davenport, ed., *A Diary of the French Revolution by Gouverneur Morris, 1752–1816* (Boston: Houghton Mifflin, 1939), 1:107.

11. Theodore Roosevelt, *Gouverneur Morris* (Boston: Houghton, Mifflin and Company, 1890), 108–109.

12. On Morris's role in the Revolutionary War, see Mintz, *Gouverneur Morris and the American Revolution*; and Mary-Jo Kline, *Gouverneur Morris and the New Nation, 1775–1788* (New York: Arno Press, 1978).

13. One biographer who was somewhat hostile to Morris went so far as to call him an "incorrigible Tory." See Daniel Walther, *Gouverneur Morris: Witness of Two Revolutions*, trans. Elinore Denniston (New York: Funk and Wagnalls, 1934), v.

14. See, for instance, Gouverneur Morris, "Oration on the Necessity for Declaring Independence from Britain" (1776), in *Writings*, 13–24.

15. On the Morris-Washington relationship, see Mary-Jo Kline, "Gouverneur Morris and George Washington: Prodigal Son and Patient Father," in *Sons of the Father: George Washington and His Protégés*, ed. Robert M. S. McDonald (Charlottesville: University of Virginia Press, 2013).

16. For the most detailed study of Morris's contributions to the first New York state

constitution, see Arthur Paul Kaufman, "The Constitutional Views of Gouverneur Morris" (PhD diss., Georgetown University, 1992), 176–261. Also useful is Kline, *Gouverneur Morris and the New Nation*, chap. 3. For more broadly focused studies of the formation of the constitution, see Charles Z. Lincoln, *The Constitutional History of New York* (Rochester: Lawyers Cooperative, 1906), vol. 1, chap. 2; Bernard Mason, *The Road to Independence: The Revolutionary Movement in New York, 1773–1777* (Lexington: University of Kentucky Press, 1967), esp. chap. 7; and William A. Polf, *1777: The Political Revolution and New York's First Constitution* (Albany: New York State Bicentennial Commission, 1977). For the journal of the convention, so far as one exists, see *Journals of the Provincial Congress, Provincial Convention, and Committee of Safety and Council of Safety of the State of New-York, 1775–1776–1777* (Albany: Thurlow Weed, 1842), 1:825–931.

17. Jay's comment was quoted by Morgan Lewis in a conversation with Jared Sparks in August 1831: see Mintz, *Gouverneur Morris and the American Revolution*, 75. For a fuller discussion of the clash between Morris and Jay on the question of religious liberty within the New York constitution, see Richard Brookhiser, *Gentleman Revolutionary: Gouverneur Morris, the Rake Who Wrote the Constitution* (New York: Free Press, 2003), 32–33.

18. On Morris's religious beliefs, see Gregg Frazer, "Gouverneur Morris and Theistic Rationalism in the Founding Era," in *Faith and the Founders of the American Republic*, ed. Daniel L. Dreisbach and Mark David Hall (Oxford: Oxford University Press, 2014), 203–227.

19. Gouverneur Morris, public letter to the Carlisle Commissioners, 20 June 1778, in *Writings*, 31. See also Morris's claim in his draft for a constitution for France that "religion is the only solid basis of good morals; therefore education should teach the precepts of religion, and the duties of man towards God. . . . But each one has a right to entire liberty as to religious opinions, for religion is the relation between God and man; therefore it is not within the reach of human authority." Gouverneur Morris, "Notes on the Form for a Constitution for France" (1791?), in *Writings*, 271.

20. Gouverneur Morris, 17 April 1777, in *Journals of the Provincial Congress*, 1:887.

21. See David N. Gellman, *Emancipating New York: The Politics of Slavery and Freedom, 1777–1827* (Baton Rouge: Louisiana State University Press, 2006).

22. Max Mintz writes that by the time of the framing of the New York state constitution, "Morris's political ideas had . . . taken permanent form. He was barely twenty-five, but the record of his position in the debates at Kingston clearly foreshadows the views he was to advocate in the Constitutional Convention of 1787." Mintz, *Gouverneur Morris and the American Revolution*, 72.

23. Gouverneur Morris to John Jay, 1 February 1778, in *Selected Papers of John Jay*, ed. Elizabeth M. Nuxoll (Charlottesville: University of Virginia Press, 2010–2017), 1:505.

24. See Kline, *Gouverneur Morris and the New Nation*, 105.

25. Quoted in Sparks 1:217.

26. As William Howard Adams notes, the instructions that Morris drew up for Franklin constituted "the first such directive to be sent to an American minister at a foreign post." Adams, *Gouverneur Morris*, 112. For Morris's responses to the Carlisle Commission, see Gouverneur Morris, public letters to the Carlisle Commissioners (1778), in *Writings*, 25–51.

27. John Jay to Robert R. Livingston, 16 February 1779, in *John Jay, the Making of a Revolutionary: Unpublished Papers, 1745–1780*, ed. Richard B. Morris (New York: Harper and Row, 1975), 2:557.

28. Gouverneur Morris, letter to the *Pennsylvania Packet*, 11 April 1780, in *Writings*, 148.

29. Gouverneur Morris to Nathanael Greene, 24 December 1781, in Sparks 1:239.

30. See, for instance, Gouverneur Morris, "Proposal to Congress Concerning the Management of the Government" (1778), in *Writings*, 53–65; Gouverneur Morris, "Report of the Committee on the Treasury" (1778), in *Writings*, 67–72; and Gouverneur Morris, "Some Thoughts on the Finances of America" (1778), in *Writings*, 73–85.

31. William Duer to Robert R. Livingston, 10 March 1778, quoted in Kline, "Gouverneur Morris and George Washington," 174.

32. William Churchill Houston to Phillip Schuyler, 15 May 1780, quoted in Melanie Randolph Miller, *An Incautious Man: The Life of Gouverneur Morris* (Wilmington, DE: Intercollegiate Studies Institute, 2008), 44.

33. Sparks 1:224.

34. John Jay to Robert Morris, 16 September 1780, in *Selected Papers of John Jay*, 2:250.

35. On Robert Morris, see Charles Rappleye, *Robert Morris: Financier of the American Revolution* (New York: Simon and Schuster, 2010); and Clarence L. Ver Steeg, *Robert Morris: Revolutionary Financier* (New York: Octagon Books, 1972).

36. Robert Morris to John Jay, 3 January 1783, in *Selected Papers of John Jay*, 3:300; and Robert Morris to John Jay, 4 November 1783, in *Selected Papers of John Jay*, 3:507.

37. Gouverneur Morris to John Jay, 31 March 1781, in *Selected Papers of John Jay*, 2:413.

38. Ver Steeg, *Robert Morris*, 124.

39. William Michael Treanor, "The Case of the Dishonest Scrivener: Gouverneur Morris and the Creation of the Federalist Constitution," *Michigan Law Review* 120, no. 1 (2021), 13n58.

40. On the series of events that have come to be known as the Newburgh conspiracy, see David Head, *A Crisis of Peace: George Washington, the Newburgh Conspiracy, and the Fate of the American Revolution* (New York: Pegasus Books, 2019); and Richard H. Kohn, *Eagle and Sword: The Federalists and the Creation of the Military Establishment in America, 1783–1802* (New York: Free Press, 1975), chap. 2

41. Gouverneur Morris to John Jay, 1 January 1783, in *Selected Papers of John Jay*, 3:296–297. As Richard Brookhiser comments, this letter "is among the worst things [Morris] ever wrote. How could such an admirer of George Washington have behaved so unlike him?" Brookhiser, *Gentleman Revolutionary*, 72–73.

42. Gouverneur Morris to William Hill Wells, 24 February 1815, in Sparks 3:339.

43. Treanor, "Dishonest Scrivener," 14.

44. Brookhiser comments that the essays that Hamilton, Madison, and Jay wrote for *The Federalist* "are clear, earnest, and intelligent, often ringing, but they have made their way without Morris's sparkle." Brookhiser, *Gentleman Revolutionary*, 93. Similarly, William Treanor remarks that "*The Federalist*, for all of its intellectual contributions and

historical significance, lacks the rhetorical power and eloquence that Morris could have brought to the project." Treanor, "Dishonest Scrivener," 14.

45. Gouverneur Morris to George Washington, 20 October 1787, in *The Papers of George Washington: Confederation Series*, ed. W. W. Abbot (Charlottesville: University Press of Virginia, 1992–1997), 5:400. The following year, when Washington showed some hesitance about the possibility of becoming the first president, Morris reiterated the point: "I have ever thought, and said that you *must* be the President. No other Man can *fill* that Office. No other Man can draw forth the Abilities of our Country into the various Departments of civil Life. You alone can awe the Insolence of opposing Factions, & the greater Insolence of assuming Adherents. . . . You will become the Father to more than three Millions of Children." Gouverneur Morris to George Washington, 6 December 1788, in *The Papers of George Washington: Presidential Series*, ed. Dorothy Twohig et al. (Charlottesville: University Press of Virginia, 1987–2016), 1:165–166.

46. See George Washington, diary entries of 19 and 21 November 1787, in *The Diaries of George Washington*, ed. Donald Jackson and Dorothy Twohig (Charlottesville: University Press of Virginia, 1976–1979), 5:217–218.

47. This poem is in Morris's hand on an invitation from Marshall to join him for dinner; it is unclear whether the invitation or the poem was written first. John Marshall to Gouverneur Morris, 11 June 1788, in *The Papers of John Marshall*, ed. Herbert A. Johnson (Chapel Hill: University of North Carolina Press, 1974), 1:271–272.

48. See George Washington, diary entries of 12 and 15 July 1788, in *Diaries of George Washington*, 5:360–361.

49. George Washington to Chastellux, 27 November 1788, in *Papers of George Washington: Presidential Series*, 1:131.

50. Clinton Rossiter, *1787: The Grand Convention* (New York: Macmillan, 1966), 325.

51. The best version of Morris's diary during his time in France is currently *A Diary of the French Revolution by Gouverneur Morris, 1752–1816*, ed. Beatrix Cary Davenport, 2 vols. (Boston: Houghton Mifflin, 1939), though unfortunately these volumes were edited with a heavier hand than the recent editions of his later diaries: *The Diaries of Gouverneur Morris: European Travels, 1794–1798*, ed. Melanie Randolph Miller (Charlottesville: University of Virginia Press, 2011); and *The Diaries of Gouverneur Morris: New York, 1799–1816*, ed. Melanie Randolph Miller (Charlottesville: University of Virginia Press, 2018). For a digital edition of the French diary with a new introduction and some added corrections, see https://rotunda.upress.virginia.edu/founders/GRMS.html.

52. On the importance of Morris's diary for understanding the French Revolution, see Marie-José Fassiotto, "Gouverneur Morris, peintre oublié de la Révolution française," *French Review* 62, no. 6 (May 1989), 997–1007. Theodore Roosevelt claimed that "as an American statesman [Morris] has many rivals, and not a few superiors; but as a penetrating observer and recorder of contemporary events, he stands alone among the men of his time." Roosevelt, *Gouverneur Morris*, 169.

53. Gouverneur Morris to George Washington, 12 November 1788, in *Papers of George Washington: Presidential Series*, 1:103.

54. On Morris's and Jefferson's activities in, and views of, France in 1789, during the

first phase of the Revolution, see Philipp Ziesche, "Exporting American Revolutions: Gouverneur Morris, Thomas Jefferson, and the National Struggle for Universal Rights in Revolutionary France," *Journal of the Early Republic* 26, no. 3 (Fall 2006), 419–447.

55. This was reported by William Short: see Charles J. Ingersoll, *Recollections Historical, Political, Biographical, and Social* (Philadelphia: J. B. Lippincott, 1861), 1:453.

56. Gouverneur Morris, diary entry of 12 June 1789, in *Diary of the French Revolution*, 1:xl.

57. Gouverneur Morris to George Washington, 24 January 1790, in *Papers of George Washington: Presidential Series*, 5:53–54.

58. Gouverneur Morris, diary entry of 18 September 1789, in *Diary of the French Revolution*, 1:223. Morris's report of a conversation with Lafayette earlier that summer is telling: "At Dinner I sit next to Monsr. de La Fayette who tells me I injure the Cause, for that my Sentiments are continually quoted against the good Party. I seize this Opportunity to tell him that I am opposed to the Democracy from Regard to Liberty. That I see they are going Headlong to Destruction and would fain stop them if I could. That their Views respecting this Nation are totally inconsistent with the Materials of which it is composed, and that the worst Thing which could happen would be to grant their Wishes. He tells me that he is sensible his Party are mad, and tells them so, but is not the less determined to die with them. I tell him I think it would be quite as well to bring them to their Senses and live with them." Gouverneur Morris, diary entry of 23 June 1789, in *Diary of the French Revolution*, 1:121.

59. Gouverneur Morris, diary entry of 6 June 1789, in *Diary of the French Revolution*, 1:108.

60. Gouverneur Morris to George Washington, 24 January 1790, in *Papers of George Washington: Presidential Series*, 5:51.

61. Gouverneur Morris, diary entry of 26 September 1789, in *Diary of the French Revolution*, 1:234.

62. On Flahaut and her salon, see Marie-José Fassiotto, "La Comtesse de Flahaut et son cercle: Un example de salon politique sous la Révolution," *Studies on Voltaire and the Eighteenth Century* 303 (1992), 344–348.

63. For a scholarly study of Morris's sexual exploits during his time in Europe, see Thomas Foster, "Reconsidering Libertines and Early Modern Heterosexuality: Sex and American Founder Gouverneur Morris," *Journal of the History of Sexuality*, 22, no. 1 (January 2013), 65–84.

64. See Miller, *An Incautious Man*, 97.

65. The other three were Antoine de Rivarol, Pierre Victor Malouet, and Jacques Mallet-du-Pan. See Hippolyne Taine, *Derniers essais de critique et d'histoire* (Paris: Librarie Hachette, 1894), 189.

66. Gouverneur Morris to William Carmichael, 25 February 1789, in *Diary of the French Revolution*, 1:xl. Morris later read Burke's *Reflections* as well as Thomas Paine's response to Burke in *Rights of Man* and commented in his diary, "there are good Things in the Answer [i.e., Paine] as well as in the Book [i.e., Burke]." Gouverneur Morris, diary entry of 8 April 1791, in *A Diary of the French Revolution*, 2:156.

67. Gouverneur Morris to George Washington, 29 April 1789, in *Papers of George Washington: Presidential Series*, 2:146.

68. Gouverneur Morris to William Carmichael, 10 July 1789, in Sparks 2:75.

69. See Gouverneur Morris, "Observations on Government, Applicable to the Political State of France" (1789), in *Writings*, 231–238.

70. For the fullest elaboration of Morris's vision for a French constitution, see Gouverneur Morris, "Notes on the Form for a Constitution for France" (1791?), in *Writings*, 269–284.

71. Gouverneur Morris to George Washington, 30 September 1791, in *Papers of George Washington: Presidential Series*, 9:32; and Gouverneur Morris to George Washington, 27 December 1791, in *Papers of George Washington: Presidential Series*, 9:335.

72. See Gouverneur Morris, "Memoir Written for the King of France, Respecting the New Constitution" (1791), in *Writings*, 239–250; and Gouverneur Morris, "Observations on the New Constitution of France" (1791), in *Writings*, 251–268.

73. For background on Morris's mission, see Stanley Elkins and Eric McKitrick, *The Age of Federalism* (Oxford: Oxford University Press, 1993), 212–223.

74. Julian Boyd argues that Morris's standing in London was also undermined by some backroom machinations by Alexander Hamilton: see Julian P. Boyd, *Number 7: Alexander Hamilton's Secret Attempts to Control American Foreign Policy* (Princeton, NJ: Princeton University Press, 1964), chaps. 2 and 6.

75. Gouverneur Morris to John Parish, 20 January 1801, in Sparks 3:146, 145.

76. On Morris's service as the minister to France, see Adhémar Esmein, *Gouverneur Morris: Un témoin américain de la Révolution francaise* (Parise: Hachette, 1906); Jean-Jacques Fiechter, *Un diplomate américain sous la Terreur: Les années européennes de Gouverneur Morris, 1789–1798* (Paris: Fayard, 1983); Melanie Randolph Miller, *Envoy to the Terror: Gouverneur Morris and the French Revolution* (Dulles, VA: Potomac Books, 2005); and Serge Ricard, "Memoir of a Republican Royalist: Gouverneur Morris, Chronicler and Actor of the French Revolution," *Canadian Review of American Studies* 47, no. 3 (2017), 353–372.

77. Sherman's speech was recorded by Rufus King: see *The Life and Correspondence of Rufus King*, ed. Charles R. King (New York: G. P. Putnam's Sons, 1894), 1:420.

78. George Washington to Gouverneur Morris, 28 January 1792, in *Papers of George Washington: Presidential Series*, 9:516. Many of these objections sprang from false stories that Hamilton circulated about Morris: see Boyd, *Number 7*, chaps. 2 and 6.

79. Gouverneur Morris to George Washington, 6 April 1792, in *Papers of George Washington: Presidential Series*, 10:223.

80. See Miller, *Envoy to the Terror*, 133.

81. Gouverneur Morris to George Washington, 14 February 1793, in *Papers of George Washington: Presidential Series*, 12:143.

82. Gouverneur Morris, "Oration on Europe's Deliverance from Despotism" (1814), in *Writings*, 626.

83. For the fullest account of this episode, see Miller, *Envoy to the Terror*, 147–160.

84. Gouverneur Morris to Edmund Randolph, 19 August 1794, in Sparks 2:454; and Gouverneur Morris to Robert R. Livingston, 23 April 1803, in Sparks 3:180.

85. This comment came in Washington's (often angry) marginal notes to James Monroe's public defense of his actions as minister to France. See George Washington, "Comments on Monroe's *A View of the Conduct of the Executive of the United States*," March 1798, in *The Papers of George Washington: Retirement Series*, ed. W. W. Abbot (Charlottesville: University Press of Virginia, 1998–1999), 2:196.

86. Roosevelt, *Gouverneur Morris*, 257, 364, 294. More recently, William Howard Adams has written that "more than Jefferson, Franklin, and certainly Adams, [Morris] was the most effective American in Paris." Adams, *Gouverneur Morris*, xiv.

87. Gouverneur Morris to Samuel Ogden, 2 February 1796, in Sparks 3:75. See also Gouverneur Morris to Robert Morris, 27 March 1794, in Sparks 3:49.

88. Alexander Hamilton to Rufus King, 2 October 1798, in *The Papers of Alexander Hamilton*, ed. Harold C. Syrett and Jacob Cooke (New York: Columbia University Press, 1961–1987), 22:192.

89. Robert Troup to Rufus King, 19 April 1799, in *Life and Correspondence of Rufus King*, 2:598.

90. See Gouverneur Morris to George Washington, 9 December 1799, in *Papers of George Washington: Retirement Series*, 4:452–453.

91. See Gouverneur Morris, "Oration on the Death of George Washington," 31 December 1799, in *Writings*, 293–301.

92. Gouverneur Morris to the Princess de la Tour et Taxis, 14 December 1800, in Sparks 3:130.

93. Gouverneur Morris to Alexander Hamilton, 19 December 1800, in *Papers of Alexander Hamilton*, 25:267. See also Gouverneur Morris to Robert R. Livingston, 20 February 1801, in Sparks 3:154.

94. For Jefferson's recollection of this episode, according to which Morris proposed a deal that he (Jefferson) refused to accept, see Thomas Jefferson, "Notes on Aaron Burr," 15 April 1806, in *FO*. For Morris's rather cagier recollection of the episode, see Gouverneur Morris to Timothy Pickering, 16 February 1809, in Sparks 3:249–250.

95. See Gouverneur Morris, "Letters to the New York *Evening Post* on the Louisiana Purchase" (1803), in *Writings*, 333–352.

96. Gouverneur Morris to John Parish, 14 January 1803, in Sparks 3:177.

97. Gouverneur Morris, diary entry of 6 April 1802, in *Diaries of Gouverneur Morris: New York, 1799–1816*, 224.

98. Gouverneur Morris to Alexander Hamilton, 11 March 1802, in *Papers of Alexander Hamilton*, 25:560.

99. See Gouverneur Morris, "Speeches in the Senate on the Repeal of the Judiciary Act of 1801" (8 and 14 January 1802), in *Writings*, 303–332.

100. Manasseh Cutler, diary entries of 8 January and 1 February 1802, in *Life, Journals and Correspondence of Rev. Manasseh Culter, LL.D.*, ed. William Parker Culter and Julia Perkins Cutler (Cincinnati, OH: Robert Clarke and Co., 1888), 2:59, 74.

101. Alexander Hamilton to Gouverneur Morris, 29 February 1802, in *Papers of Alexander Hamilton*, 25:545.

102. Gouverneur Morris, diary entry of 8 January 1802, in *The Diaries of Gouverneur Morris: New York, 1799–1816*, 207.

103. See Gouverneur Morris, diary entry of 3 January 1803, in *Diaries of Gouverneur Morris: New York, 1799–1816*, 263.

104. Elizabeth's comment was recorded by David Bayard Ogden, an eyewitness and one of Morris's nephews: see Melanie Miller, editor's introduction in *Diaries of Gouverneur Morris: New York, 1799–1816*, xxviii.

105. Gouverneur Morris, diary entry of 12 July 1804, in *Diaries of Gouverneur Morris: New York, 1799–1816*, 357.

106. See Gouverneur Morris, "Funeral Oration for Alexander Hamilton" (1804), in *Writings*, 353–356.

107. Gouverneur Morris to Madame de Damas, 1 December 1809, in Sparks 1:494.

108. On the development of Manhattan's grid layout and Morris's contributions to it, see Gerard Koeppel, *City on a Grid: How New York Became New York* (Boston: Da Capo, 2015).

109. Gouverneur Morris to John Parish, 20 January 1801, in Sparks 3:144.

110. Gouverneur Morris to Russell Atwater, 21 February 1816, in Sparks 3:347.

111. On the planning and construction of the canal, see Peter L. Bernstein, *Wedding of the Waters: The Erie Canal and the Making of a Great Nation* (New York: W. W. Norton, 2005); and Gerard Koeppel, *Bond of Union: Building the Erie Canal and the American Empire* (Cambridge, MA: Da Capo, 2009).

112. For the full story of Nancy Randolph's life, see Alan Pell Crawford, *Unwise Passions: A True Story of a Remarkable Woman—and the First Great Scandal of Eighteenth-Century America* (New York: Simon & Schuster, 2000).

113. On the alleged scandal of Nancy Randolph's youth, see Cynthia A. Kierner, *Scandal at Bizarre: Rumor and Reputation in Jefferson's America* (New York: Palgrave Macmillan, 2004).

114. Gouverneur Morris, diary entry of 25 December 1809, in *Diaries of Gouverneur Morris: New York, 1799–1816*, 622.

115. Gouverneur Morris to Gertrude Meredith, 10 January 1810, in *The Diary and Letters of Gouverneur Morris*, ed. Anne Cary Morris (New York: Charles Scribner's Sons, 1888), 2:516.

116. Gouverneur Morris to John Parish, 6 July 1816, in Sparks 1:495.

117. Gouverneur Morris to John Parish, 6 July 1816, in Sparks 1:495.

118. See Rufus King to Christopher Gore , 5 November 1816, in *Life and Correspondence of Rufus King*, 6:35.

CHAPTER 2. A MOST SPLENDID PART: MORRIS AT THE CONVENTION

1. General accounts of the Convention's proceedings are legion, but see, among others, Richard Beeman, *Plain, Honest Men: The Making of the American Constitution* (New

York: Random House, 2009); Carol Berkin, *A Brilliant Solution: Inventing the American Constitution* (Boston: Mariner Books, 2003); Catherine Drinker Bowen, *Miracle at Philadelphia: The Story of the Constitutional Convention, May to September 1787* (Boston: Little, Brown, 1966); Christopher Collier and James Lincoln Collier, *Decision in Philadelphia: The Constitutional Convention of 1787* (New York: Ballantine Books, 1986); Michael J. Klarman, *The Framers' Coup: The Making of the United States Constitution* (Oxford: Oxford University Press, 2016); Clinton Rossiter, *1787: The Grand Convention* (New York: Macmillan, 1966); and David O. Stewart, *The Summer of 1787: The Men Who Invented the Constitution* (New York: Simon & Schuster, 2007).

2. Gouverneur Morris, "Speech in the Senate on the Repeal of the Judiciary Act of 1801," 8 January 1802, in *Writings*, 311.

3. James Madison, 26 June: *Debates*, 146; *Records* 1:423.

4. Alexander Hamilton, 26 June: *Debates*, 146; *Records* 1:424.

5. Rufus King, 30 June: *Debates*, 173; *Records* 1:490.

6. James Wilson, 25 June: *Debates*, 140; *Records* 1:405.

7. Gouverneur Morris, 5 July: *Debates*, 185; *Records* 1:529.

8. James Madison to Jared Sparks, 8 April 1831, in *FO*; and John Marshall, *The Life of George Washington* (Philadelphia: C. P. Wayne, 1807), 5:134.

9. Theodore Roosevelt, *Gouverneur Morris* (Boston: Houghton, Mifflin and Company, 1890), v; and Henry Cabot Lodge, "Gouverneur Morris," in *Historical and Political Essays* (Boston: Houghton, Mifflin, and Company, [1886] 1892), 83.

10. Max Farrand, *The Framing of the Constitution of the United States* (New Haven, CT: Yale University Press, 1913), 21. For a similar, slightly later statement, see Max Farrand, *The Fathers of the Constitution: A Chronicle of the Establishment of the Union* (New Haven, CT: Yale University Press, 1921), 112.

11. See Rossiter, *1787*, 247.

12. On Wilson's role at the Convention, see George W. Carey, "James Wilson's Political Thought and the Constitutional Convention," *Political Science Reviewer* 17 (1987), 49–107; and William Ewald, "James Wilson and the Drafting of the Constitution," *University of Pennsylvania Journal of Constitutional Law* 10 (June 2008), 901–1009. On the positions that Washington took at the Convention, so far as we can know them, see Glenn A. Phelps, *George Washington and American Constitutionalism* (Lawrence: University Press of Kansas, 1993), esp. 99–111.

13. Rossiter, *1787*, 248.

14. Gouverneur Morris to Henry Knox, 9 January 1787, quoted in Max M. Mintz, *Gouverneur Morris and the American Revolution* (Norman: University of Oklahoma Press, 1970), 177.

15. Quoted in Melanie Randolph Miller, *An Incautious Man: The Life of Gouverneur Morris* (Wilmington, DE: Intercollegiate Studies Institute, 2008), 61.

16. See John R. Vile, "Lodging of the Delegates," in *The Constitutional Convention of 1787: A Comprehensive Encyclopedia of America's Founding* (Santa Barbara, CA: ABC-CLIO, 2005), 1:424.

17. See Beeman, *Plain, Honest Men*, 64.

18. Thomas Jefferson to John Adams, 30 August 1787, in *The Papers of Thomas Jefferson*, ed. Julian P. Boyd et al. (Princeton, NJ: Princeton University Press, 1950–2017), 12:69; and James Madison, *Federalist #37*, 11 January 1788, in Alexander Hamilton, John Jay, and James Madison, *The Federalist*, ed. George W. Carey and James McClellan (Indianapolis: Liberty Fund, 2001), 185.

19. Jared Sparks quotes this letter "to a gentleman in France" that Morris wrote during his time in Virginia, but he gives neither the correspondent's name nor the letter's date. See Sparks 1:290–291.

20. See Beeman, *Plain, Honest Men*, 52–54.

21. This line was included in a draft version of William Michael Treanor, "The Case of the Dishonest Scrivener: Gouverneur Morris and the Creation of the Federalist Constitution," *Michigan Law Review* 120, no. 1 (2021). Although the wording was removed in the final version, Treanor stands by the claim (personal correspondence with author).

22. See Mintz, *Gouverneur Morris and the American Revolution*, 174, 185.

23. Roger Sherman, 2 July: *Debates*, 178; *Records* 1:511.

24. Gouverneur Morris, 2 July: *Debates*, 178–180; *Records* 1:511–514.

25. On the Independence Day celebration, see Beeman, *Plain, Honest Men*, 190–193.

26. On the Committee of Detail, see William Ewald, "The Committee of Detail," *Constitutional Commentary* 28, no. 2 (Fall 2012), 197–285.

27. See George Washington, diary entries of 30–31 July 1787, in *The Diaries of George Washington*, ed. Donald Jackson and Dorothy Twohig (Charlottesville: University Press of Virginia, 1976–1979), 5:178–179; and George Washington to Elizabeth Powel, 30 July 1787, in *The Papers of George Washington: Confederation Series*, ed. W. W. Abbot (Charlottesville: University Press of Virginia, 1992–1997), 5:280.

28. See George Washington, diary entries of 3–5 August 1787, in *Diaries of George Washington* 5:180.

29. Randolph and Wilson both had a higher percentage of their motions pass than Morris—72 percent and 58 percent, respectively, compared to Morris's 56 percent—but each of them still had four fewer motions pass than he did. On the number of motions made and passed, see Keith L. Dougherty and Jac C. Heckelman, "A Pivotal Voter from a Pivotal State: Roger Sherman at the Constitutional Convention," *American Political Science Review* 100, no. 2 (May 2006), 300.

30. On the crucial decisions that were made by committees throughout the Convention, see John R. Vile, "The Critical Role of Committees at the U.S. Constitutional Convention of 1787," *American Journal of Legal History* 48, no. 2 (April 2006), 147–176.

31. William Pierce, "Characters in the Convention of the States Held at Philadelphia, May 1787," in *American Historical Review* 2, no. 3 (January 1898), 331, 327, 326.

32. Pierce, "Characters in the Convention," 329.

33. James Madison to Jared Sparks, 8 April 1831, in *FO*; and James Madison, "Explanations in Regard to His Report of Hamilton's and Morris's Speeches in the Federal Convention," 27 September 1834, in Henry S. Randall, *The Life of Thomas Jefferson* (New York: Derby and Jackson, 1858), 3:595.

34. Stewart, *Summer of 1787*, 35–36, 187; and Richard Brookhiser, *Gentleman Revolutionary: Gouverneur Morris, the Rake Who Wrote the Constitution* (New York: Free Press, 2003), 80.

35. James Madison to Jared Sparks, 8 April 1831, in *FO*.

36. Gouverneur Morris, 20 July: *Debates*, 267; *Records* 2:68.

37. William Paterson and Gouverneur Morris, 7 July: *Debates*, 197–198; *Records* 1:551.

38. Gouverneur Morris to Timothy Pickering, 22 December 1814, in Sparks 3:322.

39. David Nichols argues that "Morris always kept his ultimate goals in mind, changing positions on particular issues in light of how those decisions would fit into a larger whole. Particularly in the debate on the presidency but also throughout the Convention, Morris in debate is like the master of a complex Rubik's cube. His positions appear random only to those who have no conception of the whole he envisions." David K. Nichols, "Gouverneur Morris and the Creation of American Constitutionalism," in *Natural Right and Political Philosophy: Essays in Honor of Catherine Zuckert and Michael Zuckert*, ed. Ann Ward and Lee Ward (Notre Dame, IN: University of Notre Dame Press, 2013), 253–254.

40. For Morris's invocation of the Spartan ephors, see Gouverneur Morris, 15 August: *Debates*, 376; *Records* 2:299. For the Aulic Council, see Gouverneur Morris, 7 July: *Debates*, 199; *Records* 1:553. For the German Diet, see Gouverneur Morris, 7 July: *Debates*, 198; *Records* 1:552. For the Polish Diet, see Gouverneur Morris, 17 July: *Debates*, 243; *Records* 2:31. For the book of Ecclesiastes, see Gouverneur Morris, 26 July: *Debates*, 300; *Records* 2:122. For King Rehoboam, see Gouverneur Morris, 25 July: *Debates*, 294; *Records* 2:113.

41. Gouverneur Morris to George Washington, 24 January 1790, in *The Papers of George Washington: Presidential Series*, ed. Dorothy Twohig et al. (Charlottesville: University Press of Virginia, 1987–2016), 5:50.

42. Gouverneur Morris, diary entry of 9 November 1790, in Beatrix Cary Davenport, ed., *A Diary of the French Revolution by Gouverneur Morris, 1752–1816* (Boston: Houghton Mifflin, 1939), 2:54.

43. See Gouverneur Morris, "Political Enquiries" (1776), in *Writings*, 5–11.

44. Benjamin Franklin and Gouverneur Morris, 26 July: *Debates*, 298: *Records* 2:120.

45. Elbridge Gerry and Gouverneur Morris, 7 September: *Debates*, 493–494; *Records* 2:536–537.

46. Gouverneur Morris, 9 August: *Debates*, 340; *Records* 2:238.

47. This version of the story comes in a nineteenth-century biography of Jefferson, whose author claimed that it passed from Hamilton to John Fine, a member of the House of Representatives from New York, and then from him to Martin Van Buren. See James Parton, *Life of Thomas Jefferson* (Boston: James R. Osgood and Company, 1874), 369. For another, slightly different version of the story from a few years earlier, see William Thompson Read, *Life and Correspondence of George Read, A Signer of the Declaration of Independence* (Philadelphia: J. B. Lippincott, 1870), 29.

48. For Jackson's descriptions of the committee, see *Records* 2:547, 581, 582, 610. For Madison's, see *Debates*, 504, 511, 528, 529, 530; *Records* 2:553, 581, 585, 607, 608, 612. For

McHenry's, see *Records* 2:554. For Pinckney's, see Charles Pinckney, 10 September: *Debates*, 511; *Records* 2:564.

49. See Mary Sarah Bilder, "How Bad Were the Official Records of the Federal Convention?" *George Washington Law Review* 80, no. 6 (November 2012), 1648.

50. See *Debates*, 504; *Records* 2:553. Although we lack hard evidence, it appears that the members of most of the committees at the Convention—the various "committees of eleven," which included one member from each state—were chosen by the state delegations, with each delegation selecting its own committee member. However, for the two most important committees, the Committee of Detail and the Committee of Style, each of which consisted of five members, the members were instead chosen by individual ballots of the whole house. See David O. Stewart, "Who Picked the Committees at the Constitutional Convention?" *Journal of the American Revolution*, 13 September 2018.

51. This imbalance is noted in Stewart, *Summer of 1787*, 229–230; and Treanor, "Dishonest Scrivener", 8–9.

52. For the Committee of Detail's drafts, see *Records* 2:129–175.

53. Jared Sparks to James Madison, 30 March 1831, in *FO*.

54. James Madison to Jared Sparks, 8 April 1831, in *FO*.

55. Gouverneur Morris to Timothy Pickering, 22 December 1814, in Sparks 3:323. While the letters of Sparks, Madison, and Morris all point toward Morris's sole authorship, there is one (somewhat dubious) piece of evidence suggesting that James Wilson also played an important role. In a diary entry from December 21, 1787, Ezra Stiles recorded that "a Committee of 5 viz. Mess. Dr. Johnson, Governeur Morris, Wilson . . . reduced it [i.e., the Constitution] to the form in which it was published. Messrs Morris & Wilson had the chief hand in the last Arrang[emen]t & Composition." Ezra Stiles, *The Literary Diary of Ezra Stiles*, ed. Franklin Bowditch Dexter (New York: Charles Scribner's Sons, 1901), 3:295. Yet this is a secondhand report of a claim by Abraham Baldwin of Georgia, who was not on the committee (as Madison and Morris were), and its other basic claim is clearly inaccurate: it only includes three of the five committee members, and one of the figures listed (Wilson) is incorrect. The associated claim that Wilson played a substantial role in penning the Constitution therefore seems rather doubtful.

56. Some of these suggestions follow those of Treanor, "Dishonest Scrivener," 13–14.

57. Brookhiser, *Gentleman Revolutionary*, xv.

58. For the Committee of Style's report, see *Debates*, 512–522; *Records* 2:590–603. For a photographic reproduction of the broadside copy that was distributed to the delegates, see http://treasures.constitutioncenter.org/index.php/document/04-committee-of-style-report/.

59. For Max Farrand's compilation of the Convention's proceedings as they were referred to the Committee of Style, see *Records* 2:565–580.

60. Gouverneur Morris to Timothy Pickering, 22 December 1814, in Sparks 3:323. In another letter Morris noted that "it has been said, that our Constitution is remarkable for the perspicuity of its language"—without noting that he was responsible for much of that language. Gouverneur Morris to Robert Walsh, 5 February 1811, in Sparks 3:267.

61. Joseph J. Ellis, *The Quartet: Orchestrating the Second American Revolution, 1783–1789* (New York: Alfred A. Knopf, 2015), 151.

62. *Debates*, 308; *Records* 2:177.

63. *Debates*, 512; *Records* 2:590.

64. See *Debates*, 522; *Records* 2:583–584.

65. See *Debates*, 511; *Records* 2:583n, 585.

66. See Daniel A. Farber, "The Constitution's Forgotten Cover Letter: An Essay on the New Federalism and the Original Understanding," *Michigan Law Review* 94, no. 3 (December 1995), 615–650.

67. Madison records no discussion of the letter at all. William Jackson, the Convention's secretary, reports that on September 12 the letter "was read once throughout, and afterwards agreed to by paragraphs." *Records* 2:582.

68. Treanor, "Dishonest Scrivener."

69. 4 September: *Debates*, 473, 475; *Records* 2:497, 499.

70. Entry for 19 June 1798, in *Annals of the Congress of the United States: Fifth Congress* (Washington: Gales and Seaton, 1851), 1976.

71. Entry for 19 June 1798, in *Annals of the Congress of the United States: Fifth Congress*, 1976.

72. James Madison, "Memorandum not used in letter to Mr Stevenson," 27 November 1830, in *FO*.

73. James McHenry, 6 September: *Records* 2:529–530.

74. See also the discussion in Treanor, "Dishonest Scrivener," 21–24.

75. Gouverneur Morris to Timothy Pickering, 22 December 1814, in Sparks 3:323.

76. For the Committee of Detail's version of the judicial vesting clause, see *Debates*, 316; *Records* 2:186. For Morris's version, see *Debates*, 520; *Records* 2:600.

77. See also the discussion in Treanor, "Dishonest Scrivener," 89–93.

78. See Gouverneur Morris, 18 July: *Debates*, 253; *Records* 2:46.

79. Gouverneur Morris, "Speech in the Senate on the Repeal of the Judiciary Act of 1801," 14 January 1802, in *Writings*, 317.

80. Gouverneur Morris to Henry W. Livingston, 4 December 1803, in Sparks 3:192.

81. See *Debates*, 521; *Records* 2:602.

82. For the addition of the territories clause, see 30 August: *Debates*, 460–461; *Records* 2:466. For the Committee of Detail's stipulation, see *Debates*, 318; *Records* 2:188. For the striking down of this stipulation, see 29 August: *Debates*, 454–455; *Records* 2:454.

83. When the Louisiana Purchase was completed, Morris publicly suggested that "having purchased and paid for the country, we ought to have the right of governing it in the manner most suitable to our interest. It may, perhaps, be most convenient to hold *as colonies* those districts which from time to time we may deem it expedient to settle; but whether it be or not, we should have the sovereign right to give or to withhold a participation in our *national councils*. It is a strange policy to call in Frenchmen, Spaniards, and Indians, (for they also are inhabitants of the ceded territory) to decide on our highest concerns." Gouverneur Morris, "Letters to the New York *Evening Post* on the

Louisiana Purchase" (1803), in *Writings*, 351. See also Gouverneur Morris to Jonathan Dayton, 7 January 1804, in Sparks 3:203–204.

84. See also the discussions in Vasan Kesavan and Michael Stokes Paulsen, "Is West Virginia Unconstitutional?" *California Law Review* 90, no. 2 (March 2002), 392–395; and Treanor, "Dishonest Scrivener," 99–102.

85. Treanor, "Dishonest Scrivener," 118.

86. See *Debates*, 511; *Records* 2:582, 585.

87. See, respectively, *Debates* 525, 528 and 538–540, 532, 540, 543, 544, 548; *Records* 2:587, 607 and 624–626, 614, 626, 630, 631, 644.

88. See *Debates*, 546; *Records* 2:633.

89. See William Howard Adams, *Gouverneur Morris: An Independent Life* (New Haven, CT: Yale University Press, 2003), 164; and Beeman, *Plain, Honest Men*, 360.

90. Benjamin Franklin, 17 September: *Debates*, 547; *Records* 2:643.

91. *Debates*, 547; *Records* 2:643. Slightly later, when Edmund Randolph announced his refusal to sign the Constitution, Morris reiterated that "the signing, in the form proposed, related only to the fact that *the States* present were unanimous." Gouverneur Morris, 17 September: *Debates*, 549; *Records* 2:645.

92. On Morris's "Machiavellianism" at the Convention more generally, see John Patrick Coby, "America's Machiavellian: Gouverneur Morris at the Constitutional Convention," *Review of Politics* 79, no. 4 (Fall 2017), 621–648.

93. William Blount, 17 September: *Debates*, 549; *Records* 2:646.

94. Edmund Randolph and Elbridge Gerry, 17 September: *Debates*, 550; *Records* 2:646–647.

95. Charles Cotesworth Pinckney, 17 September: *Debates*, 551; *Records* 2:647.

96. See John R. Vile, "Signing of the Constitution," in *Constitutional Convention of 1787*, 2:721.

97. George Washington, diary entry 18 September 1787, in *Diaries of George Washington* 5:186.

98. Jackson's journal has long been the subject of derision. For an attempt to (at least partially) rehabilitate its reputation, see Bilder, "How Bad Were the Official Records of the Federal Convention?"

99. On the reliability of the various notes taken at the Convention, see James H. Hutson, "The Creation of the Constitution: The Integrity of the Documentary Record," *Texas Law Review* 65 (November 1986), 1–39.

100. Gouverneur Morris to Timothy Pickering, 22 December 1814, in Sparks 3:322.

101. Gouverneur Morris to Henry W. Livingston, 25 November 1803, in Sparks 3:185.

102. On Madison's revisions, see Mary Sarah Bilder, *Madison's Hand: Revising the Constitutional Convention* (Cambridge, MA: Harvard University Press, 2015), though Bilder's claims should be tempered by Jack Rakove, "A Biography of Madison's Notes of Debates," *Constitutional Commentary* 23 (2016), 317–349.

103. However, for a discussion of some minor shifts in emphasis in Madison's records of a few of Morris's comments, see Bilder, *Madison's Hand*, 194–195.

104. James Madison, "Origin of the Constitutional Convention," ca. 1835, in *FO*.

105. Madison, "Origin of the Constitutional Convention."

106. James Madison, "Explanations in Regard to His Report of Hamilton's and Morris's Speeches in the Federal Convention," 27 September 1834, in Randall, *Life of Thomas Jefferson*, 3:595.

CHAPTER 3. A REPRESENTATIVE OF AMERICA: FEDERALISM

1. On the government produced by the Articles, see George William Van Cleve, *We Have Not a Government: The Articles of Confederation and the Road to the Constitution* (Chicago: University of Chicago Press, 2017).

2. Forrest McDonald counts among "those whose nationalism was undiluted or nearly so" George Clymer, Thomas Fitzsimons, Nathaniel Gorham, Alexander Hamilton, Rufus King, Gouverneur Morris, Robert Morris, George Read, George Washington, James Wilson, "probably" William Davie and Benjamin Franklin, "perhaps" William Pierce, and "in several respects" James Madison and Charles Pinckney. Forrest McDonald, *Novus Ordo Seclorum: The Intellectual Origins of the Constitution* (Lawrence: University Press of Kansas, 1985), 186–187.

3. Alexander Hamilton, 18 June: *Records* 1:297. This quotation comes from the version of the speech recorded by Hamilton's New York colleague Robert Yates. Madison's version has Hamilton proclaiming that "the General power, whatever be its form, if it preserves itself, must swallow up the state powers. Otherwise, it will be swallowed up by them. . . . If [the state governments] were extinguished, he was persuaded that great economy might be obtained by substituting a General Government. He did not mean, however, to shock the public opinion by proposing such a measure. On the other hand, he saw no *other* necessity for declining it. They are not necessary for any of the great purposes of commerce, revenue, or agriculture." Alexander Hamilton, 18 June: *Debates*, 96–97; *Records* 1:287. These comments apparently caused a stir, for the next day Hamilton tried to correct a potential misunderstanding: he had not meant to suggest that the states should be entirely *abolished*, he now insisted—only reduced to insignificance. The federal government must have "indefinite authority," since "if it were limited at all, the rivalship of the States would gradually subvert it." The states could remain as "subordinate jurisdictions," as long as they remained essentially toothless. Alexander Hamilton, 19 June: *Debates*, 109; *Records* 1:323. For an older but still very useful study of Hamilton's role at the Convention, see Clinton Rossiter, *Alexander Hamilton and the Constitution* (New York: Harcourt, Brace and World, 1964), esp. chap. 2.

4. John C. Hamilton, *Life of Alexander Hamilton* (Boston: Houghton, Osgood and Company, 1879), 3:284.

5. George Read, 11 June: *Debates*, 70–71; *Records* 1:202. For similar statements, see George Read, 6 June: *Debates*, 48; *Records* 1:136, 143; and 29 June: *Debates*, 161; *Records* 1:463, 471.

6. Pierce Butler, 6 June: *Records* 1:144.

7. On the nationalism of Morris and Wilson, and for an argument that their visions taken together constitute a "lost Constitution" that stands as a challenge to recent interpretive trends, see Jonathan Gienapp, "The Lost Constitution: How a Transformative Vision of Sovereignty and National Power was Embedded in the American Constitution, and Then Forgotten" (unpublished manuscript, July 10, 2021), Microsoft Word file. I am grateful to Gienapp for sharing his essay with me prior to publication.

8. Richard Brookhiser similarly writes that "Morris was a passionate nationalist. . . . There were other nationalists at the Convention: Madison; Wilson; Hamilton, when he chose to speak; Washington, though he hardly spoke at all. None were as rhapsodic as Morris." Richard Brookhiser, *Gentleman Revolutionary: Gouverneur Morris, the Rake Who Wrote the Constitution* (New York: Free Press, 2003), 84.

9. Gouverneur Morris, 5 July: *Debates*, 186, 185; *Records* 1:530, 529.

10. Gouverneur Morris, 5 July: *Debates*, 185; *Records* 1:529.

11. Gouverneur Morris, 7 July: *Debates*, 198; *Records* 1:552.

12. Quoted in William Howard Adams, *Gouverneur Morris: An Independent Life* (New Haven, CT: Yale University Press, 2003), 50.

13. See Gouverneur Morris, "Oration on the Necessity for Declaring Independence from Britain" (1776), in *Writings*, 21–22.

14. See, for instance, Gouverneur Morris, "Proposal to Congress Concerning the Management of the Government" (1778), in *Writings*, 53–65; Gouverneur Morris, "Report of the Committee on the Treasury" (1778), in *Writings*, 67–72; and Gouverneur Morris, "Some Thoughts on the Finances of America" (1778), in *Writings*, 73–85.

15. Morris, "Some Thoughts on the Finances of America" (1778), in *Writings*, 74.

16. See Gouverneur Morris, public letters to the Carlisle Commissioners (1778), in *Writings*, 33, 37, 44. Other pseudonyms that Morris used—though not nearly as frequently as "An American"—included "A Citizen" and "An Observer." See Gouverneur Morris, "Righteousness Establisheth a Nation" (1780), in *Writings*, 170; and Gouverneur Morris, "Essays for the Examiner" (1814), in *Writings*, 605, 608, 615, 622.

17. See Gouverneur Morris, "To the Bank Directors of New-York" (1816), in *Writings*, 660.

18. Gouverneur Morris to John Jay, 10 January 1784, in *Selected Papers of John Jay*, ed. Elizabeth M. Nuxoll (Charlottesville: University of Virginia Press, 2010–2017), 3:542.

19. Gouverneur Morris to Robert Walsh, 5 February 1811, in Sparks 3:261.

20. See Edmund Randolph, 29 May: *Debates*, 9; *Records* 1:21.

21. Richard Beeman, *Plain, Honest Men: The Making of the American Constitution* (New York: Random House, 2009), chap. 3.

22. Edmund Randolph, 29 May: *Debates*, 7–8; *Records* 1:20.

23. Gouverneur Morris, 30 May: *Records* 1:38.

24. Edmund Randolph, 30 May: *Debates*, 11; *Records* 1:33.

25. Gouverneur Morris, 30 May: *Debates*, 11; *Records* 1:34.

26. Gouverneur Morris, 30 May: *Records* 1:43.

27. 30 May: *Debates*, 12; *Records* 1:35.

28. 20 June: *Debates*, 111; *Records* 1:336.

29. See *Debates*, 562; *Records* 2:663.

30. *Debates*, 522; *Records* 2:584.

31. See George Read, 6 June: *Records* 1:143; and Rufus King, 19 June: *Debates*, 109; *Records* 1:323, 328. James Madison also commented favorably about the prospect of the states being "more . . . consolidated into one nation," at least with respect to military defense. James Madison, 23 August: *Debates*, 421; *Records* 2:387.

32. On the nationalist implications of this "cover letter," see Daniel A. Farber, "The Constitution's Forgotten Cover Letter: An Essay on the New Federalism and the Original Understanding," *Michigan Law Review* 94, no. 3 (December 1995), 615–650.

33. For a recent history of, and spirited attack on, this concept of sovereignty, see Don Herzog, *Sovereignty, RIP* (New Haven, CT: Yale University Press, 2020).

34. Gouverneur Morris, 20 July: *Debates*, 267; *Records* 2:69; and 23 July: *Debates*, 281; *Records* 2:92. Later, while serving as minister to France, Morris declared that "the Corner Stone of our own Constitution is the Right of the People to establish such Government as they think proper." Gouverneur Morris to William Short, 20 September 1792, in *The Papers of Alexander Hamilton*, ed. Harold C. Syrett and Jacob Cooke (New York: Columbia University Press, 1961–1987), 12:465.

35. Gouverneur Morris, 2 July: *Debates*, 180; *Records* 1:514.

36. Gouverneur Morris, 7 July: *Debates*, 198; *Records* 1:552.

37. Gouverneur Morris, 5 July: *Debates*, 185–186; *Records* 1:529–531.

38. Gouverneur Morris, 10 July: *Debates*, 204; *Records* 1:567.

39. See James Madison, 11 July: *Debates*, 213; *Records* 1:584.

40. This is a key theme of the oft-cited essay that Madison composed in preparation for the Convention: James Madison, "Vices of the Political System of the United States" (April 1787), in *The Papers of James Madison*, ed. William T. Hutchinson et al. (Chicago: University of Chicago Press and Charlottesville: University Press of Virginia, 1962–1991), 9:345–358.

41. Gouverneur Morris, 7 July: *Debates*, 199; *Records* 1:553. William Paterson's version of this speech has Morris saying, "We must have it in View eventually to lessen and destroy the State Limits and Authorities." Gouverneur Morris, 7 July: *Records* 1:556. If Morris did indeed say something like this, it is the closest that he ever came to suggesting that the state governments could or should be abolished altogether.

42. Gouverneur Morris, 7 July: *Debates*, 198; *Records* 1:552.

43. Gunning Bedford, 30 June: *Debates*, 175; *Records* 1:492.

44. Gouverneur Morris, 5 July: *Debates*, 185–186; *Records* 1:530. For William Paterson's version of this line, see *Records* 1:537. For John Lansing's version, see James H. Hutson, ed., *Supplement to Max Farrand's Records of the Federal Convention of 1787* (New Haven, CT: Yale University Press, 1987), 150.

45. Gouverneur Morris, 5 July: *Debates*, 186; *Records* 1:530. For John Lansing's version of this line, see Hutson, ed., *Supplement to Max Farrand's Records of the Federal Convention of 1787*, 150.

46. Edmund Randolph, 29 May: *Debates*, 8; *Records* 1:21.

47. See Roger Sherman and James Wilson, 17 July: *Debates*, 239; *Records* 2:25–26.

48. Gouverneur Morris, 17 July: *Debates*, 239; *Records* 2:26.
49. See *Debates*, 312–313; *Records* 2:181–182.
50. See James Madison and Charles Pinckney, 18 August: *Debates*, 388–389; *Records* 2:324–326.
51. Gouverneur Morris, 20 August: *Debates*, 397; *Records* 2:336.
52. See *Debates*, 312; *Records* 2:182.
53. Gouverneur Morris, 17 August: *Debates*, 386; *Records* 2:317.
54. Elbridge Gerry, 17 August: *Debates*, 386; *Records* 2:317.
55. Gouverneur Morris, 17 August: *Debates*, 386; *Records* 2:317.
56. See *Debates*, 8; *Records* 1:21.
57. James Madison, 8 June: *Debates*, 57; *Records* 1:164. Madison's claim here echoed one that he had made in a letter to Washington prior to the Convention, in which he declared that "a negative *in all cases whatsoever* on the legislative acts of the States . . . appears to me to be absolutely necessary, and to be the least possible encroachment on the State jurisdictions." James Madison to George Washington, 16 April 1787, in *Papers of James Madison*, 9:383.
58. Gouverneur Morris, 17 July: *Debates*, 240; *Records* 2:27.
59. Gouverneur Morris, 17 July: *Debates*, 241; *Records* 2:28.
60. Gouverneur Morris, 17 July: *Debates*, 241; *Records* 2:28.
61. Herbert Storing remarks that viewing the Convention as a struggle between the large states and small states "is by no means simply wrong, but it is flat, lacking in perspective. Of course, the delegates recognized that clashes of interest were involved; but they also saw beyond that. We might say, for example, that the 'interest' of the small states was to maintain a degree of influence in the affairs of the Union disproportionate to the number of people they contained; and that the 'interest' of the large states was to use their greater population to dominate the Union. The delegates were sufficiently realistic to recognize these narrow interests; but they were also keen enough to see that these narrow interests were defensible only insofar as they were the carriers of certain broad principles of free government in the United States. The large states stood, not just for the large states, but for certain principles associated with *Union*; the small states stood, not just for small states, but for certain principles associated with *states* as such." Herbert J. Storing, *Toward a More Perfect Union: Writings of Herbert J. Storing*, ed. Joseph M. Bessette (Washington, DC: AEI Press, 1995), 21.
62. David Brearly, 9 June: *Debates*, 63; *Records* 1:177.
63. For Franklin's suggestion, see Benjamin Franklin, 28 June: *Debates*, 157–158; *Records* 1:450–452. The anecdote about Hamilton's response comes from an 1825 letter that attributes it to Jonathan Dayton, who was a delegate from New Jersey. See William Steele to Jonathan D. Steele, September 1825, in *Records* 3:472.
64. See Madison's note to the 28 May debate in *Debates*, 5; *Records* 1:11
65. William Paterson, 16 June: *Debates*, 87; *Records* 1:250.
66. See George Read, 30 May: *Debates*, 13; *Records* 1:37.
67. Gouverneur Morris, 30 May: *Debates*, 13–14; *Records* 1:37.
68. See 5 July: *Debates*, 182–183; *Records* 1:526.

69. Gouverneur Morris, 5 July: *Debates*, 185–186; *Records* 1:529–530.
70. Gouverneur Morris, 7 July: *Debates*, 198; *Records* 1:551.
71. Gouverneur Morris, 7 July: *Debates*, 198; *Records* 1:552.
72. Alexander Hamilton, 29 June: *Debates*, 163; *Records* 1:466.
73. See 16 July: *Debates*, 234; *Records* 2:15.
74. Edmund Randolph, 16 July: *Debates*, 236; *Records* 2:17–18.
75. Gouverneur Morris, 17 July: *Debates*, 238; *Records* 2:25.
76. Gouverneur Morris, 23 July: *Debates*, 282; *Records* 2:93.
77. See Jack N. Rakove, *Original Meanings: Politics and Ideas in the Making of the Constitution* (New York: Alfred A. Knopf, 1996), 385n21.
78. See Gouverneur Morris and Rufus King, 23 July: *Debates*, 282; and *Records* 2:94.
79. See 23 July: *Debates*, 282–283; *Records* 2:94.
80. Luther Martin, 23 July: *Debates*, 283; *Records* 2:94.
81. Roger Sherman, 15 September: *Debates*, 542–543; *Records* 2:629–630.
82. Gouverneur Morris, 15 September: *Debates*, 544; *Records* 2:631.
83. The only potential rival here is the provision barring any amendment that would affect the slave trade clause—but that was set to expire in 1808. See *Debates*, 561; and *Records* 2:663.

CHAPTER 4. CHECKING AMERICA'S ARISTOCRACY: THE SENATE

1. For Franklin's partiality for a unicameral model, see Benjamin Franklin, 31 May: *Debates*, 14–15; *Records* 1:48. For the unicameral legislature in the New Jersey Plan, see 15 June: *Debates*, 83; *Records* 1:242–243. For statements in support of unicameralism from the New Jersey Plan's supporters, see William Paterson, 16 June: *Debates*, 88; *Records* 251; John Lansing, 20 June: *Debates*, 111–112; *Records* 1:336; Luther Martin, 27 June: *Records* 1:439; Oliver Ellsworth, 16 June: *Debates*, 91; *Records* 1:255; and Roger Sherman, 20 June: *Debates*, 116; *Records* 1:341. For the vote in favor of a second branch, see 21 June: *Debates*, 121; *Records* 1:358.
2. On the fashioning of the Senate at the Convention, see Daniel Wirls and Stephen Wirls, *The Invention of the United States Senate* (Baltimore: John Hopkins University Press, 2004).
3. The origin of this (likely apocryphal) conversation seems to be Moncure D. Conway, *Republican Superstitions as Illustrated in the Political History of America* (London: Henry S. King and Co., 1872), 47–48.
4. Gouverneur Morris, 2 July: *Debates*, 178–180; *Records* 1:511–514. For Robert Yates's version of this speech, see *Records* 1:517–519. For John Lansing's version, see James H. Hutson, ed., *Supplement to Max Farrand's Records of the Federal Convention of 1787* (New Haven, CT: Yale University Press, 1987), 142.
5. Gouverneur Morris, 20 July: *Debates*, 267; *Records* 2:69.
6. Gouverneur Morris to Thomas Penn, 20 May 1774, in Sparks 1:25.
7. Gouverneur Morris to Thomas Penn, 20 May 1774, in Sparks 1:23. See also Melanie

Randolph Miller, *An Incautious Man: The Life of Gouverneur Morris* (Wilmington, DE: Intercollegiate Studies Institute, 2008), 18.

8. Gouverneur Morris, "Observations on Government, Applicable to the Political State of France" (1789), in *Writings*, 238, 237.

9. See Gouverneur Morris, "Notes on the Form for a Constitution for France" (1791?), in *Writings*, 270, 277.

10. Morris, "Observations on Government, Applicable to the Political State of France," 234.

11. Gouverneur Morris to Thomas Jefferson, 1 August 1792, in *The Papers of Thomas Jefferson*, ed. Julian P. Boyd et al. (Princeton, NJ: Princeton University Press, 1950–2017), 24:276. See also Gouverneur Morris to Robert Walsh, 5 February 1811, in Sparks 3:262.

12. Gouverneur Morris, "Speech in the Senate on the Repeal of the Judiciary Act of 1801," 8 January 1802, in *Writings*, 312.

13. Gouverneur Morris, "Speech in the Senate on the Repeal of the Judiciary Act of 1801," 14 January 1802, in *Writings*, 315, 314.

14. Gouverneur Morris to Uriah Tracy, 5 January 1804, in Sparks 3:201.

15. See 2 July: *Debates*, 177; *Records* 1:510.

16. See Charles Cotesworth Pinckney, 2 July: *Debates*, 177–178; *Records* 1:511.

17. Gouverneur Morris, 2 July: *Debates*, 178; *Records* 1:511.

18. See 7 June: *Debates*, 56; *Records* 1:156; and 25 June: *Debates*, 142; *Records* 1:408

19. See 26 June: *Debates*, 148–149; *Records* 1:426–427.

20. Gouverneur Morris, 2 July: *Debates*, 178; *Records* 1:512.

21. Morris in fact argued that the Senate should not be too small: "He wished the Senate to be a pretty numerous body," he remarked at one point. "If two members only should be allowed to each State, and a majority be made a quorum, the power would be lodged in fourteen members, which was too small a number for such a trust." Gouverneur Morris, 23 July: *Debates*, 282–283; *Records* 2:94.

22. Gouverneur Morris, 2 July: *Debates*, 178; *Records* 1:512; and James Madison, *Federalist #51*, 6 February 1788, in Alexander Hamilton, John Jay, and James Madison, *The Federalist*, ed. George W. Carey and James McClellan (Indianapolis: Liberty Fund, 2001), 268. Mary Bilder suggests that Morris's argument here—about balancing one set of vices against another—may have even helped to inspire Madison's famous argument about factions checking one another. See Mary Sarah Bilder, *Madison's Hand: Revising the Constitutional Convention* (Cambridge, MA: Harvard University Press, 2015), 105, 117.

23. Gouverneur Morris, 21 July: *Debates*, 271; *Records* 2:76. Morris also assumed that the Senate would be "more capable than the first branch" of "digesting and proposing money bills." Gouverneur Morris, 6 July: *Debates*, 194; *Records* 1:545; see also Gouverneur Morris, 8 August: *Debates*, 333–334; *Records* 2:224

24. Gouverneur Morris, 2 July: *Debates*, 178–179; *Records* 1:512–513.

25. See, for instance, Benjamin Franklin, 2 June: *Debates*, 25–28; *Records* 1:81–85; and 26 June: *Debates*, 149; *Records* 1:427.

26. Gouverneur Morris, 2 July: *Debates*, 178–179; *Records* 1:512–513.

27. Gouverneur Morris, 2 July: *Debates*, 179; *Records* 1:513.

28. Gouverneur Morris, 2 July: *Debates*, 179–180; *Records* 1:513–514.

29. Gouverneur Morris, 2 July: *Debates*, 179; *Records* 1:513.

30. Roger Sherman, 31 May: *Debates*, 15; *Records* 1:48. Elbridge Gerry, 31 May: *Debates*, 15; *Records* 1:48. (On the last day of the Convention Gerry went so far as to call democracy "the worst . . . of all political evils." Elbridge Gerry, 17 September: *Debates*, 550; *Records* 2:647.) Edmund Randolph, 31 May: *Debates*, 17; *Records* 1:51. George Mason, 4 June: *Debates*, 36; *Records* 1:101. Alexander Hamilton, 18 June: *Records* 1:299. James Madison, 26 June: *Debates*, 145; *Records* 1:422. John Francis Mercer, 7 August: *Debates*, 326; *Records* 2:205.

31. See 31 May: *Debates*, 17; *Records* 1:50; 6 June: *Debates*, 49; *Records* 1:137–138; 21 June: *Debates*, 123; *Records* 1:360.

32. Charles Cotesworth Pinckney, 26 June: *Debates*, 148–149; *Records* 1:426. Abraham Baldwin, 29 June: *Debates*, 166; *Records* 1:469–470. Pierce Butler, 26 June: *Records* 1:434. John Dickinson, 7 June: *Debates*, 51–52; *Records* 1:150; see also John Dickinson, 6 June: *Debates*, 47–48; *Records* 1:136. Alexander Hamilton, 18 June: *Debates*, 97; *Records* 1:288. James Madison, 7 June: *Records* 1:158. James Madison, 26 June: *Records* 1:431.

33. See Donald S. Lutz, "The Theory of Consent in the Early State Constitutions," *Publius* 9, no. 2 (Spring 1979), 22.

34. For the vote for a seven-year term, see 12 June: *Debates*, 76–77; *Records* 1:219. For the switch to six years, see 26 June: *Debates*, 148; *Records* 1:426.

35. James Madison, 26 June: *Records* 1:431. James Madison, 26 June: *Debates*, 146–147; *Records* 1:423. James Wilson, 26 June: *Debates*, 148; *Records* 426.

36. See Charles Pinckney, 7 June: *Debates*, 56; *Records* 1:155. Alexander Hamilton, 18 June: *Debates*, 98; *Records* 1:289–290. George Read, 25 June: *Debates*, 143; *Records* 1:409. George Read, 26 June: *Debates*, 144; *Records* 1:421. Robert Morris, 25 June: *Debates*, 143; *Records* 1:409.

37. See John Jay to George Washington, 7 January 1787, in *Selected Papers of John Jay*, ed. Elizabeth M. Nuxoll (Charlottesville: University of Virginia Press, 2010–2017), 4:468–469.

38. Alexander Hamilton, 18 June: *Debates*, 98; *Records* 1:289–290.

39. Charles Cotesworth Pinckney, 26 June: *Debates*, 149; *Records* 1:426–427. Pierce Butler and John Rutledge, 12 June: *Debates*, 77; *Records* 1:219. For the vote, see 26 June: *Debates*, 149; *Records* 1:427.

40. George Read, 7 June: *Debates*, 52; *Records* 1:151.

41. James Madison, "Explanations in Regard to His Report of Hamilton's and Morris's Speeches in the Federal Convention," 27 September 1834, in Henry S. Randall, *The Life of Thomas Jefferson* (New York: Derby and Jackson, 1858), 3:595; and James Madison to Jared Sparks, 8 April 1831, in FO.

42. Charles Pinckney, 25 June: *Debates*, 134; *Records* 1:398.

43. Gouverneur Morris, 6 July: *Debates*, 194; *Records* 1:545.

44. Gouverneur Morris, 2 July: *Debates*, 180; *Records* 1:512–513.

45. Gouverneur Morris, 19 July: *Debates*, 256; *Records* 2:52. Similarly, Robert Yates records Morris as stating that "history proves, I admit, that the men of large property will uniformly endeavor to establish tyranny." Gouverneur Morris, 2 July: *Records* 1:517.

46. Gouverneur Morris, 2 July: *Debates*, 180; *Records* 1:514.

47. Gouverneur Morris, 2 July: *Debates*, 178–179; *Records* 1:512.

48. Gouverneur Morris, 2 July: *Debates*, 179; *Records* 1:513.

49. Gouverneur Morris, "Observations on Government, Applicable to the Political State of France" (1789), in *Writings*, 234. As one scholar notes, "While Morris's plan for a new French government was ostensibly tailored to the French people's particular needs and capabilities, its basic principles"—particularly with regard to the rich and well-born—"bore a striking resemblance to those he had formulated in Philadelphia two years earlier." Philipp Ziesche, "Exporting American Revolutions: Gouverneur Morris, Thomas Jefferson, and the National Struggle for Universal Rights in Revolutionary France," *Journal of the Early Republic* 26, no. 3 (Fall 2006), 436.

50. On the distinction between these two ideas, see Martin Diamond, "The Separation of Powers and the Mixed Regime," in *As Far as Republican Principles Will Admit: Essays by Martin Diamond*, ed. William A. Schambra (Washington, DC: AEI Press, 1992), 58–67.

51. This is a key theme of Christopher Bissex, "Institutionalizing Class Conflict: Gouverneur Morris on Mediating Class Warfare through Separation of Powers" (PhD diss., Baylor University, 2014). For a much shorter but helpful discussion by the advisor of this dissertation, see David K. Nichols, "Gouverneur Morris and the Creation of American Constitutionalism," in *Natural Right and Political Philosophy: Essays in Honor of Catherine Zuckert and Michael Zuckert*, ed. Ann Ward and Lee Ward (Notre Dame, IN: University of Notre Dame Press, 2013), especially 256–264.

52. John Adams, *Defence of the Constitutions of Government of the United States of America*, vol. 1, in *The Works of John Adams*, ed. Charles Francis Adams (Boston: Charles C. Little and James Brown, 1851), 4:290. On Adams's attempts to limit the problems posed by aspiring aristocrats and oligarchs, see Luke Mayville, *John Adams and the Fear of American Oligarchy* (Princeton, NJ: Princeton University Press, 2016). A similar argument—which Morris may have known—had been made a decade earlier by Benjamin Rush in the context of a discussion of the Pennsylvania state constitution. See Benjamin Rush, *Observations Upon the Present Government of Pennsylvania* (Philadelphia: Styner and Cist, 1777), Letter 2. I thank Jonathan Gienapp for calling this pamphlet to my attention.

53. C. Bradley Thompson, *John Adams and the Spirit of Liberty* (Lawrence: University Press of Kansas, 1998), 263. On the influence of Adams's *Defence* at the Convention more broadly, see Thompson, *John Adams and the Spirit of Liberty*, 251–258; and Eric Nelson, *The Royalist Revolution: Monarchy and the American Founding* (Cambridge, MA: Belknap Press of Harvard University Press, 2014), 335–336n125.

54. Gouverneur Morris, 24 July: *Debates*, 288; *Records* 2:104.

55. Gouverneur Morris, "To the Quakers, Bethlemites, Moderate Men, Refugees, and Other the Tories Whatsoever, and Wheresoever, Dispersed" (1779), in *Writings*, 90.

56. See, for instance, Gouverneur Morris to George Washington, 9 March 1791, in *The Papers of George Washington: Presidential Series*, ed. Dorothy Twohig et al. (Charlottesville: University Press of Virginia, 1987–2016), 7:531; and Gouverneur Morris to Rufus King, 4 June 1800, in Sparks 3:128.

57. This apparent contradiction has also been noted by, among others, John Patrick Coby, "America's Machiavellian: Gouverneur Morris at the Constitutional Convention," *Review of Politics* 79, no. 4 (Fall 2017), 632–633; Jennifer Nedelsky, *Private Property and the Limits of American Constitutionalism: The Madisonian Framework and Its Legacy* (Chicago: University of Chicago Press, 1990), 80–81; and Nathan Tarcov, "The Social Theory of the Founders," in *Confronting the Constitution*, ed. Allan Bloom (Washington, DC: AEI Press, 1990), 177.

58. Gouverneur Morris, 2 July: *Debates*, 179–180; *Records* 1:513–514.

59. Gouverneur Morris, 19 July: *Debates*, 256; *Records* 2:52.

60. Gouverneur Morris, 2 July: *Records* 1:517. One scholar writes that "perhaps . . . Morris was attempting to co-opt a portion of the rich, installed as permanent lawmakers, to police the remainder of the rich, busy with moneymaking in the private economy—that is, a quasi aristocracy recruited from the oligarchical class. Extracting good from bad, and not just preventing bad, was a small, but real, part of Morris's constitutional thinking. In the main, though, Morris put his faith in vice rather than virtue." Coby, "America's Machiavellian," 633.

61. Edmund Randolph, 2 July: *Debates*, 180; *Records* 1:514.

62. Gouverneur Morris to Alexander Hamilton, 11 March 1802, in *The Papers of Alexander Hamilton*, ed. Harold C. Syrett and Jacob Cooke (New York: Columbia University Press, 1961–1987), 25:561; and Gouverneur Morris to Henry W. Livingston, 25 November 1803, in Sparks 3:185–186.

63. Gouverneur Morris to Robert Walsh, 5 February 1811, in Sparks 3:266.

CHAPTER 5. PROPERTY AND THE PEOPLE'S BRANCH: THE HOUSE OF REPRESENTATIVES

1. For these votes, see 21 June: *Debates*, 123; *Records* 1:360; 21 June: *Debates*, 125; *Records* 1:362; and 22 June: *Debates*, 127–128; *Records* 1:374–375.

2. Jennifer Nedelsky, *Private Property and the Limits of American Constitutionalism: The Madisonian Framework and Its Legacy* (Chicago: University of Chicago Press, 1990), chap. 3.

3. See Gouverneur Morris, "Political Enquiries" (1776), in *Writings*, 5–11. For the closest examination of this short piece, see Arthur Paul Kaufman, "The Constitutional Views of Gouverneur Morris" (PhD diss., Georgetown University, 1992), 39–79. Also useful is Forrest McDonald, "The Political Thought of Gouverneur Morris," *The Imaginative Conservative*, May 18, 2013.

4. Morris, "Political Enquiries," 8–10.

5. Thomas Jefferson, *Notes on the State of Virginia*, ed. William Peden (Chapel Hill: University of North Carolina Press, 1955), 165.

6. Morris, "Political Enquiries," 7, 10–11.

7. Edmund Randolph, 29 May: *Debates*, 8; *Records* 1:20.

8. Gouverneur Morris, 5 July: *Debates*, 188; *Records* 1:533.

9. Gouverneur Morris, 5 July: *Debates*, 188; *Records* 1:533.

10. John Rutledge, 5 July: *Debates*, 189; *Records* 1:534. Rufus King, 6 July: *Debates*, 191; *Records* 1:541. Piece Butler, 6 July: *Debates*, 191; *Records* 1:542. Later Butler reiterated that "wealth was the great means of defence and utility to the nation," and that the new government would be "principally, for the protection of property, and . . . supported by property." Pierce Butler, 11 July: *Debates*, 210; *Records* 1:581. James Wilson, in contrast, high-mindedly declared that he "could not agree that property was the sole or primary object of government and society. The cultivation and improvement of the human mind was the most noble object." James Wilson, 13 July: *Debates*, 226; *Records* 1:605.

11. John Rutledge and Pierce Butler, 11 June: *Debates*, 66; *Records* 1:196. John Dickinson agreed with Rutledge and Butler on the basic principle, but he argued that representation should be based on the states' *actual* contributions rather than on their quotas of distribution—that is, on the taxes that they actually paid, rather than those that were assessed to them. John Dickinson, 11 June: *Debates*, 66; *Records* 1:196

12. Gouverneur Morris, 10 July: *Debates*, 204; *Records* 1:567.

13. See Kaufman, "The Constitutional Views of Gouverneur Morris," 403–404.

14. Gouverneur Morris, 10 July: *Debates*, 207; *Records* 1:571. Unsurprisingly, this is one point on which the American West–loving Theodore Roosevelt found great fault with Morris. With regard to this issue, Roosevelt complained, Morris "showed the narrowest, blindest, and least excusable sectional jealousy. . . . He actually desired the convention to commit the criminal folly of attempting to provide that the West should always be kept subordinate to the East. Fortunately he failed; but the mere attempt casts the gravest discredit alike on his far-sightedness and on his reputation as a statesman. It is impossible to understand how one who was usually so cool and clear-headed an observer could have blundered so flagrantly on a point hardly less vital than the establishment of the Union itself." Theodore Roosevelt, *Gouverneur Morris* (Boston: Houghton, Mifflin and Company, 1890), 146.

15. Gouverneur Morris, 5 July: *Debates*, 189; *Records* 1:534.

16. Gouverneur Morris, 5 July: *Debates*, 188–189; *Records* 1:533.

17. Gouverneur Morris, 11 July: *Debates*, 212l; *Records* 1:583.

18. Gouverneur Morris, 5 July: *Debates*, 189; *Records* 1:533; and 13 July: *Debates*, 225; *Records* 1:604.

19. Roosevelt, *Gouverneur Morris*, 148.

20. Gouverneur Morris, 11 July: *Debates*, 212; *Records* 1:583.

21. James Madison, 11 July: *Debates*, 213; *Records* 1:584.

22. Gouverneur Morris, 13 July: *Debates*, 225; *Records* 1:605. See also Kaufman, "The Constitutional Views of Gouverneur Morris," 414–416.

23. Morris declared at the Convention that he "did not mean to discourage the growth of the Western country. He knew that to be impossible. He did not wish, however, to throw the power into their hands." Gouverneur Morris, 29 August: *Debates*, 455; *Records* 2:454. Many years later he claimed that "I knew as well then [i.e., at the time of the Convention], as I do now, that all North America must at length be annexed to us. Happy,

indeed, if the lust of dominion stop there." Gouverneur Morris to Henry W. Livingston, 25 November 1803, in Sparks 3:185.

24. See 14 July: *Debates*, 227; *Records* 2:3.

25. For Morris's proposal, see Gouverneur Morris, 6 July: *Debates*, 190; *Records* 1:540. For the formation of the committee, see 6 July: *Debates*, 192; *Records* 1:542.

26. See 9 July: *Debates*, 199–200; *Records* 1:559.

27. For the initial vote, see 9 July: *Debates*, 201; *Records* 1:560.

28. Gouverneur Morris, 10 July: *Debates*, 207; *Records* 1:571; see also 11 July: *Debates*, 211; *Records* 1:581.

29. Gouverneur Morris, 11 July: *Debates*, 212–213; *Records* 1:583–584.

30. James Madison, 11 July: *Debates*, 213; *Records* 1:584.

31. Gouverneur Morris, 24 July: *Debates*, 288; *Records* 2:104.

32. Gouverneur Morris, 9 July: *Debates*, 201: *Records* 1:560.

33. See 9 July: *Debates*, 202; *Records* 1:562.

34. See 10 July: *Debates*, 203; *Records* 1:566.

35. For the vote affirming this apportionment, see 10 July: *Debates*, 206; *Records* 1:570.

36. See Robert J. Dinkin, *Voting in Revolutionary America: A Study of Elections in the Original Thirteen States, 1776–1789* (Westport, CT: Greenwood Press, 1982); Donald Ratcliffe, "The Right to Vote and the Rise of Democracy, 1787–1828," *Journal of the Early Republic* 33, no. 2 (Summer 2013), 219–254; and Chilton Williamson, *American Suffrage: From Property to Democracy, 1760–1860* (Princeton, NJ: Princeton University Press, 1960).

37. See James Wilson, 7 August: *Debates*, 323; *Records* 2:201; Oliver Ellsworth, 7 August: *Debates*, 323–324; *Records* 2:201; and Benjamin Franklin, 7 August: *Debates*, 326; *Records* 2:204.

38. John Dickinson, 7 August: *Debates*, 324, *Records* 2:202; and James Madison, 7 August: *Debates*, 325; *Records* 2:203–204. Rufus King recorded Madison as stating that "I am in fav[o]r of the rig[h]t of Election being confin[e]d to Freeholders." James Madison, 7 August: *Records* 2:208.

39. See Gouverneur Morris, 7 August: *Debates*, 323–325; *Records* 2:201–203. Hence Charles Beard claimed that Morris "was the leader of those who wanted to base the new system upon a freehold suffrage qualification." Charles A. Beard, *An Economic Interpretation of the Constitution of the United States*, intro. Forrest McDonald (New York: Free Press, [1913] 1986), 207. It is worth noting, however, that Morris opposed property qualifications for *officeholders*, an idea that many other delegates supported. See Gouverneur Morris, 26 July: *Debates*, 299–300; *Records* 2:121–122.

40. See *Debates*, 309; *Records* 2:178.

41. Gouverneur Morris, 7 August: *Debates*, 323; *Records* 2:201.

42. See *Journals of the Provincial Congress, Provincial Convention, and Committee of Safety and Council of Safety of the State of New-York, 1775–1776–1777* (Albany: Thurlow Weed, 1842), 1:867; and Mary-Jo Kline, *Gouverneur Morris and the New Nation, 1775–1788* (New York: Arno Press, 1978), 76.

43. Gouverneur Morris, James Wilson, and Oliver Ellsworth, 7 August: *Debates*, 323–325; *Records* 2:201–203.

44. Piece Butler, 7 August: *Debates*, 324; *Records* 2:202. James Madison similarly claimed that "a gradual abridgment" of the right to vote "has been the mode in which aristocracies have been built on the ruins of popular forms." James Madison, 7 August: *Debates*, 325; *Records* 2:203.

45. Gouverneur Morris, 7 August: *Debates*, 324; *Records* 2:202.

46. Gouverneur Morris, 7 August: *Records* 2:207.

47. Gouverneur Morris, 7 August: *Debates*, 324–325; *Records* 2:202–203. The last of Morris's lines quoted here, about only landowners truly having a "will of their own," echoes Montesquieu's claim in his famous analysis of the English Constitution that all citizens should have the right to vote "except those whose estate is so humble that they are deemed to have no will of their own." Charles de Secondat, baron de Montesquieu, *The Spirit of the Laws*, trans. Anne M. Cohler, Basia C. Miller, and Harold S. Stone (Cambridge: Cambridge University Press, [1748] 1989), 11.6, 160.

48. Although he did not spell out his reasoning, James Madison gestured in a similar direction when he expressed a worry that without a property requirement for voting, the propertyless "will become the tools of opulence and ambition." James Madison, 7 August: *Debates*, 324–325; *Records* 2:202–203.

49. Gouverneur Morris to Robert R. Livingston, 10 October 1802, in Sparks 3:172.

50. Gouverneur Morris, 7 August: *Debates*, 325; *Records* 2:203.

51. See 7 August: *Debates*, 317; *Records* 2:206.

52. James Madison, 21 July: *Debates*, 269; *Records* 2:74. James Wilson too worried about "the Legislature swallowing up all the other powers." James Wilson, 15 August: *Debates*, 377; *Records* 2:300. On the fears of "legislative tyranny" at the Convention more broadly—particularly among Madison, Morris, and Wilson—see Judith A. Best, "Legislative Tyranny and the Liberation of the Executive: A View from the Founding," *Presidential Studies Quarterly* 17, no. 4 (Fall 1987), 697–709.

53. James Madison, *Federalist* #48, 1 February 1788, in Alexander Hamilton, John Jay, and James Madison, *The Federalist*, ed. George W. Carey and James McClellan (Indianapolis: Liberty Fund, 2001), 257.

54. Elbridge Gerry, 21 July: *Debates*, 270; *Records* 2:75; and Gouverneur Morris, 21 July: *Debates*, 271; *Records* 2:76.

55. Gouverneur Morris, 19 July: *Debates*, 256; *Records* 2:52.

56. The idea that a bicameral Congress would be sufficient to prevent legislative tyranny was perhaps stated most directly by Gunning Beford, who declared that he was "opposed to every check on the Legislature" since "the branches would produce a sufficient control within the Legislature itself." Gunning Bedford, 4 June: *Debates*, 36; *Records* 1:100–101.

57. Gouverneur Morris, 19 July: *Debates*, 256; *Records* 2:52.

58. Gouverneur Morris, 16 August: *Debates*, 380; *Records* 2:307. See also Gouverneur Morris to Timothy Pickering, 22 December 1814, in Sparks 3:323.

CHAPTER 6. A RELUCTANT ARCHITECT OF THE ELECTORAL COLLEGE: PRESIDENTIAL SELECTION

1. James Madison to George Washington, 16 April 1787, in *The Papers of James Madison*, ed. William T. Hutchinson et al. (Chicago: University of Chicago Press and Charlottesville: University Press of Virginia, 1962–1991), 9:385.

2. Roger Sherman, 1 June: *Debates*, 21, 23; *Records* 1:65, 68.

3. For the provision in the New Jersey Plan, see 15 June: *Debates*, 84; *Records* 1:244. On the widespread support for the idea of a plural executive, see Forrest McDonald, *Novus Ordo Seclorum: The Intellectual Origins of the Constitution* (Lawrence: University Press of Kansas, 1985), 240.

4. Edmund Randolph, 1 June: *Debates*, 21; *Records* 1:66; and 2 June: *Debates*, 31; *Records* 1:88.

5. James Madison, 1 June: *Records* 1:70. Rufus King records Madison as suggesting that "probably the best plan will be a single Executive of long duration w[i]th a Council, with liberty to depart from their Opinion at his peril." James Madison, 1 June: *Records* 1:70. William Pierce, however, has him saying that "an Executive formed of one Man would answer the purpose when aided by a Council, who should have the right to advise and record their proceedings, but not to control his authority." James Madison, 1 June: *Records* 1:74. Just three days later Madison voted in favor of a single executive: see 4 June: *Debates*, 33; *Records* 1:97. On Madison's views regarding the presidency more generally, see Ruth W. Grant and Stephen Grant, "The Madisonian Presidency," in *The Presidency in the Constitutional Order*, ed. Joseph M. Bessette and Jeffrey Tulis (Baton Rouge: Louisiana State University Press, 1981), 31–64.

6. See 4 June: *Debates*, 33; *Records* 1:97; and 17 July: *Debates*, 241; *Records* 2:29.

7. See Shlomo Slonim, "The Electoral College at Philadelphia: The Evolution of an Ad Hoc Congress for the Selection of a President," *Journal of American History* 73, no. 1 (June 1986), 35.

8. James Wilson, 4 September: *Debates*, 477; *Records* 2:501.

9. See Elbridge Gerry, 9 June: *Debates*, 61–62; *Records* 1:175–176; 19 July: *Debates*, 260; *Records* 2:57; and 25 July: *Debates*, 291; *Records* 2:109.

10. For a comparative study of the roles that Morris and Wilson played at the Convention, see Jack Heyburn, "Gouverneur Morris and James Wilson at the Constitutional Convention," *University of Pennsylvania Journal of Constitutional Law* 20, no. 1 (October 2017), 169–197.

11. On the historical development of the presidential selection process from the founding to today, see James W. Ceasar, *Presidential Selection: Theory and Development* (Princeton, NJ: Princeton University Press, 1979).

12. David K. Nichols, "Gouverneur Morris and the Creation of American Constitutionalism," in *Natural Right and Political Philosophy: Essays in Honor of Catherine Zuckert and Michael Zuckert*, ed. Ann Ward and Lee Ward (Notre Dame, IN: University of Notre Dame Press, 2013), 267.

13. See Slonim, "The Electoral College at Philadelphia," 37.
14. See Edmund Randolph, 29 May: *Debates*, 9; *Records* 1:21; and William Paterson, 15 June: *Debates*, 84; *Records* 1:244.
15. For most of this time the process remained rather vague. It was not until late August, for instance, that the delegates discussed in detail whether the selection of the president would be by a joint ballot of both houses of Congress—which was the custom among the state legislatures that chose their state's governor, and which was preferred by many of the larger state delegates—or by a concurrent ballot, which would in effect give each house a veto over the choice. See 24 August: *Debates*, 429–431; *Records* 2:401–403. Morris appears to have preferred a joint ballot, if the selection had to be placed in the hands of the legislature: see Gouverneur Morris, 7 August: *Debates*, 319–320; *Records* 2:196–197.
16. Gouverneur Morris, 17 July: *Debates*, 242–243; *Records* 2:29–31.
17. Gouverneur Morris, 24 July: *Debates*, 288; *Records* 2:104.
18. Gouverneur Morris, 17 July: *Debates*, 242–243; *Records* 2:29–31.
19. Gouverneur Morris, 24 July: *Debates*, 288; *Records* 2:103.
20. Gouverneur Morris, 24 August: *Debates*, 431; *Records* 2:403–404.
21. James Wilson, 24 July: *Debates*, 288; *Records* 2:103.
22. Gouverneur Morris, 24 July: *Debates*, 289; *Records* 2:105.
23. Gouverneur Morris, 25 July: *Debates*, 295; *Records* 2:113.
24. George Mason, 26 July: *Debates*, 297; *Records* 2:119.
25. Gouverneur Morris, 17 July: *Debates*, 242; *Records* 2:29.
26. James Wilson, 1 June: *Debates*, 22–23; *Records* 1:68.
27. George Mason declared on June 1 that he "favors the idea [of popular election], but thinks it impracticable," but he later expressed strong opposition to the idea. George Mason, 1 June: *Debates*, 24; *Records* 1:69. See also George Mason, 17 July: *Debates*, 244; *Records* 2:31.
28. Gouverneur Morris, 17 July: *Debates*, 242; *Records* 2:29.
29. Charles Pinckney, 17 July: *Debates*, 243; *Records* 2:30.
30. See 17 July: *Debates*, 244; *Records* 2:32.
31. Gouverneur Morris, 19 July: *Debates*, 256–257; *Records* 2:52–53.
32. Gouverneur Morris, 19 July: *Debates*, 258; *Records* 2:54.
33. Roger Sherman, 17 July: *Debates*, 242; *Records* 2:29. Charles Pinckney, 17 July: *Debates*, 243; *Records* 2:30. George Mason, 17 July: *Debates*, 244; *Records* 2:31.
34. Gouverneur Morris, 17 July: *Debates*, 242; *Records* 2:29.
35. Gouverneur Morris, 19 July: *Debates*, 257; *Records* 2:53.
36. Gouverneur Morris, 17 July: *Debates*, 243; *Records* 2:30–31.
37. Gouverneur Morris, 19 July: *Debates*, 257–258; *Records* 2:54.
38. Gouverneur Morris, 19 July: *Debates*, 256–257; *Records* 2:52–53.
39. Rufus King, 19 July: *Debates*, 259; *Records* 2:55. James Madison, 19 July: *Debates*, 260; *Records* 2:56–57. James Wilson, 19 July: *Debates*, 259; *Records* 2:56.
40. Charles Pinckney, 17 July: *Debates*, 243; *Records* 2:30.
41. Gouverneur Morris, 17 July: *Debates*, 243; *Records* 2:30.

42. See Hugh Williamson, Gouverneur Morris, and James Madison, 25 July: *Debates,* 295; *Records* 2:113–114. For the vote, see 25 July: *Debates,* 296; *Records* 2:115.

43. Madison also noted that "the right of suffrage was much more diffusive in the Northern than the Southern states," which would also put the South at a disadvantage in a direct election. James Madison, 19 July: *Debates,* 260; *Records* 2:57.

44. The role that slavery played in the formation of the electoral college was long downplayed by historians but has started to garner more attention of late. See, for instance, Akhil Reed Amar, *America's Constitution: A Biography* (New York: Random House, 2005), 156–159; Paul Finkelman, "Slavery and the Constitutional Convention: Making a Covenant with Death," in *Beyond Confederation: Origins of the Constitution and American National Identity,* ed. Richard Beeman, Stephen Botein, and Edward C. Carter II (Chapel Hill: University of North Carolina Press, 1987), 191–192, 209–210; and Slonim, "The Electoral College at Philadelphia," 41, 55–56.

45. See 2 June: *Debates,* 24–25; *Records* 1:80–81. For an overview of the gradual evolution of the electoral college over the course of the Convention, see Slonim, "The Electoral College at Philadelphia."

46. See 19 July: *Debates,* 259–261; *Records* 2:56–58.

47. Ray Raphael, *Mr. President: How and Why the Founders Created a Chief Executive* (New York: Vintage, 2012), 82.

48. See 24 July: *Debates,* 286; *Records* 2:101.

49. See 24 August: *Debates,* 431–432; *Records* 2:403–404.

50. David O. Stewart, *The Summer of 1787: The Men Who Invented the Constitution* (New York: Simon & Schuster, 2007), 179. For the formation of the committee, see 31 August: *Debates,* 469; *Records* 2:481.

51. For Madison's support of presidential electors, see 19 July: *Debates,* 260; *Records* 2:57. For Carroll's, see 24 August: *Debates,* 431; *Records* 2:404. No records of the committee's deliberations were kept, but John Dickinson—who was a member of the committee—recalled, a decade and a half later, that the other committee members had settled on congressional selection of the president until he spurred them to reconsider, at which point Morris led a discussion on the matter and Madison sketched out the plan of the electoral college. See John Dickinson to George Logan, 16 January 1802, in James H. Hutson, ed., *Supplement to Max Farrand's Records of the Federal Convention of 1787* (New Haven, CT: Yale University Press, 1987), 300–301. As Ray Raphael notes, however, the idea that Dickinson helped to sway Morris and others away from congressional selection "is highly implausible, since Morris needed no convincing." Raphael, *Mr. President,* 107. Christopher Bissex suggests that in fact "there is ample evidence that it was Morris who led the Committee to accept the Electoral College. This is corroborated by the fact that it was Morris who had always been the floor leader and the parliamentary mastermind behind the popular executive movement, it was Morris who initially proposed the two-vote system, it was Morris who continually proposed a system of electors and lobbied against legislative election, and it was Morris who was chosen by the Committee to give a defense of the new system to the Convention and who responded with seeming offense to criticism of the plan.... we cannot be completely sure what happened in the Committee,

but all evidence points to the idea that Morris was the architect of the Electoral College." Christopher Bissex, "Institutionalizing Class Conflict: Gouverneur Morris on Mediating Class Warfare through Separation of Powers" (PhD diss., Baylor University, 2014), 147. See also Charles C. Thach, *The Creation of the Presidency, 1775–1789: A Study in Constitutional History* (Baltimore: Johns Hopkins Press, 1923), 136.

52. See 4 September: *Debates*, 474; *Records* 2:497–498.

53. Edmund Randolph and Charles Pinckney, 4 September: *Debates*, 476; *Records* 2:500.

54. Gouverneur Morris, 4 September: *Debates*, 476; *Records* 2:500.

55. George Mason, 4 September: *Debates*, 476; *Records* 2:500; and Charles Pinckney, 4 September: *Debates*, 477; *Records* 2:501.

56. James Wilson, 6 September: *Debates*, 486; *Records* 2:522.

57. See James Wilson, 4 September: *Debates*, 477; *Records* 2:502. For the vote against Wilson's proposal, see 5 September: *Debates*, 483; *Records* 2:513.

58. Gouverneur Morris, 4 September: *Debates*, 478; *Records* 2:502. However, one of Morris's later comments indicated that he himself may have preferred the House to the Senate as the backup option: see Gouverneur Morris, 6 September: *Debates*, 485–486; *Records* 2:522. Ray Raphael suggests that Morris "probably opposed the Senate runoff within the Committee [on Postponed Parts], but . . . was in no position to undermine committee negotiations to which he had been a party." This, he says, would explain why Morris's defense of using the Senate rather than the House as the backup—"because fewer could then say to the President, 'You owe your appointment to us'"—was so "uncharacteristically weak": "Morris himself, had he not been the one to make this argument, would probably have countered that the Senate was more likely to engage in intrigue and cabal because of its small numbers." Raphael, *Mr. President*, 111.

59. Gouverneur Morris, 5 September: *Debates*, 482; *Records* 2:512.

60. Donald L. Robinson, "Gouverneur Morris and the Design of the American Presidency," *Presidential Studies Quarterly* 17, no. 2 (Spring 1987), 325. The only other delegate who indicated that he expected the electoral college to generally settle on a candidate in the first round, at least after a time, was Abraham Baldwin: see Abraham Baldwin, 4 September: *Debates*, 477; *Records* 2:501.

61. See Roger Sherman and Hugh Williamson, 6 September: *Debates*, 485, 489–490; *Records* 2:522, 527.

62. See 6 September: *Debates*, 490; *Records* 2:527. At this point Morris suggested adding a provision stipulating that an incumbent president would only be reelected if a majority of the electors voted for him; if he received less than a majority then he would not be one of the five candidates considered by the House, even if he was among the top five vote-getters. As Madison explained in his notes, "this was another expedient for rendering the President independent of the Legislative body for his continuance in office." However, no one seconded this idea. Gouverneur Morris, 6 September: *Debates*, 490; *Records* 2:527.

63. James Madison, 12 September: *Debates*, 525; *Records* 2:587.

64. Alexander Hamilton, *Federalist* #68, 12 March 1788, in Alexander Hamilton, John

Jay, and James Madison, *The Federalist*, ed. George W. Carey and James McClellan (Indianapolis: Liberty Fund, 2001), 352.

65. See David Alvis, "The Presidency in the Constitutional Convention of 1787," in *Natural Right and Political Philosophy: Essays in Honor of Catherine Zuckert and Michael Zuckert*, ed. Ann Ward and Lee Ward (Notre Dame, IN: University of Notre Dame Press, 2013), 292; and David K. Nichols, *The Myth of the Modern Presidency* (University Park: Pennsylvania State University Press, 1994), 43–44.

66. Gouverneur Morris, 24 August: *Debates*, 431; *Records* 2:404.

67. Hamilton, *Federalist* #68, 351.

68. Gouverneur Morris to the president of the Senate and the speaker of the Assembly of New York, 25 December 1802, in Sparks 3:174. See also Gouverneur Morris to Lewis R. Morris, 10 December 1803, in Sparks 3:192–193.

69. Gouverneur Morris to the president of the Senate and the speaker of the Assembly of New York, 25 December 1802, in Sparks 3:175. See also Gouverneur Morris to Lewis R. Morris, 10 December 1803, in Sparks 3:194.

CHAPTER 7. AN OFFICE FIT FOR WASHINGTON: THE PRESIDENCY

1. Pierce Butler to Weedon Butler, 5 May 1788, in *Records* 3:302.

2. Benjamin Franklin, 4 June: *Debates*, 37; *Records* 1:103.

3. However, for an argument that the movement for a strong, independent executive at the Convention was not a repudiation but rather a fulfillment of the principles of the American Revolution, or at least a fulfillment of the vision of those rebels who saw themselves as fighting against the British Parliament but not the crown itself, see Eric Nelson, *The Royalist Revolution: Monarchy and the American Founding* (Cambridge, MA: Belknap Press of Harvard University Press, 2014), esp. chap. 5.

4. For an older but still valuable discussion, see Charles C. Thach, *The Creation of the Presidency, 1775–1789: A Study in Constitutional History* (Baltimore: Johns Hopkins Press, 1923), chap. 2.

5. On Morris's role in empowering the presidency, see Ray Raphael, *Mr. President: How and Why the Founders Created a Chief Executive* (New York: Vintage, 2012), esp. chap. 5; and Donald L. Robinson, "Gouverneur Morris and the Design of the American Presidency," *Presidential Studies Quarterly* 17, no. 2 (Spring 1987), 319–328. On Wilson's role, see Robert E. DiClerico, "James Wilson's Presidency," *Presidential Studies Quarterly* 17, no. 2 (Spring 1987), 301–317; and Daniel J. McCarthy, "James Wilson and the Creation of the Presidency," *Presidential Studies Quarterly* 17, no. 4 (Fall 1987), 689–696. For a comparative study of the views of Morris, Wilson, and Hamilton on executive power, see Jonathan Gienapp, "National Power and the Presidency: Rival Forms of Federalist Constitutionalism at the Founding," in *Political Thought and the Origins of the American Presidency*, ed. Ben Lowe (Gainesville: University Press of Florida, 2021), 127–164.

6. See DiClerico, "James Wilson's Presidency," 303.

7. Ray Raphael, for instance, notes that while Wilson "made the motion for a single executive, first introduced the notion of presidential electors, named the office, and served on the Committee of Detail, which gave the presidency some sense of definition in early August," his contributions to the formation of the presidency should not obscure those of Morris. However, he dismisses the idea that "Morris was more of a 'father' to the presidency than Wilson, or vice versa" on the grounds that "that sort of tiering is pointless and even counterproductive, concealing the collective nature of the enterprise and the interactive dialogue that fosters ideas and generates solutions." Raphael, *Mr. President*, 283–284. Christopher Bissex states more categorically that "Morris should rightly be called the Father of the American Presidency." Christopher Bissex, "Institutionalizing Class Conflict: Gouverneur Morris on Mediating Class Warfare through Separation of Powers" (PhD diss., Baylor University, 2014), 45.

8. Michael W. McConnell, *The President Who Would Not Be King: Executive Power Under the Constitution* (Princeton, NJ: Princeton University Press, 2020), 52.

9. See Arthur Paul Kaufman, "The Constitutional Views of Gouverneur Morris" (PhD diss., Georgetown University, 1992), chap. 4.

10. Gouverneur Morris to Alexander Hamilton, 16 May 1777, in *The Papers of Alexander Hamilton*, ed. Harold C. Syrett and Jacob Cooke (New York: Columbia University Press, 1961–1987), 1:253–254.

11. On the parallels between the executives outlined in the New York state constitution and the US Constitution, and for a suggestion that Morris may have deliberately modeled the latter on the former, see Joseph M. Bessette and Gary J. Schmitt, "The Powers and Duties of the President: Recovering the Logic and Meaning of Article II," in *The Constitutional Presidency*, ed. Joseph M. Bessette and Jeffrey K. Tulis (Baltimore: Johns Hopkins University Press, 2009), 39–43. Hamilton also compared the presidency to New York's governorship in *Federalist* #69. See Alexander Hamilton, *Federalist* #69, 14 March 1788, in Alexander Hamilton, John Jay, and James Madison, *The Federalist*, ed. George W. Carey and James McClellan (Indianapolis: Liberty Fund, 2001), 355–362.

12. Gouverneur Morris, 24 July: *Debates*, 289; *Records* 2:105.

13. Gouverneur Morris, 19 July: *Debates*, 256; *Records* 2:52. See also Gouverneur Morris to William Carmichael, 4 July 1789, in Sparks 2:73.

14. Gouverneur Morris to George Washington, 24 January 1790, in *The Papers of George Washington: Presidential Series*, ed. Dorothy Twohig et al. (Charlottesville: University Press of Virginia, 1987–2016), 5:49.

15. Gouverneur Morris, 19 July: *Debates*, 256; *Records* 2:52.

16. Gouverneur Morris, 20 August: *Debates*, 397–398; *Records* 2:342–343.

17. For the proposal of the Committee of Detail, see 6 August: *Debates*, 313; *Records* 2:183. For the proposal of the Committee on Postponed Parts, see 4 September: *Debates*, 475; *Records* 2:498. That Morris was responsible for this important change is suggested by his earlier remark that he "did not know that he should agree to refer the making of treaties to the Senate at all" and his later remark that "no peace ought to be made without the concurrence of the President, who was the general guardian of the national interests." Gouverneur Morris, 23 August: *Debates*, 426; *Records* 2:392; and 7 September:

Debates, 497; *Records* 2:541. For a fuller discussion of this issue, see Raphael, *Mr. President*, 113–114.

18. See Gouverneur Morris, 20 August: *Debates*, 397–398; *Records* 2:342–343. In the prior session the delegates had begun to discuss the question of an executive council, but Charles Pinckney proposed to hold off on the discussion because Morris was "not then on the floor." Charles Pinckney, 18 August: *Debates*, 392; *Records* 2:329. As Ray Raphael comments, "We do not know why Morris was absent on August 18, but we do know that his peers readily agreed to let the issue ride until he returned. At no other time during the summer of 1787 did the convention suspend discussion because of the absence of a single member." Raphael, *Mr. President*, 99.

19. Gouverneur Morris to William Carmichael, 4 July 1789, in Sparks 2:73. See also Gouverneur Morris, 23 August: *Debates*, 423; *Records* 2:389; 6 September: *Debates*, 487; *Records* 2:524; and 7 September: *Debates*, 495, 498; *Records* 2:539, 542.

20. For the original granting of these powers to the Senate, see 6 August: *Debates*, 313; *Records* 2:183. For the proposal of the Committee on Postponed Parts, see 4 September: *Debates*, 475; *Records* 2:498.

21. See 18 July: *Debates*, 249; *Records* 2:41.

22. See 6 August: *Debates*, 315; *Records* 2:185.

23. Gouverneur Morris, 24 August: *Debates*, 432; *Records* 2:405.

24. Benjamin Franklin, Roger Sherman, Pierce Butler, and George Mason, 4 June: *Debates*, 34–36; *Records* 1:99–101.

25. For Wilson's and Hamilton's proposal, see James Wilson and Alexander Hamilton, 4 June: *Debates*, 34; *Records* 1:98. For King's support of the idea, see Rufus King, 4 June: *Records* 1:105, 108. For the votes, see 4 June: *Debates*, 37–38; *Records* 1:103–104.

26. Gouverneur Morris, 15 August: *Debates*, 376; *Records* 2:299–300. The prior week Morris had also seconded a motion by George Read in favor of an absolute veto. See 7 August: *Debates*, 322–323; *Records* 2:200.

27. See 15 August: *Debates*, 378; *Records* 2:301.

28. Gouverneur Morris, 12 September: *Debates*, 524; *Records* 2:585–586.

29. See 12 September: *Debates*, 525; *Records* 2:587.

30. See 6 August: *Debates*, 315; *Records* 2:185.

31. See 12 September: *Debates*, 518; *Records* 2:597. There are striking parallels between the executive vesting clause that Morris wrote for the US Constitution and the parallel clause in the New York state constitution that he also helped to frame, which declared that "the supreme executive power and authority of this State shall be vested in a governor." See Thach, *The Creation of the Presidency*, 35.

32. See 12 September: *Debates*, 512; *Records* 2:590.

33. For the Committee of Detail's legislative vesting clause, see 6 August: *Debates*, 309; *Records* 2:177.

34. For discussion, see William Michael Treanor, "The Case of the Dishonest Scrivener: Gouverneur Morris and the Creation of the Federalist Constitution," *Michigan Law Review* 120, no. 1 (2021), 60–67.

35. For the first vote on this arrangement, see 1 June: *Debates*, 23; *Records* 1:69. This

was also the arrangement in the Committee of Detail's draft constitution: see 6 August: *Debates*, 315; *Records* 2:185.

36. Luther Martin, Elbridge Gerry, and Rufus King, 24 July: *Debates*, 287; *Records* 2:102. Madison included a footnote to King's comment in his records suggesting that "this might possibly be meant as a caricature of the previous motions, in order to defeat the object of them," but this seems unlikely, since just four days earlier King had supported the idea of the president serving for life as long as there was an effective mode of impeachment. See Rufus King, 20 July: *Debates*, 265–266; *Records* 2:67.

37. James Wilson, 24 July: *Debates*, 287; *Records* 2:102.

38. Alexander Hamilton, 18 June: *Debates*, 999; *Records* 1:290.

39. James McClurg, Gouverneur Morris, and Jacob Broom, 17 July: *Debates*, 245; *Records* 2:33. Similarly, a few days later Rufus King added that good behavior was "a tenure which would be most agreeable to him, provided an independent and effectual forum [for impeachment] could be devised." Rufus King, 20 July: *Debates*, 266; *Records* 2:67.

40. For the vote, see 17 July: *Debates*, 248; *Records* 2:36. Madison included a footnote to this vote in his records suggesting that "this vote is not to be considered as any certain index of opinion, as a number in the affirmative probably had it chiefly in view to alarm those attached to a dependence on the Executive on the Legislature, and thereby facilitate some final arrangement of a contrary tendency. The avowed friends of an Executive 'during good behavior' were not more than three or four, nor is it certain they would have adhered to such a tenure." However, this claim is belied by Madison's own report to Jefferson, soon after the Convention's close, that "as to the duration in office, a few would have preferred a tenure during good behaviour—a considerable number would have done so, in case an easy & effectual removal by impeachment could be settled." James Madison to Thomas Jefferson, 24 October 1787, in *The Papers of James Madison*, ed. William T. Hutchinson et al. (Chicago: University of Chicago Press and Charlottesville: University Press of Virginia, 1962–1991), 10:208. On this point, see also Mary Sarah Bilder, *Madison's Hand: Revising the Constitutional Convention* (Cambridge, MA: Harvard University Press, 2015), 114–115, 216–217; and Nelson, *Royalist Revolution*, 194, 326–327n57.

41. Hamilton later made this point in justifying his own position on the matter: "Though from the manner of voting, by delegations, individuals were not distinguished, it was morally certain, from the known situation of the Virginia members (six in number, two of them *Mason* and *Randolph* possessing popular doctrines) that *Madison* must have concurred in the vote of Virginia. Thus, if I sinned against Republicanism, Mr. Madison was not less guilty." Alexander Hamilton to Timothy Pickering, 16 September 1803, in *Papers of Alexander Hamilton*, 26:148. On Washington's vote, see Glenn A. Phelps, *George Washington and American Constitutionalism* (Lawrence: University Press of Kansas, 1993), 105. Rufus King recorded Madison's initial preference for the president's term as being "7 years and an exclusion for ever after—or during good behavior." James Madison, 1 June: *Records* 1:71.

42. Gouverneur Morris, 17 July: *Debates*, 245; *Records* 2:33.

43. George Mason and Gouverneur Morris, 17 July: *Debates*, 247; *Records* 2:35–36.

44. Gouverneur Morris, 19 July: *Debates*, 257; *Records* 2:53–54.

45. Gouverneur Morris, 24 July: *Debates*, 289; *Records* 2:105.

46. Gouverneur Morris, 19 July: *Debates*, 258; *Records* 2:54.

47. Gouverneur Morris, 17 July: *Debates*, 245; *Records* 2:33; 19 July: *Debates*, 257; *Records* 2:53; and 24 July: *Debates*, 289; *Records* 2:105.

48. Gouverneur Morris, 19 July: *Debates*, 257; *Records* 2:53; 24 July: *Debates*, 289; *Records* 2:104; 25 July: *Debates*, 294; *Records* 2:112–113; and 24 August: *Records* 2:407.

49. George Mason and Gouverneur Morris, 26 July: *Debates*, 298; *Records* 2:119–120.

50. See Gouverneur Morris to George Washington, 9 December 1799, in *Papers of George Washington: Retirement Series*, 4:452–453.

51. Gouverneur Morris, 19 July: *Debates*, 257, 262; *Records* 2:53, 59.

52. Gouverneur Morris, 19 July: *Debates*, 257; *Records* 2:53–54; see also 20 July: *Debates*, 264; *Records* 2:64.

53. See Charles Pinckney, 20 July: *Debates*, 263, 265; *Records* 2:64, 66; and Rufus King, 20 July: *Debates*, 265–266; *Records* 2:66–67. The initial vote on whether the president should be removable by impeachment was eight states in favor, two opposed: see 20 July: *Debates*, 267; *Records* 2:69.

54. Alexander Hamilton, 18 June: *Debates*, 101; *Records* 1:292.

55. George Mason, Benjamin Franklin, and Gouverneur Morris, 20 July: *Debates*, 264; *Records* 2:65.

56. Gouverneur Morris, 20 July: *Debates*, 267; *Records* 2:68–69; see also 24 July: *Debates*, 288; *Records* 2:103–104.

57. Gouverneur Morris, 20 August: *Debates*, 398; *Records* 2:344.

58. For discussion, see Treanor, "Dishonest Scrivener," 33–34. Treanor also offers a useful discussion of a small change that Morris made to the impeachment clause during the drafting process. Morris changed the grounds for impeachment from "treason or bribery or other high crimes and misdemeanors against the United States" to "treason, bribery, or other high crimes and misdemeanors." The question is whether dropping "against the United States" changes the meaning of the provision—in particular, whether it suggests that presidents can be impeached for offenses that are not related to the performance of their office (say, lying to a grand jury about an extramarital affair). See Treanor, "Dishonest Scrivener," 84–86.

59. For the provision as it emerged from the Committee on Postponed Parts, see 4 September: *Debates*, 475; *Records* 2:499. For the comments of Mason, Madison, and Morris, see 8 September: *Debates*, 501–502; *Records* 2:550.

60. Gouverneur Morris, 8 September: *Debates*, 502; *Records* 2:551; see also 4 September: *Debates*, 476; *Records* 2:500. Morris did, however, help to make the removal of a president by the Senate more difficult by successfully moving that a two-thirds vote would be required and that the senators would have to be under oath for the trial. See Gouverneur Morris, 2 September: *Debates*, 503; *Records* 2:552.

61. Gouverneur Morris to George Washington, 6 December 1788, in *Papers of George Washington: Presidential Series*, 1:165. See also Gouverneur Morris to George Washington, 20 October 1787, in *The Papers of George Washington: Confederation Series*, ed. W. W. Abbot (Charlottesville: University Press of Virginia, 1992–1997), 5:399–400; Gouverneur

Morris to George Washington, 7 March 1788, in *Papers of George Washington: Confederation Series*, 6:147; and Gouverneur Morris to George Washington, 12 November 1788, in *Papers of George Washington: Presidential Series*, 1:104.

CHAPTER 8. THAT FORTRESS OF THE CONSTITUTION: THE JUDICIARY

1. Clinton Rossiter, *1787: The Grand Convention* (New York: Macmillan, 1966), 241.
2. See William F. Swindler, "Seedtime of an American Judiciary: From Independence to the Constitution," *William and Mary Law Review* 17 (1976), 503–526.
3. See William Michael Treanor, "Judicial Review Before *Marbury*," *Stanford Law Review* 58, no. 455 (2005), esp. 473–497.
4. See Edmund Randolph, 29 May: *Debates*, 9; *Records* 1:21; and James Madison, 13 June: *Debates*, 78; *Records* 1:232–233.
5. James Wilson, 5 June: *Debates*, 38–39; *Records* 1:119; and 18 July: *Debates*, 249; *Records* 2:41.
6. See 18 July: *Debates*, 249, 251; *Records* 2:41, 44.
7. See 18 July: *Debates*, 251; *Records* 2:44.
8. Gouverneur Morris, 21 July: *Debates*, 275; *Records* 2:82.
9. Gouverneur Morris and Oliver Ellsworth, 21 July: *Debates*, 275–276; *Records* 2:81–82.
10. See 4 September: *Debates*, 475; *Records* 2:498.
11. Gouverneur Morris, 7 September: *Debates*, 495; *Records* 2:539.
12. See 7 September: *Debates*, 496; *Records* 2:539.
13. See Gouverneur Morris, 20 August: *Debates*, 397; *Records* 2:342; and 27 August: *Debates*, 440; *Records* 2:427.
14. Gouverneur Morris, 20 August: *Debates*, 397; *Records* 2:342.
15. See Edmund Randolph, 29 May: *Debates*, 9; *Records* 1:21.
16. James Wilson, 21 July: *Debates*, 268; *Records* 2:73.
17. Gouverneur Morris, 21 July: *Debates*, 270–271; *Records* 2:75–76.
18. Gouverneur Morris, 15 August: *Debates*, 375; *Records* 2:299.
19. Gouverneur Morris, 21 July: *Debates*, 273; *Records* 2:78–79.
20. Gouverneur Morris, 21 July: *Debates*, 270; *Records* 2:75.
21. In fact, the council of revision never received the support of more than three state delegations. For the closest that it ever came to passing, see 21 July: *Debates*, 274; *Records* 2:80.
22. See Michael J. Klarman, *The Framers' Coup: The Making of the United States Constitution* (Oxford: Oxford University Press, 2016), 160–161.
23. William Michael Treanor, "The Case of the Dishonest Scrivener: Gouverneur Morris and the Creation of the Federalist Constitution," *Michigan Law Review* 120.1 (2021), 36.
24. It should also be noted that two years earlier Morris had expressed a hint of skepticism about the idea of judicial review on the state level. He noted that "a law was once passed in New Jersey, which the judges pronounced to be unconstitutional, and therefore void" and then remarked that "surely no good citizen can wish to see this point decided

in the tribunals of Pennsylvania. Such power in judges is dangerous." He did go on to say, however, that "unless [this power] somewhere exists, the time employed in framing a bill of rights and form of government was merely thrown away." Gouverneur Morris, "Address to the Assembly of Pennsylvania on the Abolition of the Bank of North America" (1785), in *Writings*, 184.

25. Gouverneur Morris, 17 July: *Debates*, 241; *Records* 2:28. A week later, Morris also commented on the power of state courts to exercise the power of judicial review under the Articles of Confederation: see Gouverneur Morris, 23 July: *Debates*, 281; *Records* 2:92.

26. Gouverneur Morris, 15 August: *Debates*, 376; *Records* 2:299.

27. Gouverneur Morris to Lewis R. Morris, 10 December 1803, in Sparks 3:195.

28. See 6 August: *Debates*, 313; *Records* 2:183; and, for a slight revision of this provision (while still incorporating the "supreme law of the several States" language), see John Rutledge, 23 August: *Debates*, 423; *Records* 2:389. The New Jersey Plan had stipulated that laws passed by Congress would be "the supreme law of the respective States, so far forth as [they] shall relate to the said States or their citizens; and that the Judiciary of the several States shall be bound thereby in their decisions, any thing in the respective laws of the individual States to the contrary notwithstanding." See 15 June: *Debates*, 85; *Records* 1:245.

29. See 12 September: *Debates*, 522; *Records* 2:603.

30. For discussion, see Treanor, "Dishonest Scrivener," 93–96.

31. For Morris's early essay stressing the primacy of civil liberty over political liberty, see Gouverneur Morris, "Political Enquiries" (1776), in *Writings*, 5–11.

32. William Howard Adams, *Gouverneur Morris: An Independent Life* (New Haven, CT: Yale University Press, 2003), 142. On Morris's views of rights and liberty, see also J. Jackson Barlow, "Of Rights and Revolutions: Liberty and Equality in the Political Thought of Gouverneur Morris," paper presented at the American Political Science Association annual meeting, Seattle, WA, September 2011.

33. On bills of attainder, see Gouverneur Morris, 22 August: *Debates*, 418; *Records* 2:376. On religious tests for public office, see Gouverneur Morris, 30 August: *Debates*, 462; *Records* 2:468. On the suspension of habeas corpus, see Gouverneur Morris, 28 August: *Debates*, 445; *Records* 2:438.

34. See 12 September: *Records* 2:582, 588.

35. Gouverneur Morris to Robert Walsh, 5 February 1811, in Sparks 3:266.

36. Gouverneur Morris to Robert Walsh, 5 February 1811, in Sparks 3:266–267. Morris had made a similar point two decades earlier in a speech that he wrote for King Louis XVI: "There seems . . . to be some inconvenience in joining [a declaration of the rights of man] to a constitution, because if the constitution secures those rights, whatever they may be, it is unnecessary, and otherwise it is useless; but there is in every case the risk of seeming contradictions. Controversies may thence arise, and whoever may be the judge of such controversies, becomes thereby arbiter of the constitution." Gouverneur Morris, "Observations on the New Constitution of France" (1791), in *Writings*, 253.

37. Gouverneur Morris to Robert Walsh, 5 February 1811, in Sparks 3: 267–268.

38. Gouverneur Morris, "Remarks upon the Principles and Views of the London Corresponding Society" (1795), in *Writings*, 288.

39. John Rutledge, 5 June: *Debates*, 42; *Records* 1:124. Edmund Randolph, 18 July: *Debates*, 253; *Records* 2:46.

40. Madison simply recorded that Morris "urged also the necessity of such a provision." Gouverneur Morris, 18 July: *Debates*, 253; *Records* 2:46.

41. For the vote to "empower" (but not require) Congress to establish lower courts, see 18 July: *Debates*, 253; *Records* 2:46. For discussion, see Klarman, *The Framers' Coup*, 165–166.

42. For the Committee of Detail's version of the judicial vesting clause, see *Debates*, 316; *Records* 2:186. For Morris's version, see *Debates*, 520; *Records* 2:600. For Morris's admission that this shift in language was deliberate, see Gouverneur Morris to Timothy Pickering, 22 December 1814, in Sparks 3:323. See also the discussion in Treanor, "Dishonest Scrivener," 89–93.

43. See Kathryn Turner, "Federalist Policy and the Judiciary Act of 1801," *William and Mary Quarterly* 22, no. 1 (January 1965), 3–32.

44. Gouverneur Morris to Robert R. Livingston, 20 February 1801, in Sparks 3:153–154.

45. Thomas Jefferson to John Dickinson, 19 December 1801, in *The Papers of Thomas Jefferson*, ed. Julian P. Boyd et al. (Princeton, NJ: Princeton University Press, 1950–2017), 36:165–166.

46. On Morris's opposition to the repeal of the Judiciary Act, see J. Jackson Barlow, "Representation Unbound: Gouverneur Morris on the 'Revolution of 1800,'" paper presented at the American Political Science Association annual meeting, New Orleans, LA, September 2012.

47. Gouverneur Morris, "Speech in the Senate on the Repeal of the Judiciary Act of 1801," 14 January 1802, in *Writings*, 317. See also Gouverneur Morris, "Speech in the Senate on the Repeal of the Judiciary Act of 1801," 8 January 1802, in *Writings*, 311.

48. See Edmund Randolph, 29 May: *Debates*, 9; *Records* 1:21.

49. John Dickinson and Gouverneur Morris, 27 August: *Debates*, 441; *Records* 2:428. For the vote, see 27 August: *Debates*, 442; *Records* 2:429.

50. Gouverneur Morris, "Observations on the New Constitution of France" (1791), in *Writings*, 263.

51. Gouverneur Morris, "Notes on the Form for a Constitution for France" (1791?), in *Writings*, 271.

52. Morris, "Speech in the Senate on the Repeal of the Judiciary Act of 1801," 8 January 1802, in *Writings*, 308.

53. Morris, "Speech in the Senate on the Repeal of the Judiciary Act of 1801," 8 January 1802, 307.

54. Morris, "Speech in the Senate on the Repeal of the Judiciary Act of 1801," 8 January 1802, 312–313.

55. Morris, "Speech in the Senate on the Repeal of the Judiciary Act of 1801," 14 January 1802, in *Writings*, 331–332.

CHAPTER 9. THE CURSE OF HEAVEN: SLAVERY

1. See, respectively, Sean Wilentz, *No Property in Man: Slavery and Antislavery at the Nation's Founding* (Cambridge, MA: Harvard University Press, 2018), 76; John Patrick Coby, "America's Machiavellian: Gouverneur Morris at the Constitutional Convention," *Review of Politics* 79, no. 4 (Fall 2017), 648; Melanie Randolph Miller, *An Incautious Man: The Life of Gouverneur Morris* (Wilmington, DE: Intercollegiate Studies Institute, 2008), 73; see also 78–79; Noah Feldman, *The Three Lives of James Madison: Genius, Partisan, President* (New York: Random House, 2017), 158; David O. Stewart, *The Summer of 1787: The Men Who Invented the Constitution* (New York: Simon & Schuster, 2007), 192; David K. Nichols, "Gouverneur Morris and the Creation of American Constitutionalism," in *Natural Right and Political Philosophy: Essays in Honor of Catherine Zuckert and Michael Zuckert*, ed. Ann Ward and Lee Ward (Notre Dame, IN: University of Notre Dame Press, 2013), 257; and John Dickerson, *The Hardest Job in the World: The American Presidency* (New York: Random House, 2020), 447.

2. Abraham Lincoln, "Address at Cooper Institute," 27 February 1860, in *The Collected Works of Abraham Lincoln*, Roy P. Basler (New Brunswick, NJ: Rutgers University Press, 1953–1955), 3:531.

3. Henry Cabot Lodge, "Gouverneur Morris," in *Historical and Political Essays* (Boston: Houghton, Mifflin, and Company, [1886] 1892), 84.

4. Gouverneur Morris, 13 July: *Debates*, 225; *Records* 1:604; and 8 August: *Debates*, 333; *Records* 2:223.

5. Jack Heyburn, "Gouverneur Morris and James Wilson at the Constitutional Convention," *University of Pennsylvania Journal of Constitutional Law* 20, no. 1 (October 2017), 190; and Richard Beeman, *Plain, Honest Men: The Making of the American Constitution* (New York: Random House, 2009), 211.

6. See David N. Gellman, *Emancipating New York: The Politics of Slavery and Freedom, 1777–1827* (Baton Rouge: Louisiana State University Press, 2006), 33–34; James J. Kirschke, *Gouverneur Morris: Author, Statesman, and Man of the World* (New York: St. Martin's Press, 2005), 61, 163; and Max M. Mintz, *Gouverneur Morris and the American Revolution* (Norman: University of Oklahoma Press, 1970), 7, 14–15, 76.

7. See Gouverneur Morris, diary entries of 4 March 1799, 9 March 1799, and 14 June 1803, in *The Diaries of Gouverneur Morris: New York, 1799–1816*, ed. Melanie Randolph Miller (Charlottesville: University of Virginia Press, 2018), 10–11, 286.

8. Gouverneur Morris, 17 April 1777, in *Journals of the Provincial Congress, Provincial Convention, and Committee of Safety and Council of Safety of the State of New-York, 1775–1776–1777* (Albany: Thurlow Weed, 1842), 1:887.

9. See 19 April 1777, in *Journals of the Provincial Congress, Provincial Convention, and Committee of Safety and Council of Safety of the State of New-York, 1775–1776–1777*, 1:889.

10. See Gellman, *Emancipating New York*.

11. See Gary B. Nash and Jean R. Soderlund, *Freedom By Degrees: Emancipation in Pennsylvania and Its Aftermath* (Oxford: Oxford University Press, 1991).

12. On the Pennsylvania delegation, see Paul Finkelman, "The Pennsylvania Dele-

gation and the Peculiar Institution: The Two Faces of the Keystone State," *Pennsylvania Magazine of History and Biography* 112, no. 1 (January 1988), 49–71.

13. Luther Martin, 21 August: *Debates*, 410; *Records* 2:364. George Mason, 22 August: *Debates*, 314; *Records* 2:370.

14. Charles Pinckney, 22 August: *Debates*, 413; *Records* 2:371. John Rutledge, 21 August: *Debates*, 411; *Records* 2:364. Charles Cotesworth Pinckney, 22 August: *Debates*, 413; *Records* 2:371.

15. See George William Van Cleve, *A Slaveholders' Union: Slavery, Politics, and the Constitution in the Early American Republic* (Chicago: University of Chicago Press, 2010), 109.

16. For studies that stress the proslavery side of the Convention and the Constitution, see Paul Finkelman, *Slavery and the Founders: Race and Liberty in the Age of Jefferson*, 3rd ed. (New York: Routledge, 2014), chap. 1; Van Cleve, *A Slaveholders' Union*, chaps. 3–4; David Waldstreicher, *Slavery's Constitution: From Revolution to Ratification* (New York: Hill and Wang, 2009); and William M. Wiecek, *The Sources of Antislavery Constitutionalism in America, 1760–1848* (Ithaca, NY: Cornell University Press, 1977), chap. 3. For studies that stress the antislavery side, see Don E. Fehrenbacher, *The Slaveholding Republic: An Account of the United States Government's Relations to Slavery* (Oxford: Oxford University Press, 2001), chap. 2; Earl M. Maltz, "The Idea of the Proslavery Constitution," *Journal of the Early Republic* 17, no. 1 (Spring 1997), 37–59; and Wilentz, *No Property in Man*.

17. Gouverneur Morris, 13 July: *Debates*, 225; *Records* 1:604–605.

18. See 11 June: *Debates*, 70; *Records* 1:201. For context, see Paul Finkelman, "Slavery and the Constitutional Convention: Making a Covenant with Death," in *Beyond Confederation: Origins of the Constitution and American National Identity*, ed. Richard Beeman, Stephen Botein, and Edward C. Carter II (Chapel Hill: University of North Carolina Press, 1987), 198.

19. Gouverneur Morris, 11 July: *Debates*, 212; *Records* 1:583.

20. Gouverneur Morris, 11 July: *Debates*, 216; *Records* 1:588.

21. Charles Cotesworth Pinckney and William Davie, 12 July: *Debates*, 218; *Records* 1:592–593.

22. Gouverneur Morris, 12 July: *Debates*, 218–219; *Records* 1:593.

23. Gouverneur Morris, 13 July: *Debates*, 224–225; *Records* 1:604–605; and 8 August: *Debates*, 332–333; *Records* 2:222–223.

24. Gouverneur Morris, 12 July: *Debates*, 217; *Records* 1:592.

25. See Pierce Butler, 12 July: *Debates*, 217; *Records* 1:592.

26. See Gouverneur Morris, 12 July: *Debates*, 217–218; *Records* 1:592–593; and 8 August: *Debates*, 333; *Records* 2:223.

27. Gouverneur Morris, 24 July: *Debates*, 290; *Records* 2:106.

28. See *Debates*, 309, 313; *Records* 2:178, 182–183.

29. Gouverneur Morris, 8 August: *Debates*, 331–332; *Records* 2:221–222.

30. Gouverneur Morris, 8 August: *Debates*, 332; *Records* 2:222.

31. It is thus entirely unfair to Morris to suggest, as one (generally excellent) scholar does, that "in reviewing the controversy over the three-fifths clause, one comes away with a depressing sense of the near-total absence of anything resembling a moral dimension to

the debate. . . . Those few Northerners like Gouverneur Morris, Rufus King, or Elbridge Gerry who voiced unhappiness with the idea of counting the slave population in apportioning representation did so either out of a fear that Northern interests were being sacrificed to those of the South or, as James Wilson phrased it, the 'disgust' that their white constituents may have felt about being considered even in the same category as slaves." Beeman, *Plain, Honest Men*, 213–214.

32. Jonathan Dayton, Roger Sherman, Charles Pinckney, and James Wilson, 8 August: *Debates*, 333; *Records* 2:223.

33. See Leonard L. Richards, *The Slave Power: The Free North and Southern Domination, 1780–1860* (Baton Rouge: Louisiana State University Press, 2000), chap. 2.

34. Charles Pinckney, 21 August: *Debates*, 411; *Records* 2:364.

35. See *Debates*, 313; *Records* 2:183.

36. For Morris's arguments against a prohibition on export taxes, see Gouverneur Morris, 8 August: *Debates*, 332; *Records* 2:222; 16 August: *Debates*, 379, 380–381; *Records* 2:306, 307; and 21 August: *Debates*, 407–408; *Records* 2:360.

37. See, for instance, Charles Cotesworth Pinckney, 22 August: *Debates*, 413; *Records* 2:371.

38. Gouverneur Morris, 22 August: *Debates*, 415; *Records* 2:374.

39. See 24 August: *Debates*, 428; *Records* 2:400. For the characterization of this settlement as a "dirty compromise," see Finkelman, "Slavery and the Constitutional Convention," 214.

40. See 25 August: *Debates*, 435; *Records* 2:415.

41. Gouverneur Morris, 25 August: *Debates*, 435–436; *Records* 2:415.

42. George Mason, 25 August: *Debates*, 436; *Records* 2:415.

43. See Wilentz, *No Property in Man*, 59.

44. See 29 August: *Debates*, 454; *Records* 2:453–454.

45. See 29 August: *Debates*, 454; *Records* 2:453–454; and 12 September: *Debates*, 521; *Records* 2:577.

46. Wilentz, *No Property in Man*, 145; see also 110–111. For further discussion, see William Michael Treanor, "The Case of the Dishonest Scrivener: Gouverneur Morris and the Creation of the Federalist Constitution," *Michigan Law Review* 120, no. 1 (2021), 43, 97–98.

47. See *Debates*, 561; *Records* 2:662.

48. Luther Martin, *The Genuine Information, Delivered to the Legislature of the State of Maryland, Relative to the Proceedings of the General Convention, Held at Philadelphia, in 1787*, in *Records* 3:210.

49. Akhil Reed Amar, *America's Constitution: A Biography* (New York: Random House, 2005), 257.

50. See *Annals of Congress*, 6th Cong., 1st sess., 14 May 1800, 183.

51. Gouverneur Morris, "Speech on the Free Navigation of the Mississippi River, and the Right of Deposit within the Spanish Territories" (24 February 1803), in Sparks 3:414.

52. Richard Brookhiser writes that this part of Morris's speech "was, along with his encouragement of the Newburgh near-mutiny, the worst argument of his public life. . . . How had the man who had railed against the three-fifths rule and the slave trade, and

their corrupting effect on republican institutions, come to this point? . . . Whatever his reasons, it was a wicked argument, and if he had come to the point of saying such things, it was just as well that he was leaving public life." Richard Brookhiser, *Gentleman Revolutionary: Gouverneur Morris, the Rake Who Wrote the Constitution* (New York: Free Press, 2003), 170. On the other hand, J. Jackson Barlow points out that "even as [Morris] advocated the acquisition [of New Orleans] by appealing to southern self-interest, he took care to portray that self-interest in its ugliest light." J. Jackson Barlow, "Earning Heaven's Curse: Gouverneur Morris on Americans and the Slave Power," ms. 22. I am grateful to Barlow for sharing his essay with me prior to publication.

53. Gouverneur Morris to Charles W. Hare, 30 June 1812, in *The Diary and Letters of Gouverneur Morris*, ed. Anne Cary Morris (New York: Charles Scribner's Sons, 1888), 2:542–543.

54. Gouverneur Morris to Harrison Gray Otis, 29 April 1813, in *Diary and Letters of Gouverneur Morris*, 2:552.

CHAPTER 10. A DECLARATION OF MOTIVES: THE PREAMBLE

1. See *Debates*, 552; *Records* 2:651.
2. Akhil Reed Amar, *America's Constitution: A Biography* (New York: Random House, 2005), 471. In an attempt to rectify the lack of attention paid to the preamble, Amar devotes more than fifty pages to it: see Amar, *America's Constitution*, chap. 1.
3. Sanford Levinson, *Our Undemocratic Constitution: Where the Constitution Goes Wrong (and How We the People Can Correct It)* (Oxford: Oxford University Press, 2008), 13.
4. Gouverneur Morris, "Speech in the Senate on the Repeal of the Judiciary Act of 1801," 14 January 1802, in *Writings*, 316.
5. Amar, *America's Constitution*, 471.
6. See https://malegislature.gov/laws/constitution.
7. *Records* 2:137.
8. *Records* 2:138.
9. For the initial proposal by Randolph and Morris to establish "a *supreme* Legislative, Executive and Judiciary," see 30 May: *Debates*, 11; *Records* 1:33.
10. See *Debates*, 522–523; *Records* 2:583–584.
11. *Debates*, 308; *Records* 2:177. For earlier drafts of Wilson's preamble, see *Records* 2:150, 152, 163.
12. See 7 August: *Debates*, 319; *Records* 2:193, 196, 209.
13. David Lefer, *Founding Conservatives: How a Group of Unsung Heroes Saved the American Revolution* (New York: Sentinel, 2013), 322.
14. See *Records* 2:605.
15. Joseph J. Ellis, *The Quartet: Orchestrating the Second American Revolution, 1783–1789* (New York: Alfred A. Knopf, 2015), 151. For a similar statement, see Joseph J. Ellis, *American Dialogue: The Founders and Us* (New York: Alfred A. Knopf, 2018), 239.

16. Amar, *America's Constitution*, 5. On the other hand, another scholar conducted a detailed study of how the phrase "the people" was used in various contexts, both during the founding period and in later years, and concluded that the "We, the people" in the Constitution's preamble was initially understood to include only eligible voters, and only later expanded to include the entire American populace. See Morris Forkosch, "Who Are the 'People' in the Preamble to the Constitution?" *Case Western Reserve Law Review* 19 (January 1968), 644–712.

17. See John W. Welch and James A. Heilpern, "Recovering our Forgotten Preamble," *Southern California Law Review* 91, no. 6 (September 2018), 1050–1051.

18. Patrick Henry, speech in the Virginia state ratifying convention, 4 June 1788, in *The Anti-Federalist: Writings by the Opponents of the Constitution*, ed. Herbert J. Storing (Chicago: University of Chicago Press, 1985), 297.

19. Samuel Adams to Richard Henry Lee, 3 December 1787, in *The Writings of Samuel Adams*, ed. Harry A. Cushing (New York: G. P. Putnam's Sons, 1904–1908), 4:324.

20. 15 June: *Debates*, 83; *Records* 1:242. In this, the New Jersey Plan followed the call for the Philadelphia Convention, which stated that its purpose was to "render the constitution of the Federal Government adequate to the exigencies of the Union." See Address of the Annapolis Convention, 14 September 1786, in *The Papers of Alexander Hamilton*, ed. Harold C. Syrett and Jacob Cooke (New York: Columbia University Press, 1961–1987), 3:689.

21. See Amar, *America's Constitution*, 36.

22. Abraham Lincoln, "First Inaugural Address," 4 March 1861, in *The Collected Works of Abraham Lincoln*, Roy P. Basler (New Brunswick, NJ: Rutgers University Press, 1953–1955), 4:265.

23. Catherine Drinker Bowen, *Miracle at Philadelphia: The Story of the Constitutional Convention, May to September 1787* (Boston: Little, Brown, 1966), 241.

24. See, for instance, Isaiah Berlin, "The Pursuit of the Ideal," in *The Proper Study of Mankind: An Anthology of Essays*, ed. Henry Hardy (New York: Farrar, Straus and Giroux, 1997), 1–16.

25. 29 May: *Debates*, 7–8; *Records* 1:20. The next day, Morris and Edmund Randolph jointly proposed a motion "that a union of the States merely federal will not accomplish the objects proposed by the Articles of Confederation, namely, common defence, security of liberty, and general welfare." 30 May: *Debates*, 11; *Records* 1:33.

26. See 4 September: *Debates*, 473, 475; *Records* 2:497, 499.

27. For the Pennsylvania constitution, see https://avalon.law.yale.edu/18th_century/pa08.asp. For Morris's oration, see Gouverneur Morris, "Oration on the Necessity for Declaring Independence from Britain" (1776), in *Writings*, 21.

28. Morris, "Speech in the Senate on the Repeal of the Judiciary Act of 1801," 14 January 1802, in *Writings*, 316.

29. See James Wilson, 18 July: *Debates*, 255; *Records* 48–49.

30. James Monroe, "Observations Upon the Proposed Plan of Federal Government" (1788), in *The Writings of James Monroe*, ed. Stanislaus Murray Hamilton (New York: G. P. Putnam's Sons, 1898), 1:356.

31. Brutus #12, 7 February 1788, in *The Anti-Federalist*, 169–170.

32. James Wilson, remark at the Pennsylvania ratifying convention, 28 November 1787, in *The Documentary History of the Ratification of the Constitution*, ed. Merrill Jensen et al. (Madison: Wisconsin Historical Society Press, 1976), 2:383–384.

33. Alexander Hamilton, *Federalist* #84, 28 May 1788, in Alexander Hamilton, John Jay, and James Madison, *The Federalist*, ed. George W. Carey and James McClellan (Indianapolis: Liberty Fund, 2001), 445.

34. See Jonathan Gienapp, "The Myth of the Constitutional Given: Enumeration and National Power at the Founding," *American University Law Review* 69, no. 183 (2020), esp. 194–209; and William Michael Treanor, "The Case of the Dishonest Scrivener: Gouverneur Morris and the Creation of the Federalist Constitution," *Michigan Law Review* 120, no. 1 (2021), 54–58.

35. James Madison, "The Bank Bill," 8 February 1791, in *The Papers of James Madison*, ed. William T. Hutchinson et al. (Chicago: University of Chicago Press and Charlottesville: University Press of Virginia, 1962–1991), 13:384.

36. James Madison to Robert S. Garnett, 11 February 1824, in *The Papers of James Madison: Retirement Series*, ed. David B. Mattern et al. (Charlottesville: University Press of Virginia, 2009–2016), 3:216.

37. See *Chisholm v. Georgia*, 2 U.S. 419 (1793), 463, 471; *Martin v. Hunter's Lessee*, 14 U.S. 304, 324–325; and *McCulloch v. Maryland*, 17 U.S. 316, 403–405.

38. On the Supreme Court's occasional use of the preamble in constitutional interpretation, see Dan Himmelfarb, "The Preamble in Constitutional Interpretation," *Seton Hall Constitutional Law Journal* 2, no. 1 (Fall 1991), 127–209; and Welch and Heilpern, "Recovering our Forgotten Preamble." On the concept of a constitutional preamble and the roles that preambles play in constitutional interpretation in the United States and around the world, see Liav Orgad, "The Preamble in Constitutional Interpretation," *International Journal of Constitutional Law* 8, no. 4 (October 2010), 714–738.

39. *Jacobson v. Massachusetts*, 197 U.S. 11 (1905), 22.

40. Joseph Story, *Commentaries on the Constitution of the United States* (Boston: Hilliard, Gray, and Company, 1833), 1:445.

41. Story, *Commentaries on the Constitution of the United States*, 1:443.

42. For an account of the formation of the preamble and its impact on subsequent American history, see Peter Charles Hoffer, *For Ourselves and Our Posterity: The Preamble to the Federal Constitution in American History* (Oxford: Oxford University Press, 2013).

43. Frederick Douglass, "Change of Opinion Announced," 23 May 1851, in *The Essential Douglass: Selected Writings and Speeches*, ed. Nicholas Buccola (Indianapolis: Hackett, 2016), 43.

44. Susan B. Anthony, "Is It a Crime for a Citizen of the United States to Vote?" (1872), in Lynn Sherr, *Failure Is Impossible: Susan B. Anthony in Her Own Words* (New York: Crown, 1996), 110–111.

45. Franklin D. Roosevelt, Annual Message to Congress, 6 January 1937, in *The Public Papers and Addresses of Franklin D. Roosevelt*, ed. Samuel I. Rosenman (New York: Random House, 1938), 5:639.

46. Martin Luther King, Jr., *Why We Can't Wait* (New York: Signet Classics, [1964] 2000), 11.

47. Ronald Reagan, "Proclamation 5634: Law Day, 21 April 1987," https://www.reagan library.gov/archives/speech/proclamation-5634-law-day-usa-1987.

EPILOGUE: FROM CONSTITUTION-MAKER TO ASPIRING CONSTITUTION-BREAKER

1. Gouverneur Morris, 13 July: *Debates*, 225; *Records* 1:604; and 8 August: *Debates*, 333; *Records* 2:223.
2. George Mason and Gouverneur Morris, 31 August: *Debates*, 467; *Records* 2:479.
3. Gouverneur Morris, 17 September: *Debates*, 549; *Records* 2:645.
4. Gouverneur Morris to William Hill Wells, 24 February 1815, in Sparks 3:339.
5. Gouverneur Morris to John Dickenson, 23 May 1803, in Sparks 3:181.
6. Gouverneur Morris to William Hill Wells, 24 February 1815, in Sparks 3:339.
7. James J. Kirschke, *Gouverneur Morris: Author, Statesman, and Man of the World* (New York: St. Martin's Press, 2005), 200.
8. Gouverneur Morris to William Carmichael, 4 July 1789, in Sparks 2:73. For a similar statement, see Gouverneur Morris to George Washington, 24 January 1790, in *The Papers of George Washington: Presidential Series*, ed. Dorothy Twohig et al. (Charlottesville: University Press of Virginia, 1987–2016), 5:49.
9. Gouverneur Morris to Rufus King, 4 June 1800, in Sparks 3:128.
10. Gouverneur Morris, "Speech in the Senate on the Repeal of the Judiciary Act of 1801," 14 January 1802, in *Writings*, 315–316; see also 331.
11. Gouverneur Morris, "Speech in the Senate on the Repeal of the Judiciary Act of 1801," 8 January 1802, in *Writings*, 311.
12. Gouverneur Morris to Robert R. Livingston, 20 March 1802, in Sparks 3:165.
13. Gouverneur Morris to Henry W. Livingston, 25 November 1803, in Sparks 3:185–186. Over a decade later, Morris had not changed his mind about the harm that had been done by the repeal of the Judiciary Act: "When, in debate on the judiciary I pronounced the Constitution to be gone, it was considered by many as a mere turn of rhetoric. I have frequently since recurred to that occasion, and repeated the same sentiment. It was and is my serious conviction. The omnipotence of legislative authority, assumed by the Congress, resides essentially in the House of Representatives, to which a pair of complaisant Presidents [i.e., Jefferson and Madison] turned over executive authority also." Gouverneur Morris to Lewis B. Sturges, 12 February 1814, in Sparks 3:302.
14. Gouverneur Morris, "Election Address" (1810), in *Writings*, 496.
15. On the war, see Donald R. Hickey, *The War of 1812: A Forgotten Conflict* (Urbana: University of Illinois Press, 2012); J. C. A. Stagg, *Mr. Madison's War: Politics, Diplomacy, and Warfare in the Early American Republic, 1783–1830* (Princeton, NJ: Princeton University Press, 1983); and Alan Taylor, *The Civil War of 1812: American Citizens, British Subjects, Irish Rebels, & Indian Allies* (New York: Vintage, 2010).

16. Gouverneur Morris to Egbert Benson, 23 June 1813, in Sparks 3:294

17. Gouverneur Morris, "The British Treaty" (1807), in *Writings*, 428. The editor of this volume, J. Jackson Barlow, deemed the authorship of this pamphlet as uncertain; for confirmation that it was written by Morris, see Melanie Randolph Miller, editor's introduction in *The Diaries of Gouverneur Morris: New York, 1799–1816* (Charlottesville: University of Virginia Press, 2018), xxxi.

18. Gouverneur Morris to James Parish, 6 March 1813, in *The Diary and Letters of Gouverneur Morris*, ed. Anne Cary Morris (New York: Charles Scribner's Sons, 1888), 2:548.

19. Gouverneur Morris to Harrison Gray Otis, 29 April 1812, in Sparks 3:290–291.

20. Gouverneur Morris to Charles W. Hare, 30 June 1812, in *The Diary and Letters of Gouverneur Morris*, 2:542.

21. Gouverneur Morris, "An Address to the People of the State of New York on the Present State of Affairs" (1812), in *Writings*, 538.

22. See also, however, Gouverneur Morris, "Oration Before the Washington Benevolent Society" (1813), in *Writings*, 584–585.

23. Gouverneur Morris to Rufus King, 23 March 1814, in *The Life and Correspondence of Rufus King*, ed. Charles R. King (New York: G. P. Putnam's Sons, 1898), 5:389–390.

24. Gouverneur Morris to Robert Oliver, 18 July 1814, in *The Diary and Letters of Gouverneur Morris*, 2:566.

25. Gouverneur Morris to Rufus King, 1 November 1814, in Sparks 3:317.

26. See Gouverneur Morris to Lewis B. Sturges, 1 November 1814, in Sparks 3:319.

27. Gouverneur Morris to David B. Ogden, 11 February 1814, in *The Diary and Letters of Gouverneur Morris*, 2:559.

28. The Hartford Convention still awaits an authoritative modern study. For an older account by the convention's secretary, see Theodore Dwight, *History of the Hartford Convention* (New York: N. and J. White, 1833). For a somewhat more recent examination of the events leading up to it, see James M. Banner, Jr., *To the Hartford Convention: The Federalists and the Origins of Party Politics in Massachusetts, 1789–1815* (New York: Alfred A. Knopf, 1970).

29. Gouverneur Morris to Harrison Gray Otis, 8 November 1814, in Sparks 3:319–321.

30. Gouverneur Morris to Timothy Pickering, 22 December 1814, in Sparks 3:324.

31. Richard Brookhiser, *Gentleman Revolutionary: Gouverneur Morris, the Rake Who Wrote the Constitution* (New York: Free Press, 2003), 204.

32. Gouverneur Morris to Rufus King, 7 January 1815, in *The Life and Correspondence of Rufus King*, 5:458–459.

33. Gouverneur Morris to Moss Kent, 10 January 1815, in Sparks 3:326.

34. Gouverneur Morris to Richard Townsend, 14 February 1815, in *The Diary and Letters of Gouverneur Morris*, 2:588.

35. Gouverneur Morris to David B. Ogden, 17 February 1815, in *The Diary and Letters of Gouverneur Morris*, 2:582.

36. Gouverneur Morris to Timothy Pickering, 22 December 1814, in Sparks 3:323.

37. Gouverneur Morris, 12 July: *Debates*, 218; *Records* 1:593.

38. Gouverneur Morris to the Committee of Correspondence, Philadelphia, 27 August 1816, in Sparks 3:361.

39. Gouverneur Morris, "An Inaugural Discourse" (1816), in *Writings*, 649–650.

APPENDIX: MORRIS'S GREAT CONVENTION SPEECHES

1. Gouverneur Morris, 2 July: *Debates*, 178–180; *Records* 1:511–514.
2. Gouverneur Morris, 19 July: *Debates*, 256–258; *Records* 2:52–54.
3. Gouverneur Morris, 8 August: *Debates*, 331–333; *Records* 2:221–223.

Index

Act of Union of 1707, 169
Adams, Abigail, 10–11
Adams, John, 1, 90–91, 120, 165
Adams, John Quincy, 29
Adams, Samuel, 168
amendments, Constitutional, 93, 120, 133, 181
"An American" (Morris), 65, 179
Anthony, Susan B., 173
Antoinette, Marie, 10
apportionment
    Congressional powers regarding, 100
    House of Representatives and, 97–98, 99–101, 153–159
    property and, 96, 97–98
    slavery and, 153–159
    tax assessment and, 154, 157
    viewpoints regarding, 155–156, 157, 159
aristocracy, 80–81, 90, 103–104
aristocratic capitalism, 94
army, condition of, 15
Article I, 51, 56–57, 128
Article II, 51, 56–57, 128
Article III, 51, 56–57, 128
Article IV, 51, 170–171
Article V, 51, 169
Article VI, 51, 67–68, 142
Article VII, 51
Articles of Confederation, 3, 16, 62, 168, 170

Baldwin, Abraham, 86
Barlow, J. Jackson, 239n52
Battle of New Orleans, 181
Bedford, Gunning, 59, 71, 223n56
Berlin, Isaiah, 170
bills of rights, 14, 143–144, 171
"Bizarre" plantation, 35
Black people, voting rights of, 101
Blackstone, William, 45
Blount, William, 58
Bodin, Jean, 68
Bowen, Catherine Drinker, 169
Brearly, David, 74, 115

bribery, impeachment for, 135
Britain, ministers to, 27
Bronck, Jonas, 11
Brookhiser, Richard, 2–3, 50, 181, 238–239n52
Broom, Jacob, 130
Burke, Edmund, 25
Burr, Aaron, 8, 31, 33, 120
Butler, Pierce
    apportionment, viewpoint of, 155, 157
    fugitive slave clause, viewpoint of, 161
    presidential veto, viewpoint of, 127
    property, viewpoint of, 96–97
    quotes of, 63, 86, 96–97, 103, 122
    Senate payment, viewpoint of, 87

cabinet, presidential, 125, 139–140
Calhoun, John C., 153
campaign finance laws, 105
Carlisle Commissioners, 64–65
Carmichael, William, 25, 26
Carroll, Daniel, 16, 115
Chief Justice of the Supreme Court, 125, 139–140
Chisholm v. Georgia, 172
citizenship, requirements for, 46
civil liberty, 46, 95, 143
civil war, 71, 132, 177, 180
Clinton, DeWitt, 34
Clinton, George, 123
Clymer, George, 40
Commentaries on the Constitution of the United States (Story), 172
Committee of Detail, 48–49, 166
Committee of Style, 47, 48, 50–51
Committee on Postponed Parts, 115, 119, 170
Confederation Congress, 52–53, 62, 66, 79, 122–123. *See also* Continental Congress
Congress
    abilities and virtue in, 83
    apportionment powers of, 100
    Constitutional amendments regarding, 181
    Constitutional Convention deliberations regarding, 53, 79

Congress, *continued*
    as envisioned in Virginia Plan, 71–72, 138
    potential selection of president of, 109–110
    powers of, 53
    presidential veto power over, 57, 108, 122, 124, 126–128
    state representation in, 74–76
    treasurer in, 57
    See also House of Representatives; Senate
Connecticut, 67, 109
Connecticut Compromise (Great Compromise), 42, 76, 82, 96
Constitution
    cover letter of, 52–53, 68
    overview of, 37
    provision streamlining in, 51–52
    punctuation use in, 53–54
    signing of, 58–59
    smuggling changes in, 53–57
    See also preamble of the Constitution; *specific articles; specific clauses*
Constitutional Convention
    break of, 42–43
    committees in, 43, 209n50
    delegate attendance in, 41
    delegates in, 42, 63
    importance of, 37
    Madison's influence regarding, 195–196n12
    Morris as peacemaker in, 45
    Morris's absence from, 41–42, 75
    Morris's committee involvement in, 43
    Morris's delegate selection in, 39
    Morris's demeanor at, 44
    opening of, 41
    speech statistics in, 43
Continental Congress, 3, 15, 16–17, 64. *See also* Confederation Congress
Contract Clause, 57
cotton, 160
council of appointment, 124
council of revision, 124, 140–141
cover letter, Constitution, 52–53, 68
currency, 19

Dailey, Mary, 40
Davie, William R., 155–156
Dayton, Jonathan, 40, 158–159

decentralized political system, during Revolutionary War, 62
decimal system, for currency, 19
Declaration of Independence, 1–2, 127, 194n4
Declaration of the Rights of Man and of the Citizen (France), 144
Defence of the Constitutions of Government of the United States (Adams), 90
Delaware, 75, 123, 130, 131
delegates, 38, 41, 42, 63, 69. *See also specific delegates*
Dickinson, John, 16, 59, 86, 102, 141
dirty compromise, 160
domestic emoluments clause, 57
Douglass, Frederick, 172–173
Dutch Republic, government structure in, 69

electoral college
    criticism regarding, 118–119
    Morris's viewpoint regarding, 174
    overview of, 115–116
    proposal of, 108–109, 115–119
    slavery role regarding, 226n44
    three-fifths compromise and, 116
elitism, 80–81, 89, 93, 98
Ellis, Joseph, 2, 52, 168
Ellsworth, Oliver, 102, 139
Embargo Act of 1807, 144, 163, 178
Engagements Clause, 57
England, government structure in, 141
Erie Canal, 4, 34, 99
Estates General, 25, 26
executive branch. *See* president/presidency

Farrand, Max, 38
Federalist, The, 3, 21
Federalist #10, 82
Federalist #39, 68
Federalist #48, 106
Federalist #68, 118
Federalist #72, 133
Federalist #84, 143, 171
Federalist Party, 31, 32, 146
federal judiciary, reorganization of, 32. *See also* judiciary; Supreme Court
financial plan, 19, 65
Fitzsimons, Thomas, 40

Flahaut, Adélaïde de, 24–25, 28
France
　conditions in, 28
　Declaration of the Rights of Man and of the Citizen, 144
　executions in, 81
　factions of, 28
　ministers to, 3–4, 16
　Morris in, 27–29
　nobility structure in, 81
　social hierarchy in, 26
Franklin, Benjamin
　as Constitutional Convention delegate, 39, 40
　at Constitution signing, 58
　Declaration of Independence and, 1
　dinner hosting by, 41
　impeachment, viewpoint of, 134
　legislature, viewpoint of, 79
　levity of, 46
　as minister to France, 3, 16, 27
　Morris and, 10
　personal life of, 6
　Philadelphia Academy and, 11–12
　preamble, viewpoint of, 172
　presidential veto, viewpoint of, 127
　quotes of, 122
　religion and, 74
　Society for Political Inquiries and, 20
　as stylist, 50
　voting, viewpoint of, 102
freehold requirement, 102, 103, 105
Fugitive Slave Clause, 57, 161–162

Gallatin, Albert, 53
Garrison, William Lloyd, 153
general welfare clause, 53–54
George III, 10, 29, 127
Georgia, 79, 101
Germany, government structure in, 69
Gerry, Elbridge
　Congress, viewpoint of, 106
　as Constitutional Convention delegate, 40
　impeachment, viewpoint of, 134
　presidency, viewpoint of, 111
　proposal of, 99
　quotes of, 73, 85–86

　signing refusal of, 58
　term limit, viewpoint of, 130
　vice president, viewpoint of, 46
Gorham, Nathaniel, 138, 155
Gouverneur, Sarah, 10
governors, 109, 122, 124, 125, 131
Great Compromise (Connecticut Compromise), 42, 76, 82, 96
Greece, government structure in, 69
Greene, Nathaniel, 16

Hamilton, Alexander
　bill of rights, viewpoint of, 143
　Committee of Style and, 48
　as Constitutional Convention delegate, 3, 40
　Constitution ratification and, 176
　death of, 33
　electoral college, viewpoint of, 117, 118, 119
　financial plan of, 19
　impeachment, viewpoint of, 134
　leadership of, 19–20
　Morris and, 4, 10
　as nationalist, 63
　prayer, viewpoint of, 74
　preamble, viewpoint of, 171
　presidency, viewpoint of, 107, 123
　presidential veto, viewpoint of, 127
　quotes of, 5, 30, 32, 37, 47, 63, 76, 86, 107, 124
　reputation of, 6
　Senate term limit, viewpoint of, 87
　term limit, viewpoint of, 130, 133
　writings of, 21, 59, 143
　writings regarding, 43
Hamilton, Elizabeth, 33
Hartford Convention, 180–181
Henry, Patrick, 21–22, 35, 168, 171
Hobbes, Thomas, 68
Houdon, Jean-Antoine, 12
House of Representatives
　abilities and virtue in, 83
　apportionment discussion regarding, 99–101, 153–159
　aristocracy and, 103–104
　Constitutional Convention deliberations regarding, 79

House of Representatives, *continued*
   election of 1800 determined by, 31
   property in apportionment formula
      regarding, 97–98
   role of, 95
   term limits for, 94, 105
   upper limit regarding, 57–58
   See also Congress; Senate
Hume, David, 45

immigrants, citizenship requirements for, 46
impeachment, 45, 125, 133–135, 147, 232n58
Impeachment Clause, 57
Ingersoll, Jared, 40
internal police, 72, 78

Jackson, Andrew, 181
Jackson, William, 59
Jacobson v. Massachusetts, 172
Jay, John, 10, 12, 14, 16, 65, 87, 124
Jefferson, Thomas
   criticism of, 32
   as Declaration of Independence writer, 1,
      194n4
   election of, 31, 120
   leadership of, 144
   as minister to France, 3, 27
   Morris and, 10, 23, 81, 221n14
   quotes of, 5, 40, 221n14
   as stylist, 50
   Supreme Court pick of, 145–146
   Virginia Declaration of Rights and, 1
Johnson, William Samuel, 48
judges
   appointment process for, 138–139
   impeachment of, 147
   midnight, 32, 146
   position rescinding of, 147–148
   term limit for, 137, 147
   See also Supreme Court
judicial vesting clause, 54–55, 56–57
judiciary
   Constitutional provisions for, 174
   executive branch and, 139–140
   Federalists and, 146
   judicial review in, 141–144
   state level review of, 233–234n24

   structure considerations regarding,
      145–146
   See also Supreme Court
Judiciary Act, 32, 55, 145–146, 147–148, 177,
      242n13

King, Martin Luther, Jr., 173
King, Rufus
   apportionment, viewpoint of, 155
   Committee of Style and, 48
   consolidation term use by, 68
   Constitutional Convention committee
      involvement of, 43
   electoral college, viewpoint of, 115
   impeachment, viewpoint of, 134
   Morris and, 177, 179
   popular election, viewpoint of, 113
   presidential veto, viewpoint of, 127
   property, viewpoint of, 96
   quotes of, 37, 96, 113
   term limit, viewpoint of, 130
   voting per capita, viewpoint of, 77
   writings of, 59
King's College, 64
Knox, Henry, 39

Lafayette, Marquis de, 10, 24, 29, 202n58
Lansing, John, 59, 67
law-of-the-land provision, 57
legislatures, state, 79
lifetime appointments, of Senate members,
      84–85, 86–87, 92
Lincoln, Abraham, 73, 150
Livingston, Henry W., 55
Livingston, Robert R., 1, 12, 14, 123–124, 177
Locke, John, 45
Lockean rights, 94–95
Lodge, Henry Cabot, 38, 150
Long, Staats, 11, 20
Louisiana Purchase, 32, 55, 210n83
Louis XVI, 10, 23–24, 26, 147
lower federal courts, 145

Madison, Dolley, 33
Madison, James
   Benjamin Franklin and, 41
   Committee of Style and, 48

Congress, viewpoint of, 106
  as Constitutional Convention delegate, 1, 3, 40
  Constitutional Convention speeches of, 43
  contributions of, 194n8
  council of revision, viewpoint of, 124
  description of, 178–179
  electoral college, viewpoint of, 115
  Federalist #10, 82
  impeachment, viewpoint of, 134, 135
  judicial review, viewpoint of, 141
  Morris and, 10
  as nationalist, 63
  national power, viewpoint of, 72
  popular election, viewpoint of, 113–114
  preamble, viewpoint of, 172
  presidency, viewpoint of, 107
  proposals of, 195n10
  quotes of, 3, 37, 38, 44–45, 47, 49, 50, 54, 58, 74, 76, 86, 87, 100, 106, 113–114, 128
  Senate, viewpoint of, 87–88
  term limit, viewpoint of, 130
  Virginia Plan and, 41, 73
  at Virginia state convention, 21–22
  voting, viewpoint of, 102
  writings of, 49, 59–61, 68
  writings regarding, 43
Manhattan, 4, 34
Marbury v. Madison, 142
Marshall, John, 10, 21–22, 35, 38, 142
Martin, Luther, 77, 130, 152, 162
Martin v. Hunter's Lessee, 172
Mason, George
  electoral college, viewpoint of, 117
  popular election, viewpoint of, 112
  presidency, viewpoint of, 111
  presidential veto, viewpoint of, 127
  quotes of, 86, 111, 112, 117, 225n27
  signing refusal of, 58
  slavery, viewpoint of, 152, 161
  term limit, viewpoint of, 130, 131, 133
  Virginia Declaration of Rights and, 1
  at Virginia state convention, 21–22
  writings of, 60
Massachusetts, 109, 165
McClurg, James, 130
McCulloch v. Maryland, 172

McHenry, James, 47, 54, 60, 67
Mercer, John Francis, 86, 141
midnight judges, 32, 146
Mifflin, Thomas, 40
Miller, Melanie, 7
Mississippi River, 163
Mississippi Territory, 162–163
mixed regime, 90
monarch, powers of, 90
Monroe, James, 10, 21–22, 171
Montesquieu, 45, 90
Montmorin, Count de, 24
"more perfect union" (preamble to the Constitution), 168–171
Morris, Gouverneur
  accolades for, 38
  accomplishments of, 3–4, 50
  antislavery efforts of, 151–152
  characteristics of, 44, 50
  as Constitution-breaker, 174–183
  cosmopolitan outlook of, 69–70
  criticism of, 17, 44–45, 53, 221n14
  death of, 4, 36
  education of, 11–12
  election of, 13
  elitism of, 80–81, 93, 98
  European diplomatic mission of, 27–29
  faith of, 15
  family of, 10–11
  fraud case against, 35–36
  home of, 11, 33
  illness/injuries of, 17–18, 33–34, 35
  as lawyer, 12
  levity of, 46
  naming of, 10
  in Paris, 23
  as passionate nationalist, 63–64
  as peacemaker, 45
  philosophical principles of, 45–46
  physical characteristics of, 12–13
  poetry writing by, 22
  political disenchantment/disillusionment of, 7, 32–33, 176–178
  private pursuits of, 20
  progressivism of, 98
  reputation of, 6, 50
  slavery history of, 151

Morris, Gouverneur, *continued*
   speeches of, 32, 61, 123, 131, 148, 150–151, 157–158
   travels of, 29
   writings of, 7, 22, 89
Morris, Gouverneur, Jr., 35
Morris, Lewis, 10, 11
Morris, Robert
   accomplishments of, 18
   as Articles of Confederation signer, 16
   Benjamin Franklin and, 41
   business ventures of, 20
   as Constitutional Convention delegate, 39, 40
   Gouverneur Morris and, 18, 39
   leadership of, 19–20
   national financial plan and, 19, 65
   quotes of, 18–19
   Senate term limit, viewpoint of, 87
Morrisana, 11, 13, 20, 30, 33
motions, statistics regarding, 207n29

National Assembly (France), 26
nationalists, 63–64
Necker, Jacques, 10, 24, 29
Newburgh conspiracy, 65
New Hampshire, 42, 109
New Jersey, 130
New Jersey Plan, 42, 63, 109, 168
new states and territories clauses, 55–56
New States Clause, 57
New York
   anti-British protest in, 80
   constitution, 3, 8, 14–15, 124
   Constitutional Convention involvement of, 42
   governor selection process in, 109, 123
   governor term limit in, 131
   Hartford Convention and, 180
   national government opposition by, 67
   Revolutionary War in, 13
   slavery in, 152
New-York Historical Society, 182–183
New York Provincial Congress, 3, 13, 14
Nichols, David, 208n39
Non-Importation Act of 1806, 163, 178
North, the, 159–160, 178

Ogden, David Bayard, 35–36
Ogden, Samuel, 30
Otis, Harrison Gray, 179, 180

Paine, Thomas, 50
Paris, 23, 81
partisanship, 91–92
Paterson, William, 45, 60, 75
Pennsylvania, 38–40, 79, 130, 152
Pennsylvania Abolition Society (Philadelphia's Society for the Relief of Free Negroes Unlawfully Held in Bondage), 152
Philadelphia, Pennsylvania, 38–39
Philadelphia Academy, 11–12
Philadelphia Convention. *See* Constitutional Convention
Pickering, Timothy, 50, 54, 180, 182
Pierce, William, 43–44, 46, 60
Pinckney, Charles
   electoral college, viewpoint of, 116, 117
   impeachment, viewpoint of, 134
   national power, viewpoint of, 72
   quotes of, 47, 88, 111, 112, 114, 117
   Senate term limit, viewpoint of, 87
   slavery, viewpoint of, 153, 159
Pinckney, Charles Cotesworth
   apportionment, viewpoint of, 155, 159
   candidacy of, 120
   committee proposition of, 82
   popular election, viewpoint of, 111, 112, 114
   quotes of, 155
   Senate, viewpoint of, 86, 87
   slavery, viewpoint of, 153, 155, 160
Pitt, William, 10, 27, 29
Place de Grève, 81
"Political Enquiries" (Morris), 94–95, 96
political parties, 117–118, 120. *See also* Federalist Party; Republican Party
popular election, 111–112, 114–115
preamble of the Constitution
   aims in, 171–172
   drafts of, 167
   grant of power in, 171–172
   impact of, 172–173
   legal weight of, 172
   "more perfect union" phrase in, 168–171

overview of, 52, 56–57, 164
quotes in, 164
Randolph's viewpoint regarding, 166
substantive aims in, 168–171
"the people of the United States" in, 167–168
writing process of, 2, 165–167
Presidential Succession Clause, 57
president/presidency
   agenda-setting role of, 126
   appointment powers of, 125, 126
   authority of, 125
   cabinet of, 125, 139–140
   Constitutional Convention deliberations regarding, 45, 107–108, 124–125
   council of revision and, 140–141
   domestic emoluments clause for, 57
   impeachment of, 45, 133–135, 232n58
   judicial branch and, 139–140
   Morris's speech regarding, 188–190
   powers of, 124–125, 174
   reelection conditions regarding, 227n62
   selection process of, 108, 109–115, 225n15
   Supreme Court appointments by, 138
   term limit for, 129–133
   treaty-making power of, 125
   vesting clause and, 128–129
   veto of, 57, 73, 126–128, 174
   See also electoral college
property rights, 94–95, 96, 97–98, 101–105

Quakers, 152
Qualifications Clause, 57
Quasi-War, 30
quotas of contribution, 95

Randolph, Ann Cary ("Nancy"), 4, 34–35
Randolph, Edmund
   Benjamin Franklin and, 41
   as Constitutional Convention delegate, 40
   Constitutional Convention speeches of, 43
   electoral college, viewpoint of, 116, 117
   impeachment, viewpoint of, 134
   judiciary, viewpoint of, 145
   motion statistics of, 207n29
   preamble, viewpoint of, 166
   presidency, viewpoint of, 107
   quotes of, 86, 93, 107
   signing refusal of, 58, 175
   term limit, viewpoint of, 130
   Virginia Plan and, 41, 66
   at Virginia state convention, 21–22
Randolph, Richard, 35
Raphael, Ray, 229n7
Read, George, 63, 68, 75, 87
rebellion clause, 72–73
Reflections on the Revolution in France (Burke), 25
removal by address, 147
Republican Party, 146, 148–149, 172
Revolutionary War, 13, 62
Rhode Island, 42, 109
Roosevelt, Franklin D., 133, 173
Roosevelt, Theodore, 38, 98
Rossiter, Clinton, 38
Rudolph, Theodorick, 35
Rutledge, John, 43, 87, 117, 145, 153

secession, 179, 182
Secretary of Commerce and Finance, 125
Secretary of Domestic Affairs, 72, 125
Secretary of Foreign Affairs, 125
Secretary of State, 125
Secretary of the Marine, 125
Secretary of War, 125
Senate
   abilities and virtue in, 83
   advice and consent of, 126
   as aristocratic body, 42, 79–80
   aristocratic discussion regarding, 86, 103–104
   citizenship requirements regarding, 46
   Constitutional Convention deliberations regarding, 42, 46, 79, 81, 83
   electoral college and, 117
   lifetime appointment discussion regarding, 84–85, 86–87, 92
   Morris's speeches regarding, 82–85, 185–187
   payment proposal regarding, 84, 87, 93, 174
   state representation in, 77, 174
   term limits in, 86–87, 93, 174
   vice president role in, 46
   wealth discussion regarding, 83–84, 86, 89, 90, 91

Senate, *continued*
    See also Congress; House of
        Representatives
separatist movement, 179
Seventeenth Amendment, 93
Sherman, Roger
    apportionment, viewpoint of, 155, 159
    as Articles of Confederation signer, 16
    Declaration of Independence and, 1
    internal police, viewpoint of, 72
    popular election, viewpoint of, 112
    presidency, viewpoint of, 107
    presidential veto, viewpoint of, 127
    quotes of, 27, 42, 85, 107, 112
    state representation, viewpoint of, 77
    work of, 54
    writings regarding, 43
slavery
    apportionment discussion regarding,
        153–159
    census and, 174–175, 237–238n31
    clauses regarding, 160–161
    Constitution references to, 52, 175
    debates regarding, 150
    dirty compromise and, 160
    electoral college and, 226n44
    fugitive slave clause, 161–162
    Mississippi Territory and, 162–163
    Morris's speech regarding, 190–192
    in New York, 152
    overseas slave trade, 159–161
    in Pennsylvania, 152
    preamble of the Constitution and, 172–173
    representation factors and, 150–151
    statistics regarding, 152
    three-fifths compromise regarding, 96
Smith, William, 12, 13
smuggling, 144
Society for Political Inquiries, 20
South, the, 159–160, 178
South Carolina, 101, 131, 160
sovereignty, indivisibility of, 68–69
Sparks, Jared, 49
Staël, Germaine de, 10, 24, 29
state conventions, 21–22
state judiciary, 137
state legislature, 105

State of the Union address, 126
states
    Constitutional Convention deliberations
        regarding, 63, 74
    Constitutional provisions regarding, 55–56
    Constitution ratification process and, 77
    governor selection process in, 109
    judicial review in, 233–234n24
    legislature roles in, 79
    Morris's work with, 65
    national legislature representation by,
        95–96
    political power of, 62
    population struggles regarding, 215n61
    problematic governments in, 70–71
    sovereignty considerations regarding, 63
    tax burdens of, 95
    veto of, 73, 195n10
    voting qualifications in, 102, 105
Stiles, Ezra, 11
Storing, Herbert, 215n61
Story, Joseph, 172
Supreme Court
    appointments for, 138
    Chief Justice of, 125, 139–140
    council of revision and, 140–141
    preamble of the Constitution and, 164, 172
    sessions of, 145
    structure of, 145
    term limits in, 137, 147
    See also judges; judiciary
supreme government, 67–68

Taine, Hippolyte, 25
Talleyrand-Périgord, Charles-Maurice de,
    10, 24
taxation/tax assessment, 150–151, 154, 157, 160
term limits
    of governors, 131
    for House of Representatives, 94, 105
    for judges, 137, 147
    for president, 129–133
    for Senate, 86–87, 93, 174
Têtard, John Peter, 11
three-fifths compromise, 96, 116
Tracy, Uriah, 82
Treanor, William, 5, 53, 56–57

treason, impeachment for, 135
treaty-making power, of the president, 125
Treaty of Ghent, 181
Trist, Nicholas, 61
Twelfth Amendment, 120
Twenty-Second Amendment, 133

universal suffrage, 104. *See also* voting

vesting clause, 56–57, 128–129
veto
   Congressional power regarding, 57, 73
   judiciary and, 142
   Madison's viewpoint regarding, 195n10
   presidential, 57, 73, 126–128, 174
   of states, 73
   two-thirds majority over, 128
vice president, 46, 119–120
Virginia, 21–22, 39, 101, 130, 160
Virginia Declaration of Rights, 1, 194n4
Virginia Plan
   aims in, 168
   debates regarding, 75
   first resolution of, 66
   introduction of, 41
   Morris's support for, 41
   overview of, 41, 65–66, 71–72
   presidential selection process in, 109
voting, 101–105, 223n47

War of 1812, 98, 163, 178
Washington, George
   Benjamin Franklin and, 41
   characteristics of, 47
   as Constitutional Convention delegate, 40
   death of, 30–31
   leadership of, 15, 42–43
   Morris and, 10, 13–14, 21
   as president, 112, 122, 136, 201n45
   quotes of, 5, 29
   resignation of, 133
   speech of, 20
   term limit, viewpoint of, 130
Watson, James, 31
wealth
   influence of, 88
   Morris's portrayal of, 92
   poverty *versus*, 104–105
   risks regarding, 89
   in the Senate, 83–84, 86, 89, 90, 91
   unity against, 89
West, the, 98–99
Wilentz, Sean, 162
Williamson, Hugh, 43, 114, 117
Wilson, James
   apportionment, viewpoint of, 155, 159
   Benjamin Franklin and, 41
   bill of rights, viewpoint of, 143
   as Constitutional Convention delegate, 39, 40
   Constitutional Convention speeches of, 43
   electoral college, viewpoint of, 117, 118
   judicial review, viewpoint of, 141
   judiciary, viewpoint of, 139
   Morris and, 39
   motion statistics of, 207n29
   as nationalist, 63
   popular election, viewpoint of, 114
   preamble of, 166
   presidency, viewpoint of, 108, 110, 123
   presidential veto, viewpoint of, 127
   quotes of, 37, 114, 140
   representation, viewpoint of, 154
   Senate term limit, viewpoint of, 87
   speeches of, 123
   term limit, viewpoint of, 130
   voting, viewpoint of, 102
   writings of, 60

Yates, Robert, 60, 87, 92

www.ingramcontent.com/pod-product-compliance
Lightning Source LLC
Chambersburg PA
CBHW070303240426
43661CB00057B/2635